BY IBRAM X. KENDI

The Black Campus Movement

Stamped from the Beginning:
The Definitive History of Racist Ideas in America

How to Be an Antiracist

Stamped: Racism, Antiracism, and You
by Ibram X. Kendi and Jason Reynolds

Antiracist Baby
by Ibram X. Kendi,
illustrated by Ashley Lukashevsky

Be Antiracist: A Journal for Awareness,
Reflection, and Action

Four Hundred Souls: A Community History
of African America, 1619–2019
edited by Ibram X. Kendi and Keisha N. Blain

Stamped (For Kids): Racism, Antiracism, and You
by Ibram X. Kendi, Jason Reynolds,
and Sonja Cherry-Paul

The Antiracist Deck: 100 Meaningful Conversations
on Power, Equity, and Justice

Goodnight Racism
by Ibram X. Kendi,
illustrated by Cbabi Bayoc

How to Raise an Antiracist

How to Raise an Antiracist

HOW TO
RAISE
AN
ANTIRACIST

IBRAM X.
KENDI

ONE WORLD

NEW YORK

Published in the United States by One World, an imprint of
Random House, a division of Penguin Random House LLC, New York.

ONE WORLD and colophon are registered trademarks of
Penguin Random House LLC.

Hardback ISBN 9780593242537
Ebook ISBN 9780593242544

Printed in the United States of America on acid-free paper

oneworldlit.com
randomhousebooks.com

2 4 6 8 9 7 5 3 1

First Edition

Book design by Jo Anne Metsch

Contents

Introduction

She noticed. First once or twice a day. Soon, two or three times a day.

It was March 2016. We lived in central Florida. Sadiqa had been pregnant with our child for twenty-three weeks. She did not have any pain. She did not notice any bleeding. But the discharge worried her. It was odd. It kept coming.

Three days after it started, Sadiqa told me about it. I could tell she felt uncomfortable sharing. We live in a body-shaming society where even pregnant women are socialized to be embarrassed about their bodies. But as a physician, Sadiqa eased her discomfort by medicalizing its source, by observing and reporting her clinical symptoms as she would a patient's. She called her obstetrician's office not long after she opened up to me and told a nurse about the discharge, its increasing volume, and her increasing worry.

"Any other symptoms?" the nurse asked.

"No, not really."

"Well, I think it's fine. There's nothing to worry about. People have symptoms like that all the time."

Not Sadiqa. It was the first symptom like that she'd experienced during the six months of her first pregnancy. And she was not reassured by the nurse. Now she had a new worry: *Is something wrong with me for thinking there is something wrong with me?* she thought. *Am I paranoid? Foolish?*

The world has a knack for causing women to question their sanity, and those questions fall especially heavily on pregnant women, and pregnant Black women perhaps most of all. The self-doubt arises from what microbiologist Sasha Ottey terms "health-care gaslighting."

In the end, Sadiqa listened to her body. But medical workers too often don't listen to Black women.

The medical establishment's disregard for Black women is one of the reasons "Why America's Black Mothers and Babies Are in a Life-or-Death Crisis"—the headline on the *New York Times Magazine* story by Linda Villarosa that broke open this crisis in 2018. That article opens with medical providers brushing aside pregnant Simone Landrum's complaints in Louisiana around the same time they brushed aside Sadiqa's complaints in Florida. Landrum had been complaining of spotting and then bleeding, pain, and fatigue, but doctors ignored her until it was too late—she nearly died delivering a premature, stillborn baby.

Even wealthy and powerful Black women like Serena Williams have faced similar disregard. In 2017, the day after giving birth by C-section to her daughter, Olympia, the legendary tennis player struggled to breathe. Williams knew it was a trademark symptom of a blood clot because she had a history of clots in her lungs. Williams also knew what the next step should be: She asked for a CT scan and a blood thinner. But the nurse told her she was wrong, that the pain medication had confused her. An ultrasound was performed on her legs instead. After finding nothing, medical workers finally performed a CT scan of her chest, and found several small blood clots in her lungs. The clots caused Williams to cough out the stitches from her C-section. While repairing the stitches, doctors discovered a hematoma in her abdomen.

"I didn't expect that sharing our family's story of Olympia's birth and all of the complications after giving birth would start such an outpouring of discussions from women—especially Black women—who have faced similar complications and women whose problems go unaddressed," Williams wrote in 2018. "EVERY mother, regardless of race or background, deserves to have a healthy pregnancy and childbirth."

Indeed, every mother deserves reproductive justice. How a society treats pregnant women is a metaphor for how a society raises its children. Every year, about seven hundred American women die from pregnancy, the highest maternal mortality rate among rich countries in the world. Two-thirds of the annual deaths from pregnancy are considered preventable. And certainly, the racial disparities in those deaths are preventable.

Black women in the United States are more than three times more likely to die from pregnancy than White women (even as the death rate for White women in the United States is absurdly high). In 2019, a Centers for Disease Control study found that between 2007 and 2016 the pregnancy-related death rate for Black women was 40.8 per 100,000 births. For Native women, it was 29.7; Asian—13.5; White—12.7; and Latinx—11.5 per 100,000 births. The racial disparities were even wider among older women and women with college degrees. Pregnant Black and Native women over thirty years old were four to five times more likely to die than White women over thirty years old. The pregnancy-related death rate for Black college graduates was 5.2 times higher than for their White counterparts. In 2016, Sadiqa had a medical degree and middle-class status, had just turned thirty-seven, and worked in the same hospital that provided her maternal care. But education, social status, wealth, age, access to premium care—none of this can assure that medical providers take the concerns of Black women seriously.

This is a problem of racism. Black mothers (10.2 percent) are more than twice as likely as White mothers to "receive later or no prenatal care." Black women are more likely to be uninsured outside of pregnancy, and to lose coverage during the postpartum period. Black women are four times more likely than White women to live in neighborhoods facing high air pollution, a risk factor for preterm births. The hospitals where Black mothers give birth tend to have fewer resources and less expertise than where White mothers typically deliver, even as Black mothers tend to have more life-threatening conditions and complications.

And that imbalance in resources and expertise matters. Let's face it: We live in societies where the mothers with the greatest needs commonly give birth in the hospitals with the greatest needs. Just like the children with the greatest needs commonly go to the schools with the greatest needs. Just like the families with the greatest needs commonly live in the communities with the greatest needs. This is the startling injustice of racial inequity. And this is all considered normal. Raising kids in this structure of racial inequity has become very normal. Raising kids to see all this racial inequity as normal—*is so very normal.*

.   .   .

Days after opening up about her discharge, Sadiqa went to work at the local children's hospital. On her feet for hours, she shuffled between small rooms and sick kids and fearful parents and wired nurses and learning trainees. Working in a pediatric emergency department is taxing on the body, let alone the pregnant body. Every time she went to the bathroom during the shift, she noticed the discharge.

After signing out, Sadiqa walked over to the nearby labor and delivery unit. She reported her symptom again. A nurse assured her there was nothing to worry about; that she was okay. She left without being examined.

Sadiqa came home. "Everybody seems to think it's fine," she told me that night. "But I'm just going to make an appointment with the OB, you know, just to have them check me, tell me I'm wrong, and we'll move on." I listened. I did not encourage or discourage her.

We were in our kitchen days later, the morning of her appointment. Fixing to leave, Sadiqa told me I didn't need to come along. She thought she'd be in and out and off to her lunch appointment. I did not go.

It was Sadiqa's first solo OB-GYN appointment. She described the day for me later.

When she left the house, she felt good. Bobbed to hip-hop on the drive over. She felt the warmth of the sun on her skin as she glided into the outpatient medical building with doctors' offices and their clinics. She trotted up the stairs with no problems; she hadn't stopped exercising during the pregnancy. Then she entered the examination room of her OB-GYN's office.

The room was dismal. No windows. No colors. A small box, lit by artificial light. Half-dressed, sheet covering her bare legs, Sadiqa sat on a table and leaned against the bare wall.

A nurse practitioner soon arrived with a nursing student. Sadiqa does not remember the nurse's name, but she remembers her blondish-brown hair, and the warmth and confidence of this bespectacled White woman.

Sadiqa repeated her symptom again. "It's probably nothing, but I figured I'd rather just come in and make sure that's the case." Sadiqa smiled in her infectious way, I imagine, and the nurse smiled back. "Yeah, you know, it's probably nothing. But definitely let's examine you and make sure everything's okay."

Sadiqa lay back on the exam table. The gloved nurse pulled out a speculum to perform a pelvic exam. The speculum, ironically, is a product of the medical racism experienced by Sadiqa, Serena Williams, Simone Landrum, and countless other Black women throughout American history. J. Marion Sims invented the speculum and the field of gynecology based on painful, profoundly unethical experiments he conducted on enslaved Black women on his Alabama plantation before the Civil War.

The nurse inserted the speculum. She looked. She noticed. She took a deep breath.

"She has bulging membranes," the nurse said, turning to her student.

She looked up at Sadiqa. "I'm going to take the speculum out now and then I'll talk to you."

The nurse took the speculum out and ordered her student to call an ambulance.

"You're dilated about four to five centimeters, and your amniotic membranes are bulging," she told Sadiqa. "So we need to get you to the hospital now!"

"Well, I drove here. Like, can't I just drive there?"

"No!"

Sadiqa tried to sit up.

"No, you have to lie back on the table!"

Our baby was coming. And the nurses didn't want Sadiqa

to progress and deliver in the clinic. They didn't want her to deliver at all—not yet.

Sadiqa called me as the frantic energy of nurses engulfed her. She told me about the dilation, the ambulance. I could hear her fear. I tried to convey calm as much as I could, hoping she'd feel it, too. She did, settling down a bit. I had channeled my mother, who is the calmest amid the craziest storms.

After I hung up, I felt shipwrecked emotionally. *Why didn't I go with her? Why did I not encourage her to go sooner? What the hell was wrong with me?* I'm still raw about it all these years later. When someone tells us they don't need us, *isn't that often when they need us the most?* I'm still beating myself up about not being present for Sadiqa during one of the scariest times of her life—and the life of our coming child. But in that moment, I had to pull myself back together. It was apparent no one around Sadiqa had taken her discharge seriously, including me. I had been nothing but a passive ear for a week. Not an active supporter.

Fortunately, Sadiqa was not passive, which was why we now had a chance to save our child. Sadiqa had been scheduled to work that night, which would have required her to be in constant motion. That scary thought was what drove her to the clinic. Now the nurses did not want her to move at all. Sadiqa thought about the contrast as she lay there on the exam table, completely still.

An EMT crew arrived. Two bald White guys carefully slid Sadiqa onto the gurney. They rushed her downstairs and out of the building.

"We like delivering full-term babies, but we don't want to deliver any preemies," one said with a smile as he lifted her into the ambulance.

"Yeah, the goal is not delivery here," Sadiqa joked back.

They pulled off, going hot. Sirens blazed through red lights. Sadiqa had ridden in ambulances as a physician. Never as a patient.

And yet the kind of premature birth that Sadiqa was confronting really does constitute an emergency, one that falls heaviest on Black people. When babies are delivered at twenty-four weeks, only about 6 in 10 survive in the United States. Among survivors, most of these premature babies have chronic health challenges. Black babies (13.8 percent) were the most likely to be born premature from 2016 to 2018, more likely than Native babies (11.6 percent), Latinx babies (9.6 percent), White babies (9.1 percent), and Asian babies (8.7 percent). More premature births lead to more infant deaths. In 2018, nearly 11 Black babies died per 1,000 live births, almost tripling the infant mortality rate for Latinx (4.86), White (4.63), and Asian (3.63) babies. Black infants account for 15 percent of the births in the United States, and 29 percent of the infant deaths.

The data is clear: Racism is a mortal threat to children and parents alike during pregnancy and childbirth. But the threat does not stop there. What does racism do to the children—of all races—who survive?

Just as Sadiqa found herself in an emergency not of her own making, we also find our society in a dire, life-threatening emergency. White supremacists attacked the U.S. Capitol on January 6, 2021, to overturn the 2020 presidential election. And then GOP legislators spent the rest of the year passing thirty-four voter suppression bills in nineteen states that make it harder for all Americans to vote. Democracy and our very lives are being threatened by White supremacists whose organizing mantra has been that people of color, antiracism, and what they call "critical race theory" are harming White people. This mythology preys on vulnerable White male youth, who prey on the rest of us. In 2020, seventeen-year-old Kyle Rittenhouse killed two White antiracist demonstrators in Kenosha, Wisconsin, with an AR-15-style rifle. In 2019, twenty-one-year-old Patrick Crusius entered a Walmart in El Paso, Texas, with an AK-47-style rifle and murdered twenty-three people, claiming the "attack is a response to the Hispanic invasion of Texas." In 2018, nineteen-year-old Nikolas Cruz said "I hate jews, niggers, immigrants" in a private Instagram group chat before killing seventeen people with an AR-15 at Marjory Stoneman Douglas High School in Parkland, Florida. In 2015, twenty-one-year-old Dylann Roof killed nine Bible-studying African Americans in Charleston, South Carolina.

Strict gun safety laws can prevent these mass shootings. But the mantra of White supremacy—that White people are under attack—has greased the political wheels that rolled back gun safety laws. The United States has been flooded with high-powered rifles and racist ideas, making for a life-threatening situation for us and our children. But instead of restricting and banning ammunition and guns, GOP state legislators are restricting and banning antiracist books and education. Instead of arming teachers with expertise on how to teach about racism, our country is asking teachers to arm themselves with guns. Fears of dark bodies over the last few decades have also justified the accumulation of police and prisons, which has contributed to the defunding of public safety nets, public health, public libraries, public schools, and public universities relied on by children and families.

The situation is grave. Caregivers of children are being asked to do more with less. But like me and the nurses who ignored Sadiqa's symptoms, the American people are not willing to fully accept the gravity of the emergency. If anything, we're in even worse shape than Sadiqa: There is no ambulance in sight. Our political will isn't going hot. Our society is not headed to the hospital.

To many of our societal caregivers, even our racial disparities from health to wealth do not signify an emergency made of racist policies. No, *it's primarily a poverty or class issue,* they say, even though White high school dropouts have more wealth than Black and Latinx college graduates, even though the male millennial children of Black millionaires have higher incarceration rates than the male millennial children of the White working class. Or, in dismissing the racism, they point to behavior. Meaning if Black people are dying at higher rates than White people from COVID-19, then it's because White people are making healthier decisions than Black people. Meaning there's something behaviorally superior about White people. Meaning there's something behaviorally inferior about Black people. And therein lies the emergency—not history, not policy, not power.

And as they express these racist ideas, they likely self-identify as "not racist." But one of the core findings of my historical research on racism is this idea: There is no such thing as a "not racist." One is expressing either ideas of racial equality (as an antiracist) or ideas of racial hierarchy (as a racist). One is supporting either policies that lead to racial equity and justice (as an antiracist) or policies that lead to racial inequity and injustice (as a racist). There's no in-between equality and hierarchy; equity and inequity; justice and injustice. The defining question for the individual in any given moment: Am I upholding the structure of racism through my action or inaction (as a racist) or challenging it (as an antiracist)?

If you are actively challenging racism, congratulations, you are being an antiracist. But if you are doing nothing, while trying to claim some kind of neutral territory between racist and antiracist, you are complicit in allowing the structural problem to persist. Do you know what enslavers wanted the rest of us to do as domestic slave traders separated Black children from their parents and forced them onto plantations in the Deep South in 1818? Nothing. Do you know what settler colonialists wanted the rest of us to do as federal agents and "missionaries" separated Native children from their parents and forcibly assimilated them at Eurocentric boarding schools in 1918? Nothing. Do you know what the Trump administration wanted the rest of us to do as border officials separated Latinx children from their parents and caged them in trauma in 2018? Nothing. To do nothing in a society of injustice is to uphold racism. To do nothing in the face of racism is to be racist.

Many caregivers are doing something. They do recognize the emergency. They will tell you that they know that we live in a racist society. But are those caregivers actively seeking to protect *their children* from the racism? How many caregivers recognize their society as dangerous but let their children roam freely without protection? What happens to an unprotected child in a dangerous society?

I don't ask these questions to pass judgment. I ask these questions because they are exactly the questions I regret not asking when I contemplated becoming an educator and a parent. Of all the books I read during Sadiqa's pregnancy, none were on raising an antiracist child—and I wasn't even sure I needed such a book.

We imagine our kids *can't* be racist, so why teach them about a problem they can't possibly have? We worry that, in any event, racist ideas are too sophisticated for kids to understand. But the opposite is true: Racist ideas have spread across humanity and history precisely because they are *simple. Dark skin is bad and light skin is good.* Strikingly simple. And danger-ous.

The thought of nurturing my child to be antiracist did not sit well with me. It was uncomfortable even to think about. If anything, I wanted to shield my child from racism as long as I could. Avoid the dialogues—the so-called "talks"—as long as possible. Preserve the child's innocence—and unbounded joy. Racism can be a bloodsucker of joy. I didn't want my kid any-where near that vampire.

But if I'm being honest, was my planned avoidance about protecting my child? Or was it about protecting me? My dis-comfort? My insecurities about my ability to explain it all the right way?

In thinking racism was too hard a subject for children to handle, was that about me, too? It had been hard for me to be antiracist. And I'm an adult who has studied these issues for years! Now I have to assist a child?

That's the fear so many of us have—that I had. But after more research and reflection, I discovered the good news. Learning to be antiracist isn't as complicated for children as it is for adults. Children don't have the emotional and concep-tual baggage that we do. It is easier for children to learn the language of antiracism just as it is easier for children to learn spoken languages. Deconstructing an ingrained racist identity is much harder than constructing a fresh antiracist identity.

To be an effective caregiver requires us to sometimes do hard things for our kids, and *with* our kids. Adults can unlearn racist ideas—and learn antiracist ideas. We are likely raised on racist ideas without realizing it, and our parents probably didn't realize it, either. My parents didn't know how deeply racist ideas had burrowed into my understanding of the world as I was coming of age in the 1980s and 1990s. They did not know that by the time I graduated from high school in 2000 I thought Black people were America's racial problem—as opposed to the racism Black people were facing. I don't blame my parents or my teachers. They did not protect me from the racist messages because they did not know *to* protect me.

I have spent my entire adult life unlearning the racist ideas taught to me at my most impressionable stages of development. All this unlearning has been treacherous at times, but absolutely liberating in the end. The difficulty is fighting the reflex to deny what I have been and believed; the liberation is in discovering that I can change. Whether starting the journey at thirty years old or fifty years old or eighty years old, anyone can strive to be antiracist. Whether starting at birth, at five years old, at ten years old, at fifteen years old, any child can be raised to be antiracist.

This book is for the people doing the raising. This book is for caregivers. When I say caregiver, I mean all the people who are nurturing the environments, experiences, minds, bodies, souls, and futures of children. Biological and adopted parents. Educators and childcare workers. Doting and indefatigable grandparents. Pediatricians and pediatric nurses. Faith leaders and politicians. And all the aunts and uncles and cousins and friends and coaches and neighbors and counselors and executives and artists and creators and social workers who are part of the caregiving village that raises our children.

Raising our children to be antiracist is like dressing their minds in armor before we send them out into the world. Let's unpack two pieces of the armor:

There's nothing right about me because of the color of my skin.

Imagine if all White children are taught this antiracist idea, internalize it, and develop their sense of self through it. White children need protection from all the verbal and nonverbal messages in our society telling them they are special—not simply because they are individual, unique, and precious humans, but because they are White.

There's nothing wrong with me because of the color of my skin.

Imagine if all kids of color are taught this antiracist idea, internalize it, and develop their sense of self through it. Children of color must be protected from all those verbal and nonverbal messages telling them they are not special because they are not White.

The kind of armor our children need changes with age. Studies show that the way children and youth experience race and racism develops with age, which is why this book is structured according to the key stages in the lives of our growing children. Chapters follow development from pregnancy to newborn to infant to toddler to preschooler to kid to middle schooler to teenager. I emphasize antiracist parenting in the early chapters and antiracist teaching in the later chapters as the child goes to school. Don't worry if your child has already grown past those initial stages; it is never too late to begin raising a child to be antiracist.

I am not a pediatric medical researcher like my partner. I am not a child psychologist. I have a background in educational research. I am a historian of anti-Black racism. I am a scholar of antiracism who engages the work of medical researchers, psychologists, educational researchers, sociologists, geneticists, political scientists, economists, ethnic studies scholars, and other scholars to glean evidence-based policies and practices that can create equitable and just societies. I am a teacher at heart, striving to educate students at Boston University and beyond. I'm a parent, striving to raise a child in

Boston. This book shares my life as a parent—and my life as a child among teachers and parents—to set the table for my research on the racial development of children and youth, and the historical and structural forces shaping that development, and how we can help our children develop to be antiracist.

Raising a child to be antiracist is a journey. Every journey is different because every caregiver and child and environment is different. And so this isn't a one-way-fits-all prescriptive book. *How to Raise an Antiracist* provides critical research and insights and stories for all caregivers to shape and direct their own unique journeys no matter where their children are in their lives, from newborns to teenagers. But equipping our young people as they develop is only the beginning.

The most critical part of raising an antiracist child is not what we do with our child. It is what we do with our society. We must keep our individual children safe in this racist society, while building an antiracist society that can protect all our children. *How to Raise an Antiracist* is as much about how to raise an antiracist society for our children as it is about how to raise an individual who embraces antiracism. Because nothing raises an antiracist child more effectively than an antiracist society.

How to Raise an Antiracist

CHAPTER 1

Birth of Denial

The gravity of the emergency hit Sadiqa when she arrived at the hospital. She entered the labor and delivery unit, where days earlier a nurse told her nothing was wrong. Multiple nurses now surrounded her knowing something was very wrong. Doctors rushed into the room almost as soon as she was wheeled in. As a pediatric ER doctor, Sadiqa knew that when a mass of nurses and doctors hurry into your room, it's a problem.

She got scared.

When my mother—Ma—came into the room, Sadiqa let her tears go. "I'm really, really scared, you know," she said.

My mother was at the beauty parlor when I called. Ma put on a slumber cap and darted to the hospital. You know the situation is grave when an elderly Black woman shows herself in public with a slumber cap.

Ma cradled Sadiqa's tears and fears in prayer. She offered a fervent prayer at the bedside—overtaking the clamor of footsteps and voices and machines—enjoining the Lord Almighty to intervene. To stop the delivery.

"In the name of Jeee-sus-uh!" she closed as she always does. "Amen! Amen! Amen."

Meaning I believe! I believe! I believe.

Ma did.

"We'll get through it," Ma said, holding Sadiqa's hand. "We'll get through this okay." Sadiqa heard the conviction in Ma's voice.

Sadiqa's parents lived three hours away. I called and asked them to come. But I wasn't there yet myself! When Sadiqa and I had spoken before the ambulance arrived at the clinic, she expressed worry about the dilation, about our baby. But mostly she went on and on about her car.

"What's going to happen to it?" she asked me on the phone. "We can't leave it here. They won't let me drive it!"

She was upset. The car, her immobility—an allegory. Mostly, Sadiqa was in disbelief. She saved babies for a living. How could she entertain the thought of losing her baby? Who could?

Perhaps thoughts of the car allowed her to maintain a deeper denial as she rode to the hospital. She worried aloud about the car and kept on joking with the EMTs, laughing with them to hold off from crying.

I did not want Sadiqa worrying about the car. I called Dad and asked him to pick me up from my home. We'd get Sadiqa's car and speed to the hospital. The retrieval gave me something to do for my partner. Maybe I was in denial, too.

Picking up the car bought me time. Before I could hold her up, I needed to stop beating myself down for not accompanying her to the appointment in the first place. When we went through past medical emergencies, we were yoked, physically and emotionally. When she faltered, I faltered. When I faltered, she faltered.

Months after we wed in 2013, Sadiqa was diagnosed with invasive breast cancer. Surgery and chemotherapy cured her. We did not expect to conceive after her chemotherapy. Now we didn't know if our baby would survive. Still reeling from the terrifying scare of her cancer diagnosis, I silently battled thoughts of the worst throughout the pregnancy. Convinced myself all was good when she first noted her discharge, when it wasn't. A feigned optimism concealed a suppressed fear, and all the while kept me from a measured realism.

The tension between outward optimistic denial and inward fear is probably familiar to any caregiver. This tension applies to how we approach teaching our children about racism. Caregivers want to believe, optimistically, that their children don't need to learn about it. But that belief is often driven by a fear—the fear of having to confront the troubling truth. We convince ourselves that it is better for our children if we don't teach them about racism.

Or is it better for us? How often do we put off these hard conversations and claim it is about protecting our children when it is really about protecting ourselves? When our babies are born, is our denial born with them? The sound of that denial: *Racism is not around my child.* Or: *My child will be unaffected by the racism around them.* No matter what is in fact around our child, no matter what we don't do, no matter how the child is affected—the sound of our denial remains.

We deny the harmful structure of racism as surely as we don't want to be identified as racist. That's not who we are. But *racist* and *antiracist* don't describe who a person is in an absolute sense; they describe us from moment to moment, based on what we're doing and why we're doing it. *Racist* and *antiracist* are descriptive terms, not fixed categories, not identities, not reflections of what's in anyone's bones or heart.

The popular perception that *racist* and *antiracist* define a person rather than describe a person in any given moment doesn't account for human complexity, for individuals living in contradiction, for individuals holding both racist and anti-racist ideas. If there's anything I've learned while researching the history of racism, it's that individuals constructing or de-constructing it are deeply complex. Countless individuals ad-vocate for both racist and antiracist policies at different times. And so how can they be identified as essentially racist or anti-racist? Humans can change, moment to moment, or grow, even after being raised to be racist, as so many of us are, with-out our even realizing it. The way to account for this human complexity is to say that what we are doing or not doing in each moment determines whether we are being racist or being antiracist in that moment. When one is saying that Black peo-ple are *not* more dangerous than White people, one is being antiracist. If in the next moment, one is supporting a policy that maintains the racial wealth gap, one is then being racist.

Racist and *antiracist* describe individuality—an individual idea or policy or institution or nation or person—while *racism* and *antiracism* describe connectivity or what's systematic, struc-tural, and institutional. When an individual cop pulls me over because he suspects wrongdoing because I'm Black, this cop is being racist. If I try to hold him accountable for racially profil-ing me, I must face the power and policy structure that empow-ers and protects cops like him as they keep racially profiling, arresting, brutalizing, and killing Black people like me at the highest rates. Racism manifests itself as a powerful collection of policies that lead to racial inequity and injustice and are justified by ideas of racial hierarchy. Meanwhile, antiracism is the very opposite: a powerful collection of policies that lead to racial equity and justice and are justified by ideas of racial equality.

To construct antiracism, to be antiracist, we must admit the times we are being racist. To raise an antiracist, caregivers must first overcome that inner voice of denial. They must acknowledge the gravity of the emergency—*our society is dangerously racist*—and the gravity of their power—*I can still raise a child to be antiracist.*

How we raise a child depends, at least in part, on how we racially socialize the child. What does it mean to "racially socialize" a child? It refers to the ways that we talk about race and racial groups in verbal and nonverbal ways with our kids—often unwittingly. Caregivers commonly and perhaps unknowingly socialize their children in the way they were socialized. But the way we talk about race and racial groups with our kids matters deeply.

Caregivers deploy four predominant forms of racial socialization. Two of these forms are antiracist; two are racist. They are: *promotion of mistrust, cultural socialization, preparation for bias,* and *color blindness.* I suspect caregivers engage in different forms at different ages and times, slipping in and out of racist and antiracist modes.

The most well-known racist form of socialization is *promotion of mistrust,* which "may be communicated in parents' cautions or warnings to children about other racial groups." When decades ago caregivers might have used explicit racial language, now promoting mistrust for people of color might take a euphemistic form but still have profound effects on our kids. It appears in phrases like "be careful around *those* kids," or "stay away from *that* girl," or "no, you can't sleep over *there,*" or "*they* are ghetto," or "*their* parents don't care," or "that's a *bad* school," or "*they're* taking over," or "*she* looks grown," or "*he* looks dangerous." The subjects in these lines are typically people of color, and their institutions and neighborhoods. This degradation can happen to White people and their institutions and neighborhoods. But despite what some people believe, it is rare for Black parents to promote mistrust of White people with their kids.

It is racist to promote mistrust of any racial group of people. On the other hand, it is antiracist to promote mistrust of racist ideas, practices, policies, and behaviors. To be antiracist is to promote distrust of racism and dehumanization, while promoting trust of antiracism and humanity.

Caregivers can promote trust of humanity through perhaps the most popular form of antiracist socialization: *cultural socialization,* or "parental practices that teach children about their racial or ethnic heritage and history." It is antiracist for caregivers of Mexican American, Iranian American, Irish American, Chinese American, Nigerian American, and Ojibwe children to educate those children about their cultures. It is antiracist for caregivers of Native American, Black American, White American, Latinx American, Middle Eastern American, and Asian American children to educate those children about their racialized histories. It is antiracist for caregivers of multicultural or multiracial children to educate those children about their multiple cultures and racialized histories. This positive practice is also one that is routinely practiced by parents: About eight out of twelve Black middle-class mothers, for instance, noted the importance of teaching their children about African American history and culture.

In order for cultural socialization to be antiracist, however, it has to unfold in three crucial steps. The first is to raise a child to comprehend and appreciate what is distinct about their own culture and history. Next, we have to raise a child to comprehend and appreciate what's distinct about *other* cultures and histories. And finally, we must raise the child to comprehend and appreciate what's the *same* about their own and the other cultural groups. In the words of the classic *Ses-*

ame Street picture book, we have to teach kids that *We're Different, We're the Same.*

If a child understands the distinct features of their own culture, and is taught those things in a spirit of conveying the humanity (and not inferiority) of that culture, then the child can appreciate the strength and specificity of their cultural difference. But that can easily turn into racist ideas if we don't also teach them—in that same spirit of humanity—the things that make other cultures strong and distinct, so they can appreciate other cultures. But even that isn't enough. Those two steps alone might lead a child to thinking that however admirable their culture and the cultures of others are, there is an uncrossable chasm between them. But teaching kids that we share a common humanity is the bridge that allows us to meet each other and share our cultures. We're different. We're the same.

Cultural point of view is key, too. To raise an antiracist is to raise a child to gaze at their own culture from their own cultural point of view. A Native girl can learn the medicinal role of water in Native cultures in Carole Lindstrom's picture book *We Are Water Protectors*. To raise an antiracist is to raise a child to gaze at other cultures from the point of view of other cultures. A Latinx evangelical can learn the dignity of wearing a hijab from the story of two Muslim sisters in *The Proudest Blue,* a picture book by Olympic medalist Ibtihaj Muhammad. A White child can be exposed to modern Native cooking in *Fry Bread,* a picture book by Kevin Noble Maillard. My daughter fell in love with the Hindu festival Holi through reading *Festival of Colors,* a picture book by Kabir Sehgal and Surishtha Sehgal. Caregivers must seek to expose their child to different cultures to open their horizons to different cultures.

Caregivers can open the child's horizon to different cultures through books, and through bringing the child to cultural gatherings and spaces. Chinatowns, powwows, country music festivals, and Puerto Rican Day parades can be instructive. Cultural socialization—like learning a language—requires some level of *immersion*. But as children learn cultural conventions, they must have the freedom to defy those cultural conventions, too: Culture is a resource, not a trap. Consider the way gender conventions are defied in Jessica Love's picture book *Julián Is a Mermaid*, about a boy who desires to dress like the fabulous ladies in a mermaid parade. (Mermaids have become symbolic to transgender people.)

Cultural socialization can ensure children are fully clothed and comfortable in their own culture and history—and can recognize and respect the cultures of others. And yet cultural socialization is not enough.

The least commonly deployed form of antiracist socialization is the most protective: what scholars call *preparation for bias,* which I'll slightly modify to *preparation for racism*. As caregivers we prepare our children for all sorts of trying, uncomfortable, and menacing aspects of our world *to protect them*. When we don't, are we not being negligent? Caregivers instruct their kids to look both ways before crossing the street, preparing them and protecting them from being harmed by distracted or speeding drivers. Likewise, we must instruct our kids to notice the cars of racist ideas, preparing and protecting them from being harmed. How will they know to stay away from "dark skin is ugly" if they don't know it as a racist idea that can hit them?

Most American parents teach their adolescents about their bodies, preparing them for their sexual lives, protecting them from unplanned pregnancies and STIs. Similarly, we must teach our adolescents the relative privileges and disadvantages of their racial bodies. Because when we don't, we leave them unprepared for a world where their racial bodies will have real effects on their lives—in everything from how they're disciplined in school to how they are treated by doctors to what happens to them when they're stopped by the police. If they've been left to believe that merit alone always explains the relative treatment—and the successes and failures—of all racialized individuals and groups, we are nurturing their individual vanity or insecurity. We are nurturing their racist ideas.

Preparing children in this way influences the kind of adults they become. In one study, about three out of four White respondents whose caregivers instructed them as children about racism grow up to recognize the unequal opportunities between people of color and White Americans. By contrast, among White respondents who reported their parents "never" or "rarely" talked to them about racism as children, fewer than half see unequal opportunity. Not seeing the problem doesn't mean it doesn't exist—nor does it mean it won't be hurtful to you, your loved ones, or the people around you. It only means that you refuse to see it.

But even if caregivers prepare and protect their individual kids, their work is half-finished. We cannot neglect societal structures. Because ultimately protecting the individual child *requires* that we also address the dangers in the society they will grow up in. We understand this with other issues. We advocate for policies that provide more effective screening of violent content in our media; safer crosswalks for our streets; and laws to curb distracted driving. Likewise, when it comes to racism, we must advocate for policies that more effectively screen racist content in our media directed at children; create neighborhoods safe from economic exploitation, police violence, and food apartheid; and create opportunities for all kids no matter their zip code. Most societal caregivers have long recognized the protective importance of comprehensive sex education in schools. How can they not recognize the protective importance of comprehensive antiracist education in schools? Teaching kids about their reproductive bodies does not cause them to engage in sexual intercourse just as teaching kids about racism doesn't cause them to be racist. But not teaching our kids about either leaves them vulnerable to their own ignorance. As with misinformation about sex, children will learn misinformation about race whether or not caregivers discuss the subject. It is our job to preempt hearsay and misinformation with the facts.

As I went to pick up the car that day—while Sadiqa was in a hospital bed some distance away—somewhere inside myself I knew I'd made an error. I'd left my partner alone in a moment of vulnerability and danger. My denial caused my negligence, just as it does for so many of us in the role of caregivers. I should have gone straight to the hospital. What a grave error in judgment. Because as soon as she got to the hospital, Sadiqa stopped thinking about the car. There were bigger problems.

Sadiqa's fear started to ebb when her providers finished the ultrasound and the attending physician told her our baby didn't seem distressed. The plan was to give Sadiqa some medicine to stop her from going into labor and keep her on bed rest for as long as possible.

I arrived not long after the plan was set, Sadiqa's car parked outside. I didn't share about the car. Sadiqa didn't ask. But I did apologize for not being there with her the whole time, and for not taking the discharge seriously in the first place. I didn't think I should be forgiven, but I apologized anyway.

Sadiqa didn't think I should be apologizing, but she forgave me anyway.

Sometime later, a nurse started Sadiqa on magnesium sulfate to keep the baby parked in her womb. The magnesium sulfate—and perhaps her fear—took her breath away. It seemed to be choking her—and once again I felt helpless to stop her discomfort. She had to lie on her back and take it. She couldn't sit up or get out of bed to use the bathroom. Imagine remaining still for hours while struggling to breathe. It was awful. They gave her oxygen, which did not seem to help her breathe.

Sadiqa also suffered in ways that I could not see. As a pediatrician she knew all the challenges our baby would face if born at twenty-four weeks. No one else in our family really knew until a researcher with an eastern European accent came into our room the next day. Sadiqa was still in pain. We were still pained about the situation. But whoever let the researcher into the room didn't think that mattered.

The researcher didn't try to connect with us. Didn't read distress in our unfamiliar faces and come back another day. Instead, she launched into her tortured and torturous pitch to recruit our baby for a study. On and on about all the neurodevelopmental issues our baby could have if she were delivered at twenty-four weeks and how useful that would be to study. She was completely oblivious about how her words were making us feel. A lack of empathy. She never asked how we felt. By the time she finally stopped and left the room, we all could barely breathe. The room, thick with fear.

Some caregivers are similarly oblivious to racism—and how their obliviousness makes others feel. This obliviousness causes them to reject attempts at antiracist socialization. Rather than leaning into opportunities for cultural socialization and preparation for racism, they reject those opportunities—they consider these solutions to be the problem. "[My kids] never seemed to notice or care what race someone was, until they came home from school after Martin Luther King, Jr., Day last year. Then all of a sudden, they were talking about people's race all the time," one White parent told Jennifer Harvey, a scholar of White antiracism. "And I felt like they actually might have been better off without that celebration. Because I really don't think it's good for them to focus on people's race and put them in boxes! Isn't that the opposite of what we should be trying to do?" The delusion that talking about race puts people into boxes diminishes our ability to explain how racism puts people into unequal boxes. Caregivers cannot explain to children the mirage of race—and the realness of racism—by ignoring it and teaching children to do the same.

This parent's response shows symptoms of the fourth mode of racial socialization: *color blindness,* whereby caregivers actively "avoid any mention of race in discussions with their children." Color-blind caregivers think they can stop their kids—or themselves—from seeing race. But they are only stopping their kids from seeing racism.

Color-blind caregiving is in many ways the most dangerous form of racial socialization. How can a society ever abolish racism if caregivers deny its existence and indoctrinate their kids into denying its existence? If we pretend that race—and therefore racism—doesn't exist, how will we be able to name and quantify its effects and find ways to dismantle it? We will be in the midst of a problem that no one will be able to identify and quantify, even as the problem festers and worsens.

Color-blind caregiving is no different from Sadiqa's medical providers and me not recognizing the seriousness of her condition, worsening it, threatening her life and the life of our child. A problem undiagnosed is a problem untreated. Color-blind caregivers routinely say, "I don't see color." And like its twin, "I'm not racist," the mantra thumps to the heartbeat of racism: denial.

My parents did not often talk to me about racism or being antiracist. My parents were not alone. Around the time of my birth in 1982, only 8.2 percent of Black parents stressed "the presence of racial restrictions and blocked opportunities" to their children. When I was fourteen years old in 1997, "only a small minority" of Black parents of children between four and fourteen frequently discussed race and racism with their children. Black parents of millennials like me were much more likely to stress the importance of hard work (22.2 percent) or emphasize racial pride in being Black (17.2 percent). By 2008, only a sixth of Black middle-class mothers of children between the ages of three and six taught their children about racism.

Yes, the main reason why parents don't teach about racism is that when those parents were kids their parents didn't teach them about racism. But are parents also more inclined to emphasize the positives of our world—and downplay the negatives? I know I am. We want our children to feel good. We want our children to dream and imagine and believe they have the freedom to shape their lives. We don't want them to worry and feel distress about the structural forces inhibiting lives like theirs. If we tell them that there are racist policies holding them back or propelling them, then will they push themselves in life or become lethargic in their racial deprivation or privilege? But I started wondering, what happens to kids *if we don't* explain racism to them? What will happen to my kid?

Black kids, like me, were like kids who had to cross the street without anyone having informed us that cars might come speeding toward them. We were left exposed to racism because no one told us it was coming. And yet Black children like me were better off than kids of other races, who were even less protected. Black parents are still more likely than any other racial group to discuss race and racism with their kids. Black parents (61 percent), Asian parents (56 percent), and Latinx parents (46 percent) "often or sometimes" talk to their kids about racism. White parents (26 percent) are the least likely to engage their kids about racism. White parents are the most likely to engage in color-blind socialization. In a survey of more than two thousand adults in 2020 in Chicago, Los Angeles, New Orleans, and New York City, about two-thirds of White respondents said their parents "never" or "rarely" facilitated "conversations with them about racism when they were children."

This ignoring of racism by color-blind socializers has echoes in the era of slavery. Everyone laments American slavery now, but if you were a White child being raised around the violently racist institution, how were you socialized to understand it? Then, as now, it was through the racial fairy tales you were told by the adults around you. One such story was *Little Eva,* a popular children's picture book published around 1853.

The story's protagonist, Little Eva, is an eight-year-old White girl from Alabama, "the only daughter of a wealthy planter, who owned many slaves." Little Eva and the enslaved people on her father's plantation share an idyllic existence. The enslaver's young daughter teaches the enslaved children the alphabet and Scripture. The relationship is portrayed as mutually satisfying—the enslaved children "all love Eva, and would do anything to please her," while Eva "takes a great deal of pleasure in teaching them and making them happy."

The climax of this bucolic tale arrives when an enslaved

boy named Sam—who appears to be Eva's age—saves her from drowning. At the end of the story, Eva's parents free Sam as a reward, but he "never left them, he loved them all too well." *Little Eva* encouraged a fantasy: that Black people enjoyed their enslavement and White enslavers were benevolent toward them. This fantasy produced its own popularity, a fantasy about slavery that endures. For example, in December 2021, Republican state representative Jim Olsen introduced a bill that would prohibit Oklahoma state agencies and public school districts from teaching "that one race is the unique oppressor" during American slavery or "another race is the unique victim in the institution of slavery."

Little Eva and recent Republican laws consoled children—unlike the truth that Black people hated their enslavement and White people used brute force and torture to keep them enslaved. The truth felt bad. This fantasy felt good. But any parent who offered this pleasant fiction as truth was lying to their child, and leaving them completely unequipped to deal with the world as it actually was. Is making our children feel good in moments more important than raising them for a lifetime in the real world?

Parents give many reasons for color-blind socializing that aren't necessarily born of malice. "He has lots of Black friends," another White parent told scholar Jennifer Harvey. "I don't want him to start to treat them as being somehow different. I also don't want to say something to him about racism that he repeats to his friends in a way that hurts them." Speaking of her preschool-aged child, one White mother told psychologist Brigitte Vittrup: "She is just too young now." A Black mother expressed concern to psychologist Jill V. Hamm that if she talked about racism, her child would "form this kind of preconceived notion that I'm never gonna be treated right, and this is the way that all Black people are treated. And I don't think that's right." An Asian father informed researchers: "As far as to be prepared for them being teased, I cannot see what I would do."

To be fair, many color-blind caregivers correctly acknowledge that race doesn't exist biologically, and for this reason they don't want to speak of it as if it does. Indeed, there's no such thing as racial biology, or Black blood, or White purity, or Asian physicality, or Native diseases, or genetically derived Black behavior. These *segregationist* ideas are "fatal inventions," as scholar Dorothy Roberts explains. While *assimilationist* racist ideas suggest that one racial group, the target for assimilation, is culturally or behaviorally superior to another racial group, the one that must assimilate, segregationist ideas suggest that a racial group is biologically or genetically distinct and superior to another. While assimilationist ideas suggest childlike Black people can be developed only if they adopt the ways of White people, segregationist ideas suggest animal-like Black people are a different species that can never be humanized.

While race doesn't exist biologically, it does exist in human society *because of racism.* As Ta-Nehisi Coates once wrote, "race is the child of racism, not the father." It is possible to teach our children that race exists as a power construct, devised to divide people and justify exploitative practices and policies—*and* that it doesn't exist as a meaningful biological reality. It is possible to impart to our children: *Skin colors are like book covers; they don't tell us what's inside the body of the book. But some people think they do. Some people think darker people have less because they don't work as hard. But that's not true. What's true is our leaders don't work hard enough at instituting rules that are fair. Our rules are the problem, not darker people.*

Race, in this sense, has shaped our society, even as it is meaningless when it comes to the common humanity of all people. The vital distinction for antiracist parents is that in order to dismantle destructive ideas about race, and the structures these ideas support, we first have to see the mirage of race. We can't see racism if we refuse to see race.

After a while, the medicine wore off. Sadiqa regained her normal breathing. She did not go into labor. A miracle.

Sadiqa was transferred out of the labor and delivery unit. They removed the bars over her body. Which is to say, Sadiqa could now sit up. But she remained in the hospital, on bed rest.

I took up residence in her hospital room. Weeks went by. Our baby remained in place. An immobility Sadiqa now desired.

At around twenty-eight weeks, when Sadiqa had been in the hospital for nearly a month, talk began about going home. A feeling of relief rose in all of us. Sadiqa's brother came to town to stay with her one night, allowing me to go home and sleep on a bed for the first time in weeks. Of course, the next morning Sadiqa's water broke.

I rushed back to the hospital. No detours this time. They gave her magnesium sulfate again. She suffered horribly again. Our baby remained in place again.

But this time, not for long. A week and a half later, I stood over Sadiqa as she squirmed in pain from contractions and squeezed my hands tighter than ever. I admired her courage. Sadiqa had been on bed rest for nearly five and a half weeks, a herculean, life-giving effort. Delivering a baby at twenty-nine and a half weeks compared with twenty-four weeks can be the difference between life and death.

As daylight faded from the window, a no-nonsense attending physician stormed into the room. It was my first time seeing her, all seriousness and poise. Her conviction and confidence, in a moment of uncertainty, settled Sadiqa, settled us all. She stood over Sadiqa and uttered, "It's time."

CHAPTER 2

Newborn Nature

Sadiqa had grimaced in intense pain from her C-section. But as I rolled her into the neonatal intensive care unit, or NICU, a bright smile stretched across her face. Moments later, she smiled even brighter as she held our baby for the first time.

"She likes Mommy," I said softly as Sadiqa cradled our newborn daughter.

"Hey, baby," she said. Their faces were as close as they could be without touching.

Hospital-gowned but looking regal, Sadiqa turned to the camera I was holding. I asked her if she wanted to say something.

"I'm just happy she's okay."

Sadiqa glanced back down at our baby who, the nurses told us, had been pulling out her tubes. "Such a cute and feisty little peanut," Sadiqa said.

The word stuck. *Peanut* became Sadiqa's nickname for our little caramel one.

After weeks of anguish, Sadiqa probably had never been happier than in this moment, giving her Peanut "kangaroo care," which is holding an infant skin-to-skin on one's chest. We had learned about the benefits of kangaroo care for our preemie: stabilizing heart and breathing rates, improving oxygen saturation rates, regulating body temperature, and conserving calories.

We named our baby girl *Imani,* meaning "faith" in Swahili, an East African language. We had chosen the name before Sadiqa dilated at twenty-four weeks. Imani held on for five weeks. She overcame the odds. She will always inspire me to overcome the odds and keep the faith, including my faith in our power to nurture our children to be antiracist. Being racist is not our unchangeable nature; it is not our inevitable destiny.

It was nearly noon on April 26, 2016. Imani, not even a day old. She sneezed. We jumped. We eased.

"You going to hold her, too?" Sadiqa asked me, looking up.

"You think I should?"

"Yeah."

"I'm going to have to take off my shirt," I said, serious about kangaroo care.

"Yeah, the ladies in here will enjoy it," Sadiqa said, amused.

I smiled. As Sadiqa looked back down at Imani, I frowned, scared.

I'd never contemplated holding anyone so precious, so fragile, so . . . small. Three pounds, two ounces, Imani was smaller than a football. I was afraid I might break her. Sadiqa and Imani had endured so much together to arrive at this moment. I trusted Imani in Sadiqa's arms more than my own.

.   .   .

On April 12, 2016, two weeks before Imani's birth, my second book, *Stamped from the Beginning*, was born. From my research on the history of racist ideas, I had tried to construct fresh language adults could use to describe its effects on our world. But at that point, I did not have the language for children at different ages. Imani had not arrived yet, but my thinking about sharing with her what I learned about race had already frozen me. I did not know what to say, how to say it, when to say it. I did not want to say the wrong thing at the wrong time in the wrong way. Without consciously articulating it to myself, I'd already decided: I would say nothing. Like many caregivers, I simply stumbled into color-blind socializing.

Even though I didn't strive to be an antiracist dad from the beginning, I did strive, unsuccessfully, to be a feminist dad from the beginning. I strove to share the caregiving duties. I strove to constantly empower and encourage Imani. I strove not to impose sexist views of girls and women onto Imani, while also working to smash the patriarchy in society. Indeed, most parents are more comfortable addressing gender than race with their kids, instead of addressing both and their intersection. This *intersectionality* is "a lens, a prism, for seeing the way in which various forms of inequality often operate together and exacerbate each other," explains Kimberlé Crenshaw, who coined the term.

I had fled the scariness of raising a child to be antiracist, but I did not want to flee the scariness of caregiving a newborn. Then again, I didn't know what to do. I had never held a newborn before. But my excitement to hold our baby had been growing ever since Sadiqa called me to say she was pregnant. I was out of town, I believe in New York City, in a tiny hotel room. Sadiqa's early morning call woke me up. I had to use the bathroom. I scurried to the bathroom, where I heard the news. I couldn't tell whether I was dreaming or not when I got off the phone and got back in the bed. When the excitement stopped me from returning to sleep, I knew it was real.

Now our baby was here, before me, not even one day old. I sat down. Locs tied back. Blue jeans and a V-neck gray T-shirt on me. Sadiqa cradled Imani and stood above me. I did not take off my shirt. Instead, I pulled and stretched out the V-neck to do kangaroo care. Sadiqa placed our newborn inside my shirt, on my chest. My body stiffened.

"Loosen up," Sadiqa admonished.

I took deep breaths. Told myself if my body was stiff, Imani would not be comfortable on my chest. That did the trick. As I relaxed, Imani relaxed onto me. Her head poked out of my shirt, inches from my lips as I tilted my head in adoration. A beige cover blanketed her for extra warmth. But nothing in that moment was warmer than my heart.

Her eyes stayed closed. She wasn't sleeping.

"Hey, Imani," I whispered.

I listened, not expecting a reply.

But then she cooed back at me! Quickly, ever so quietly amid the loud and long hum of NICU machines. Only I heard the coo. I translated the adorable sound.

"Hey, Daddy" is what I heard.

The coo is the first milestone in human communication. Imani's first coo came ten weeks before she was supposed to be born. Typically, babies coo about eight weeks after their full-term births. Which is to say Imani cooed eighteen weeks earlier than most babies. It didn't mean anything. But as caregivers, if we are being honest, we are always on the hunt for early signs of advanced skills. Was I seeing a sign that our baby had been born with advanced communication skills?

I wanted to believe it. After all, her doctor mom communicates complex ailments to pediatric patients and their caregivers during emergencies. Her professorial daddy communicates the complexities of history, racism, and being antiracist to students, scholars, the general public, and their policymakers. I wanted to believe our communication skills rested in our genetic code and we passed them on. I wanted to believe that her talents were in her blood. Inherent.

I did not want to believe that we birthed Imani into an unusually privileged situation in a deeply unequal society—that even the fact of her survival owed not just to her mother's resilience and our family's support but to our access to care and enough status and information to insist on it. Why would I prefer *not* to see those privileges—or the flip side of them, the deprivations that other people in our situation would face? That's rather normal, especially for caregivers of young children. But to raise an antiracist is to recognize the child's racial privileges (and deprivations), which are intersectional and subject to change over time. Though she'll face racism and sexism, Imani likely won't face their intersection with poverty. She likely won't face the deprivation of hunger or homelessness or incarcerated parents and grow up in densely impoverished and exploited neighborhoods, and attend overcrowded, overpoliced, and under-resourced schools with overworked teachers, like disproportionate numbers of Black kids. As a Black girl, she likely won't escape the deprivation of being hypersexualized, being deemed angry, and being overly scrutinized. She won't wield the presumed innocence of a White girl—a racialized privilege that creates its own harmful distortions. She won't have a lifetime of other White privileges, like appearing unthreatening even when armed. She won't be born into the sorts of White privileges that lead to longer life spans for White people in the United States. But since her parents are a doctor and a professor, she'll have the economic privileges of resources and opportunities that newborns of all races born into low-income households won't have. And perhaps, *because of all of us,* by the time she is an adult, she'll be able to escape the deprivations assigned at birth to Black people, and Black girls specifically. That can only happen if we manage to free the world from the domineering structures of racism and sexism, and from other forms of bigotry.

Children inherit the privileges and deprivations of their parents and other caregivers. But how many caregivers engage in color-blind socialization and refuse to recognize these racial privileges and deprivations? Take literacy for example: How many privileged caregivers want to believe their child's extensive vocabulary is hereditary—not the result of an extensive (and expensive) home or school library? But on the other hand, how often are deprived caregivers told to ignore the decisive role the lack of opportunities and resources plays in their child's plight? How many privileged caregivers want to believe their child is special—not that she has special privileges? How many deprived caregivers are led to believe their child is especially problematic—not that he is especially deprived? Of course, some children don't take advantage of their privileges, and some overcome their deprivations—but for the color-blind caregivers these are not exceptions to the rule but the rule itself. For the color-blind ideal to be true it requires us to erase the impact of all preexisting privilege, in part because caregivers need to justify their children's abilities as being the pure fruit of their inherent talents. It is not enough for them to say my child is special *like* every other child. Instead, caregivers want to believe their child is special *in relation to* every other child.

And even on my first day of parenting, I wanted to believe that, too. My denial had me thinking that Sadiqa and I had made a naturally gifted child. We supplied the genetic gifts. Isn't that what the online articles told me? One article listed five things "to know about the DNA you pass on to your children." The five: appearance, medical history, intelligence, talkativeness, and "special talents." Without linking to any evidence, the article stated "sixty percent of our ability to learn comes from our parents." This shouldn't come as a surprise. *Talent* and *aptitude* are defined today as "natural" in most dictionaries.

That coo from Imani did not mean I'd passed on advanced communication skills to her through my genes. But American parental culture had passed on to me one of the most horrific ideas in modern history.

The cousin of biologist Charles Darwin was an English polymath named Francis Galton. Like intellectuals throughout the Western world in the late nineteenth century, Galton received intellectual direction from his cousin's *On the Origin of Species,* published in 1859. Known as the father of modern statistics, Galton pioneered methods to study whether variation in human skills is hereditary—or not. Nature or nurture? He argued nature.

Galton considered the linchpin skill to be intelligence. For his 1869 book, *Hereditary Genius,* Galton contended human eminence came from the inheritance of intelligence. This inheritance of intelligence extended from eminent individuals to eminent classes, nations, genders, and races. "The average intellectual standard of the negro race is some two grades below our own," Galton wrote. According to Galton's logic, European elites had more wealth than poor Europeans and the peoples of the Global South, not because of colonialism and enslavement and the industrial emergence of racial capitalism, not because of the power and capital accumulated (and reinvested) and bequeathed and inherited over the centuries from land stealing, body stealing, and labor stealing abroad and at home—but because European elites were superior.

Galton argued that parents passed traits on to their children and warned that the lower "stock" of people were having more children than the higher "stock." He pushed for policies that reversed this trend. In 1883, Galton called his intellectual and political movement *eugenics,* from a Greek root word meaning "good in birth."

Yesterday's eugenicists are some of today's geneticists, like James Watson, who won the Nobel Prize in 1962 for outlining the double helix structure of DNA. In 2007, Watson told a British reporter with *The Sunday Times* that "all our social policies are based on the fact that African intelligence is the same as ours, whereas all the testing says not really." Days later, in a statement to the Associated Press, Watson backtracked: "There is no scientific basis for such a belief." However, when asked for a PBS documentary in 2019 if his views on race and intelligence and genetics had changed, Watson responded, "There would [have to be] new knowledge, which says that your nurture is much more important than nature. But I haven't seen any knowledge."

If he hadn't seen any, it was because he had no interest in looking. New knowledge has already disproved that IQ scores are a reliable measure of intelligence. New knowledge has disproved the long-standing idea of genetic distinctions between races. Geneticists have found more genetic variation *within* Africa than between the continental African people and the rest of the world. Scientists the world over have yet to establish a causal link between genetics and race *or* genetics and IQ scores, let alone genetics and IQ scores and race, let alone standardized tests and intelligence.

Even so, researchers keep trying. They've been trying in the United States for more than a century. A Harvard-trained biologist at the University of Chicago named Charles Davenport ushered Galton's eugenics into the United States. In 1904, Davenport became director of the Cold Spring Harbor Laboratory, which reigns today as one of the leading basic science research institutions in the world. Interestingly, after airing his racist ideas, James Watson was removed as chancellor of this very Cold Spring Harbor Laboratory in 2007. After the PBS documentary aired, the laboratory's president and the chair of the board of trustees stated: "The Laboratory condemns the misuse of science to justify prejudice."

From his perch directing the laboratory and the Eugenics Record Office he established there in 1910, Charles Davenport misused science for decades to justify prejudice. At the time, White Anglo-Saxon elites in the United States feared that Black and Jewish Americans, immigrants from Asia and southern and eastern Europe, and members of the working class, especially working women, were poisoning the purity of American "civilization." Among the most horrific outgrowths of the eugenics movement was the genocide in the 1930s and 1940s of millions of European Jews and other so-called "undesirables" by Nazis inspired by American eugenicists.

Positive eugenics encouraged the breeding of the supposedly superior groups. *Negative* eugenics discouraged the breeding of the purportedly inferior groups. Eugenicists now cast the best "breeders" as wealthy, White, able-bodied, Anglo-Saxon women. "Eugenics is the science of the improvement of the human race by better breeding," Davenport stated in his 1911 movement manifesto, *Heredity in Relation to Eugenics*. Granddaughters of the formerly prized breeders—the Black women who had been forced to grow the enslaved populations (and American wealth) from 1619 to 1865—were now discouraged and sometimes prevented from having children, along with Native and Asian and Latinx women, low-income women, non-Christian women, and any woman who had or was perceived as having a disability. Eugenicists pushed federal immigration restrictions, state laws prohibiting interracial marriage, segregationist policies, and sterilization laws in more than thirty states. "Sterilization protects future generations, while segregation safeguards the present as well," wrote Chicago municipal judge Harry Olson in the preface to *Eugenical Sterilization in the United States* (1922), authored by Eugenics Research Association secretary Harry Laughlin.

The nation's first adoption agencies opened between 1910 and 1930 in the crucible of eugenics in the United States. Adoption agencies replaced orphanages, and prospective parents contacted these new adoption agencies seeking children of what they believed to be superior racial, ethnic, religious, and national "stock." "Not babies merely, but better babies, are wanted," said Henry Dwight Chapin, a pediatrician and the husband of Alice Chapin, an early adoption agency founder. Meanwhile, Better Baby contests, first introduced in Louisiana in 1908, spread throughout the United States. These contests often took place at agricultural fairs, with biological parents showing off their White children, who were scrutinized like livestock.

After all these years, biological parents are still engaging in their own private better baby contests. Many biological parents still believe that they pass on good and bad traits to their offspring—the foundational idea of eugenics. There's still a widely held belief that there's such a thing as isolated *behavior genes* that biological parents pass on to their offspring: a smart gene, a violence gene, a funny gene, or in Imani's case, an expressive gene. Geneticists have spent decades and untold amounts of time and money searching for a genetic basis for specific behaviors. They speculate that intelligence correlates to over five hundred genes; that aggression is tied to forty genes; that spoken language is related to several genes, and in "rare" cases, involves mutations of genes; that sexual orientation is influenced by "many" genes. But geneticists also often caution that these vast assemblages of genes are typically only partly responsible for particular traits and behaviors. No race has more or less of these purported assemblages of genes. Geneticists today have yet to scientifically prove that a smart or violent or hardworking or humorous parent will have a smart or violent or hardworking or humorous child—let alone that there are smart or unwise races. Instead, modern geneticists—whose field has historically done more than any other to assert the biological basis of behavior—often point us to environmental explanations for inequities between groups and often between individuals. But the common belief persists that specific behaviors are inherent—and even for those of us who know better. The reflex to attribute positive behaviors in our children to their genetic inheritance, in other words, to us, as their parents, is hard to resist. It was hard for me to resist.

This all left me thinking: How can I raise an antiracist child if a eugenicist idea raised me as a parent? To be fair, when I wondered if I passed on an expressive gene to my newborn, I did not wonder if Black parents and thereby Black children were genetically superior. I did not make that racist leap to eugenics. My eugenics was more personalized than grouped. But personalized ideas—*my baby is genetically gifted*—are the conceptual pathway to group eugenics—*my racial group is genetically gifted and should be encouraged to reproduce.*

Caregivers: Let's be honest. We know how we are. Once we start thinking a kid is naturally talented in some way, we perceive what we didn't before. If we think a child is inherently smarter than other children, we start to see signs of it everywhere, from their coos to their finger paintings. We become convinced. For many privileged caregivers, if the child excels, then it's due to the natural talent she inherited, not the unnatural privileges she inherited. For many deprived parents, if she falters, then she is to blame, not the unnatural deprivations she inherited. If privileged and deprived parents believe that their kids are better or worse by nature, then they are bound to impart these ideas to those same kids. That makes those kids vulnerable to racist ideas of inherent superiority.

Don't get me wrong: I think every parent and teacher should think their child is a genius *in her own way*. We should imagine our child can one day become a head of state, or lead NASA, or cure a disease, or lead the revolution. Every parent and teacher should think their child is gifted and beautiful. Beauty and giftedness are considered relative and relational. But they don't have to be for our kids. We can convey to our child that she is beautiful in her own right—not in comparison with other children. We can convey to our child that he has gifts—because every human being has gifts for the world if only the world is fortunate enough to open them. I think parents and teachers should admire every inventive, creative, intelligent, kind, and incredible thing that their kid does. But that doesn't mean caregivers have to *express* admiration to the child for every single thing (or tell them they are better than other children). We don't want the child to view our admiration of them as conditional, as transactional—*as coming only when they do something good.* We want them to know we value them no matter what. Simply by virtue of being human and in community with other humans, they are of immeasurable intrinsic value. They matter because they matter. Not because other people don't matter. Every child on earth should feel this way. Every caregiver on earth should be making their child feel this way. Feel loved. Cared for. Valued always.

At the end of the day, we don't really know what genes and biology contribute to what we think of as intelligence or talent. But we do know it's not a useful way to approach parenting and teaching. We do know that it is, in fact, destructive.

Like thinking being racist is inherited. Some, though certainly not all, implicit bias scholars argue that "bias" is biological: in our human nature. Some psychologists who study implicit social cognition have challenged the "assumption that implicit intergroup cognition emerges through the slow-learning of environmental regularities," and hypothesized that implicit bias is derived from an innate "evaluative or attitudinal system" that is "fundamental to an organism's survival."

History does not verify that *racial* bias is human nature. Baby studies don't verify natural racial bias. As I held one-day-old Imani, she had no conception of race nor its father, racism; nor its mother, power. For newborns, the colors on skins are as meaningless as the colors of clothing covering skins. Newborns demonstrate "no spontaneous preference for faces from either their own or other [race] groups," according to a team of psychologists. Racial "bias" is not rooted in nature. Racial "bias" is rooted in racist ideas. Racist ideas and constructions of color-coded *races* did not begin to emerge until the fifteenth century, when the Portuguese began justifying the racist policies behind the transatlantic slave-trading of African peoples. As Nelson Mandela once stated, "No one is born hating another person because of the color of his skin, or his background, or his religion. People must learn to hate, and if they can learn to hate, they can be taught to love, for love comes more naturally to the human heart than its opposite."

I love Mandela's quote. But I'm not sure love in this sense comes more naturally to the human mind than hate. Babies seem to have no conception of love or hate. They learn to love or hate themselves, their racial groups, or other racial groups from their caregivers and the environment they are raised in.

In those early days in the NICU, we were overly worried about Imani's protection. I came to learn that in NICUs, machines and nurses monitor the immature bodies of preemies for As, Bs, and Ds. A is for apnea: when a preemie stops breathing. B is for bradycardia: when a preemie's heart rate decreases. D is for desaturation: when a preemie's oxygen level drops. As, Bs, and Ds can all be deadly.

After seven weeks in the NICU, Imani continued to have Bs and Ds. But they occurred less and less frequently, and then rarely, which intensified our lobbying for Imani to come home. We longed to leave the hospital with her. It was a longing two months in the making. Adding Sadiqa's month of bed rest, it was a longing three months in the making. It felt like we had been wandering as a family. We wanted home.

A NICU doctor told us if Imani went three straight days without an apnea, bradycardia, or desaturation, then she could go home with a monitoring machine.

Wednesday, Thursday, and Friday went by. No A, B, or D! But on Saturday, June 18, 2016, our hopes of going home crashed.

CHAPTER 3

Baby Nurture

A new attending doctor came on call in the NICU. When he refused to follow the discharge plan of his predecessor, Sadiqa transfigured into the *real* Dr. Kendi. She called the doctor and challenged his decision, but he wouldn't budge on letting Imani go home.

It wasn't malpractice. It was mistrust. Dr. Kendi took it personally. Her Yale medical degree, residency in New York City, fellowship at Children's Hospital of Philadelphia, one of the nation's top children's hospitals. Her years of experience. Her ER work resuscitating pediatric patients at *that* very hospital. And still. She had been distrusted as a pregnant patient and now as a mother and a pediatrician. Would he have trusted a White pediatric ER physician to take his baby home?

Maybe there's no one he would have trusted that Father's Day weekend of 2016. But we couldn't help thinking: *Is it us?* That enduring question nagging at Black people. Is it me? I don't know. What I do know: To be a Black parent in America is to be distrusted. From nature to nurture. America neglects us and calls us neglectful. Our credentials and love don't matter.

Though celebrated in the NICU, my first Father's Day lifted our spirits in 2016. Sadiqa clothed Imani in a pink onesie decorated with the words "Happy 1st Father's Day. I love you." But Imani gave me the sweetest gift when I did kangaroo care: She smiled in her sleep, and she kept smiling, lying on my chest, in my arms. I asked Sadiqa to freeze the moment in time with a picture.

When Sadiqa and I came back to the hospital the next day, we were prepared to wait more days, after having waited for months. At nearly 9 A.M., the time Imani normally fed, we were standing over her crib when a NICU nurse came by.

"We have great news," she said. "They're okay with your baby being discharged."

"Wait, what?" Sadiqa responded.

"She can go home today," the nurse said matter-of-factly, wholly unaware of our emotional roller coaster, or hardly caring. Indeed, from Sadiqa's discharge to Imani's discharge, we'd felt neglected. Things happened to us, not with us. But at this point, we stopped caring about the neglect. We just wanted to leave.

"That's great news," I responded in a snarky tone Sadiqa knew.

"Yeah, so great," Sadiqa said, looking at me and smirking.

When the nurse left, our anger and shock left with her. Sadiqa lifted Imani out of the crib. We embraced as a family. That is, until Imani let us know it was time for her to eat. Now.

.　　.　　.

Our house became a home on June 20, 2016. We were fortunate enough to have an extra bedroom for Imani. We bought her a rich dark brown crib that we could eventually break down into a toddler's bed. We secured a matching dresser with a table on top for changing her clothes and diapers. We brought in a bright-red sofa where we planned to feed and read to her. We positioned family photos and hung African-print curtains to ensure the room captured the light of her ancestry. Her closet filled up with blankets people had made for her, tiny clothes her grandmothers picked up, and a war chest of diapers.

Getting the baby's room together was only the beginning. Dr. Kendi is a passionate and astute medical researcher in the field of pediatric injury prevention. Unintentional injuries—not the flu or gun violence—are the number one cause of death in children, from drownings to window falls to poisonings to motor vehicle crashes. It gnaws at her that societal caregivers accept all these injuries, all this death, as normal, when waging a war against childhood injury, through changes in policy, education, our built environment, and the affordability and accessibility of safety products could dramatically reduce the number of children dying from unintentional injuries. Those kinds of changes have already done wonders in other countries, like Sweden. If policy is our love language, as Congresswoman Ayanna Pressley tells us it should be, then the Swedes love their children. Do Americans?

Dr. Kendi does. She's on a mission to childproof communities and nations. And before Imani came home in June 2016, Sadiqa brought that mission home. She went around installing covers on electrical outlets. She instructed me to put covers on the oven knobs, locks on all the cabinets, and protectors on the sharp corners of tables. To prevent drowning, we fenced in our pool. Sadiqa and her younger brother Cha worked together on installing the fence, racing to get their portions done first. Sadiqa won. She hates to lose.

For poison control, Sadiqa had me putting our medicines and cleaning supplies out of reach and view of Imani, which is as important as locking away guns and storing bullets separately. In Imani's room, I attached pieces of furniture to walls to ensure they would not tip over onto her. And Sadiqa tutored all Imani's potential caregivers—from her grandparents to her uncles to me—on CPR and reminded us to never leave buckets of water sitting around the house or to put anything in Imani's crib with her as she slept. No pillow. No blanket or bedsheet covering her. No stuffed animals. Not even crib bumpers. Just Imani, swaddled on her back on top of a sheet firmly tucked under the mattress. Sadiqa said having things in the crib increased the likelihood of SIDS (sudden infant death syndrome), or as it's being called now, SUID (sudden unexpected infant death).

We knew that childproofing a house prevents unintentional injuries. But we didn't yet know that preventing racial injury requires childproofing our environment, too.

In 1954, psychologist Gordon Allport released his very influential book, *The Nature of Prejudice*. Allport maintained that parental influence is *the* major element in a child's "socialization." But recent research has scaled back the socializing influence of parents and even teachers. Sociologists Debra Van Ausdale and Joe R. Feagin dismissed the popular belief that children are "empty vessels into which adults put their own ideas, concepts, and attitudes." Children actively apply specific racial knowledge to their own environments.

Psychologist Beverly Daniel Tatum describes a racist environment as the "smog" our children breathe. "If we live in a smoggy place, how can we avoid breathing the air?" she asks. Sadiqa and I went about creating a safe physical environment for Imani. But we did not go about creating a safe *racial* environment for Imani. Why not? Did we assume she'd naturally grow to be antiracist? Did we believe in nature over nurture? I should not say *we*. I should say *I*. Dr. Kendi deployed her research expertise to shield Imani as much as possible from unintentional injuries—but I didn't deploy my research expertise to protect our baby as much as possible from being injured by racism. I had published a book about the power of racist ideas, but somehow still underestimated the power of racist ideas on my own child.

Imani was nearly two months old when we brought her home (if we're not correcting her age as a preemie). By three months of age, the face-processing skills of babies "are starting to become proficient," according to developmental neurocognition experts Sandy Sangrigoli and Scania de Schonen. In a study of White infants in Israel and Black infants in Israel and Ethiopia, another group of researchers found "preference for own-race faces is present as early as 3 months of age." Meaning three-month-olds can distinguish between own-race and other-race faces of adults.

Researchers seemingly considered "own-race face" to be when, let's say, a baby of African descent recognizes another person of African descent as having a face similar to their own. But there are people of African descent who identify as "Black" who may not be racialized as Black by the general public. It doesn't appear that researchers showed babies multiracial or "racially ambiguous" faces in these studies. It appears researchers showed babies racially unambiguous faces that are generally identified with a particular race. And researchers found that infants tend to show a partiality for their own "race faces." All of which is to say: At birth, babies don't see color, but as early as three months, some babies do. And some babies are partial to their own color.

This partiality isn't fixed in nature. It is nurture-dependent, or "experience-dependent." Partiality for their own-race faces is greatest among infants who live in "predominantly homogenous own-race environments," according to psychologists at Tel Aviv University and a physician based in Ethiopia. White babies are the most likely to live in predominantly homogeneous own-race environments in the United States. A team of psychologists in the United States, the United Kingdom, and China found that three-month-old White infants demonstrate "significant preference for faces from their own-[race] group." But this preference can be quickly reversed.

Experts in developmental neurocognition assembled three-month-old White infants who had no regular contact with Asian people. At first, the White babies were able to recognize an individual White face but not an individual Asian face. In a second experiment, after several different Asian faces were presented, the White infants were able to recognize an individual Asian face. Which makes sense. If babies are exposed to different faces, whether living, in photographs, in books, or on screens, then they can come to know the beautiful rainbow of human faces. But in the United States, how many infants are regularly exposed to the human rainbow?

Between three and six months of age, babies rapidly increase their face-processing skills—and apparently their race-processing skills. By six months of age, due to their socialization, infants typically "have preverbal concepts of both gender and race," according to social-developmental psychologist Phyllis A. Katz. By nine months of age, infants are clearly identifying racial groups. Infants at this age can categorize own-race faces, but are less able to distinguish between faces of other racial groups. Predominantly homogeneous racial environments and the smog of racist ideas are the main culprits. Diversified racial environments and the clarity of antiracist ideas are the main solutions.

Psychologist Linda Tropp examined 515 studies in thirty-eight countries over six decades and found "approximately ninety-four percent of cases in our analysis show a relationship such that greater contact is associated with lower prejudice," because it "reduces our anxiety in relation to other groups and enhances our ability to empathize with other groups." It may strike a lot of Americans as counterintuitive, but raising our children in predominantly homogeneous environments endangers them.

In 1900, the majority of Black Americans lived in the rural South, while the majority of White Americans lived in the urban North. Black people started migrating out of rural counties to western and northern cities during the Great Migration that lasted until 1970. The public and private sectors hardly helped migrants find homes. Quite the opposite. Starting in the 1930s, the federal government and the private sector colored neighborhoods with Black residents, even middle-class neighborhoods, in stop-sign red on city maps. The red lines were for mortgage lenders, mythologizing that Black neighborhoods were risky investments, which in turn justified conventional loans not being offered to Black residents in redlined neighborhoods, which led to lower homeownership, depressed wealth, and predatory lending.

Meanwhile, the people already living in the north and west depicted Black migrants as "invaders," much as many border-state residents today frame Latinx immigrants as "invaders." Back then, these residents attempted to block this Black "invasion" through erecting the border walls of restrictive covenants, homeowner associations, and segregationist policies for suburban developments. Opponents of desegregated neighborhoods and schools imagined they were protecting "their sweet little girls" from being "required to sit in schools alongside some big black buck," as President Dwight D. Eisenhower quipped to a Supreme Court justice before the *Brown* case in 1954.

All this housing and educational racism over the years resulted in Americans, especially White Americans, living in relatively homogeneous neighborhoods. From 2014 to 2018 in the hundred largest metropolitan areas, the neighborhood of the average Black resident was 45 percent Black; the neighborhood of the typical Latinx resident was 47 percent Latinx. By comparison, the neighborhood of the average White resident was 71 percent White. In the smaller metropolitan areas, the neighborhood of the average White resident was 79 percent White. Outside of metropolitan areas, the average rural White resident lived in a neighborhood that was *85 percent White*. No wonder a recent poll found that 21 percent of White Americans "seldom or never" interact with any people of color. As policy expert Heather McGhee writes, "White people are the most segregated people in America."

Today, White Americans remain the most resistant to integration. They are striving to maintain their segregation through gated communities, private schools, restricted use areas, border walls, and corrupt politicians pledging to make America "great" again. Rages of "White flight" are especially high among middle-income White residents fleeing Latinx and Asian neighbors with similar incomes. During his 2020 reelection campaign, Donald Trump discontinued an Obama-era program designed to desegregate America's suburbs.

"People living their Suburban Lifestyle Dream" should "no longer be bothered or financially hurt by having low-income housing built in your neighborhood," he tweeted. "It's been hell for suburbia." The implication: Integration is hell for White people. On the campaign trail in 2016, Trump repeatedly said, "African Americans are living in hell in the inner cities." White people should be afraid, was the message: Hell was migrating to their communities.

Trump kept evoking this Black hell because he knew many White voters feared it. Despite White people saying they prefer to live in a neighborhood that is about 47 percent White, when they look for a new home, they typically search in neighborhoods that are 68 percent White, and end up in neighborhoods that are 74 percent White. When researchers show videos of neighborhoods where everything is the same except their racial composition, White viewers rate the racially mixed and Black neighborhoods as less desirable than White neighborhoods.

White children live in slightly Whiter neighborhoods than White adults, sociologist Ann Owens discovered in a study of a hundred metropolitan areas. White parents tend to believe that "a good school is in a good neighborhood, and a good neighborhood is a wealthier and whiter neighborhood."

The racist myth: the Whiter the space, the better for the White child. The reality: the Whiter the space, the worse for the White child. This is not hyperbole. When shown photos of people doing things like stealing money, not sharing toys, cheating on a test, and pushing someone off a swing, White seven- and ten-year-olds attending predominantly White schools rate Black perpetrators more harshly when compared with White children attending diverse schools. Test scores aren't lower for White students in racially diverse schools. In fact, researchers have found that White students in diverse schools score higher on standardized tests than their counterparts in predominantly White schools. But even so, test scores aren't the measure of our children or the skills they need. Psychologists, economists, and neuroscientists tell us that standardized tests don't capture the most important skills children should be learning in the twenty-first century. These skills—critical thinking, problem-solving, communication, cross-cultural collaboration, empathy, and, yes, antiracism— are best fostered in diverse classrooms. Graduates of diverse schools are more effective in their careers and are more likely to thrive within our multiracial, multicultural world. The mounting evidence is clear: Diverse schools make all our kids smarter.

Racial segregation is typically framed as a tragedy for people of color. It is a tragedy for White people, too. White caregivers might think that living in predominantly White neighborhoods is only natural or even beneficial to their children. But that is a myth. The truth is, segregated environments are harmful to their babies. Caregivers of color are more likely to strive to protect their babies from White racism. But who is going to protect White babies from White racism?

I was not thinking about childproofing the racial environment when we brought Imani home. We were thinking about how to keep our newborn baby alive, fed, clean, comforted, and occasionally entertained.

After three months away from work, Sadiqa returned to her job a week after Imani came home. She had no paid maternity leave. Unlike other wealthy nations, the United States had zero weeks of federally guaranteed paid maternity leave in 2016. Only 16 percent of private U.S. employees have access to paid maternity leave. The societal neglect of mothers like Sadiqa begins during pregnancy and extends after birth.

With Sadiqa back at work, I primarily took care of Imani, with help from Imani's grandparents. And I also had to take care of my anxiousness. Not over the routine tasks. I found a gas mask and gloves and hazmat suit and scented candles for changing diapers. (In all seriousness, I did find a scented trash can that worked wonders.) We fed Imani every three hours, which was impossible to forget because she sounded off like an alarm clock when it was time. Rocking her to sleep was my specialty. I'd hold her over my heart, sway to my heartbeat, and sometimes strike a melody. When I did sway or sing to her liking, she'd smile—and sometimes coo.

But anxiety dominated it all. Imani was so small, so precious. I did not want to harm her. When one time I strapped her diaper on too tight and slightly scratched her, I beat myself up. I had no problem when Imani's other caregivers made mistakes, but I didn't give myself that grace. Whenever I picked her up out of her crib to feed her, to change her, to rock her, or to hang out with her during those early weeks, my body still stiffened. I relaxed only when I told myself, "She'll feel more relaxed if I relax." Over and over, I repeated it; aloud when alone, in my head when in company.

I worried over Imani's physical health but ignored her racial health. I didn't give a second thought to the diversity of the faces she was seeing. My body never stiffened to stop me from dropping her into a predominantly homogeneous racial environment.

There's no hard or fast or exact rule on how diverse our neighborhoods or schools should be to protect our children. White people were on to something when they commonly told a researcher they prefer a neighborhood about 47 percent White. But I don't think White people should be the largest racial group in *all* integrated neighborhoods or schools (or institutions). Always being in the minority is unattractive to many people of color. All groups should be able to build or maintain integrated neighborhoods, institutions, and spaces where they are the largest group, where their group is not starved of power and resources, where their cultures can flourish, where their babies are immersed in their cultures, and where other groups are welcome, respected, and comprise a significant minority.

I yearn to return to those moments when Sadiqa and I started thinking about having a child. I would have started childproofing early by supporting policies that can lead to integrated and antiracist schools and neighborhoods. But it's never too late to start childproofing environments for our newborns, our kids, our teenagers. There are so many policy outcomes familial and societal caregivers can pursue in our local communities that can power integration and antiracism. Policy outcomes that create more affordable housing in middle- and upper-income neighborhoods. Ensure equitable access to federal housing programs. Expand tenants' rights to prevent evictions. Provide legal resources to challenge those evictions. Invest in local job creation programs, basic income programs, and employee-owned companies. Radically change public funding policies so schools and institutions with the greatest needs receive the most funding. Provide reparations and alternatives to prison and police. Appropriately value homes owned by people of color to ensure equity in wealth, schools, and infrastructure.

But, as important as living in racially diverse neighborhoods and schools, childproofing the total environment also includes regulating the media our newborns consume. We limited Imani's television consumption, having learned that watching TV before eighteen months can have lasting effects on her language development, reading skills, and short-term memory. Rather than staring at screens, Imani stared at board books like Innosanto Nagara's *A is for Activist*, Loryn Brantz's *Feminist Baby*, and *Homemade Love* by bell hooks. When she graduated to picture books years later, we picked Brenda J. Child's *Bowwow Powwow*, Cleo Wade's *What the Road Said*, Minh Lê's *Drawn Together*, Andrea Wing's *Watercress*, and *The Bench* by Meghan, the Duchess of Sussex. Childproofing is certifying our babies' personal libraries have books that reflect the full range of humanity and inspire antiracist action. But we still have to be intentional about the way we share these books with our children. We can't lose the opportunity to expose our child to different faces. When Black and White parents of young children read a picture book with Black and White characters, the parents often channel their child's attention to the characters of their own race. This behavior is "most pronounced" in parents of White boys.

Childproofing the books we read to our kids can be done rather quickly. Childproofing our circle of friends, by ensuring that our kids can see diversity, is a lifelong process. Suddenly seeking out friends of other races *because they are of other races* likely won't result in genuine interracial friendships. White Americans are less likely than Black, Asian, Latinx, or multiracial Americans to have interracial friendships. Asian, Latinx, and multiracial individuals are more likely than White and Black individuals to have interracial friendships. But Black people are still twice as likely as White people to have interracial friendships.

The truth is interracial friendships and relationships are not common among people of any racial group. Caregivers send a message to their children when nearly all the people with whom they regularly interact as a family or who regularly come to their homes—are White. This is a nonverbal message of who's valued, and who's not.

Childproofing our nonverbal behaviors is as important as locking up harmful weapons. Children are more influenced by *perceptions* of their parents' racial beliefs than their parents' *stated* beliefs. It is likely the same for teachers. This is, perhaps, what happens when parents and teachers fail to talk directly to their kids about what we think and believe about race. Because even when we fail to communicate verbally, we're always speaking to our kids in nonverbal ways. We are conveying racist ideas to our babies when they see us avoid eye contact with Native faces, when we stand farther away from Latinx faces, when we clutch our purses and wallets when Black faces are approaching.

Childproofing our children's environments is not a one-size-fits-all proposition. There's no single blueprint. The protective measures change with the age and growth of the child. They change depending on neighborhood and school and family and the personality and needs of our individual children. And we will, as caregivers, sometimes get it wrong. We are, and always will be, imperfect. And just like we cannot always perfectly protect our children from physical risks despite our best efforts, we can leave our child exposed to racist harms without meaning to—or sometimes without even knowing it. We may not realize the danger until our kid is harmed.

I didn't realize it—until I thought Imani was harmed.

CHAPTER 4

Infant's Doll

noticed. I didn't make much of it. The daycare was closing. I walked over to Imani, took the blue-eyed White doll out of her hands, put it to the side, picked her up off the carpet, and raised her up high. She frowned. I smiled. Her frown turned to a smile.

It was summertime in 2017. Sadiqa and I had just moved to Washington, D.C., and enrolled our one-year-old in this daycare about ten minutes from our home. We lived in the Columbia Heights neighborhood, attracted by its walkability, racial diversity, and accessibility to public transit and historic Black spaces like Malcolm X Park, Sankofa bookstore, Nu-Vegan Café, and Howard University.

Imani loved that her bedroom was next to the front door and our bedroom—and within earshot of the living room. When I put her down in her crib at night, she'd lie there and wait and listen.

"Toooooo loud!" she'd shout if she could hear Sadiqa and me, or our company, talking or laughing in the living room or the bedroom. It was her way of saying, "If you are making me go to sleep, the least you can do is not let me know you're still awake."

When Sadiqa was home, sometimes I'd put Imani down and go out the front door to get a package downstairs in our building. As I opened the front door, I'd say, "Imani, I'm just going outside for a second."

"Ooo-kay!" Imani would respond. And that was all. But when one of us didn't clear it with our toddler to leave our own home, as soon as we'd open the door, she'd erupt. "Who's that! Who's that! Who's that!"

I knew to promptly answer.

"It's just me."

"Who?"

"Daddy."

"Oh. Where?"

"Downstairs."

"Why?"

Mission accomplished. As she accumulated more words, she used them to interrogate us longer, to stay up longer past her bedtime.

We *did* want Imani to remain up longer so we could spend more time with her after our long days of work. But we were consoled by knowing that the quality of time parents spend with their children is more important than the quantity of time, according to researchers.

Sadiqa and I were strict about her bedtime. No later than 7 P.M. Imani's grandparents? Not so much. The political divide between Democrats and Republicans is nothing compared to the bedtime divide between grandparents and parents. The ability of grandparents to put their grandchildren to bed on time is nil. The refusal of grandparents to say *no* to their grandchildren is total. The spoiling—the smiles of the grandparent and grandchild as they both break the rules—knows no bounds. But as much as we complained, their relationships brought us so much joy.

Perhaps the joy filled a hole within us. Sadiqa had never met her father's parents. I had never met either of my grandfathers. But aside from the parent-child relationship—and perhaps the teacher-student, the coach-player, or the pediatrician-patient relationships—is there a more generous and generative relationship than between a grandparent and a grandchild? And the relationship is not just generative to the child. Regular time spent taking care of grandkids—one study found once a week to be ideal—boosts the health, cognitive performance, and life spans of grandparents. But too much time, like a full-time parental role, can be mentally and physically harmful for grandparents. And yet between 2.5 and 3 million grandparents are filling in as full-time parents these days. Their absent adult children are often mentally ill, incarcerated, impoverished, or addicted to substances.

We valued Imani's grandparents and they understood the valuable role they played in the life of their granddaughter. All four grandparents took a nickname their first grandchild could easily pronounce and routinely shared it to inscribe their nickname on Imani's tongue. "This is Baaa-buuu!" Dad would shout when calling. "Baa-baa is here," my father-in-law would excitedly say upon greeting Imani. "Mimi loves you," my mother-in-law would tenderly say. "Bibi missed you," Ma would say again and again.

Like Sadiqa, the grandparents were happily irate when Imani uttered her first word: "Dadda!" I mean, what can I say! From her first coo to her first word, nobody in the family could tell me nothing for weeks, both times. I talked some trash to Sadiqa. Not *too* much. Didn't want a replay of Jamaica.

I still remember the first time we competed. We walked along Seven Mile Beach in Negril, Jamaica, during our first vacation together. We sat down on a beachfront bench for a drink and to eat some freshly caught red snapper. (Well, I ate the snapper. Sadiqa was a vegetarian. We're both vegans now.)

I challenged Sadiqa to a card game: speed. I beat her. Oh, and I trash-talked! And oh, she got quiet when she lost!

"Let's play again," she mumbled, looking down.

"Are you sure? I don't want to have to punish you, *again*!" I jibed.

She looked up at me, eyes fixated like I'd never seen them before.

"Let's play again."

She proceeded to beat me three times in a row, eyes like scopes on the cards, silent the whole time.

After the third time, she asked, "Anything else you have to say?"

"No," I mumbled.

"I thought so," she said. And that was that.

It was a tough decision to move to Washington, D.C., away from Imani's grandparents in Georgia and Florida. With our flexible work schedules and grandparents helping, we had not had to put Imani into daycare during her first year of life.

The day after I picked Imani up from daycare and noticed her playing with the White doll, Sadiqa picked her up and noticed, too. She did not think too much of it either. But it struck Sadiqa enough to tell me. We laughed it off. The next day we expected her to be playing with a different doll or toy.

But she wasn't. The next day, and the day after that, one of us arrived for pickup only to see Imani playing with the same blue-eyed, blond-haired White doll. With each passing day, it became harder to pry her away from her doll to go home. Her frown on day 1 when I took the doll out of her hands turned into a sharp "No!" on day 2 when Sadiqa tried, which turned into a car ride of whining on day 3, climaxing into an all-out tantrum on day 4—as she held on firmly to her White doll, not wanting to go home. Who knew a one-year-old was that strong!

Sadiqa and I were probably unduly sensitive about the whole saga. We wondered if our Black child's attachment to a White doll could mean she had ingested the "smog" of White superiority.

Maybe our minds were ringing a false alarm. Maybe the skin color and eye color and hair texture of the doll had no bearing on why Imani became attached. I did not know. No one knows. But I *did* know where the alarms came from. I was, of course, thinking of the famous "doll test," created by one of the first scholars to examine the racial attitudes of children, psychologist Mamie Phipps Clark.

Born in 1917 during World War I, Mamie Phipps was the eldest daughter of Harold H. Phipps, a well-respected physician in Hot Springs, Arkansas. Her mother, Katy Florence Phipps, assisted Mamie's father at his medical practice. Mamie's parents were born in the late nineteenth century, when mass-produced toys first entered American homes, including toys that often played on racist and ethnocentric ideas. For instance, there were mechanical banks designed as toys for children. The kids who played with the "Always Did 'Spise a Mule" mechanical bank (1879) could push a lever and make the figure of a Black American fly off a mule, a simulation of racial violence presented as a game for children during the lynching era. Playing with the "Paddy and the Pig" mechanical bank (1882), children saw an Irishman swallowing and rolling his eyes as a pig kicks a penny into his mouth, associating Irish immigrants with animals. The "Reclining Chinaman" mechanical bank (1882) featured a supine Chinese man flashing a handful of aces with a rat at his feet, instilling in children the racist ideas that Asian immigrants ate rodents and forced honest White people out of their jobs through trickery.

As early as 1897, the father of American psychology, G. Stanley Hall, published his influential *A Study of Dolls* with Alexander Caswell Ellis. They found White dolls with "fair hair and blue eyes are the favorites." Children who played with non-White dolls only did so because their appearance made them " 'funny' or exceptional."

But for Mamie Phipps, growing up in segregated Arkansas in the 1920s, these toys were anything but humorous. "You had to have a certain kind of protective armor about you, all the time," she said about her childhood. Mamie Phipps determined she wanted to nurture children, to give them the protective armor they needed.

In 1934, she enrolled at Howard University. By chance, she met a psychology master's student named Kenneth Clark from Harlem there. He encouraged her to major in psychology. She committed herself to psychology (and to Kenneth, too, eventually).

The Clarks entered a discipline long dominated by eugenicists and their standardized testing. But as scholars increasingly identified the "race prejudice" of eugenicists, they increasingly debated the origins of racist sentiment. Were humans born prejudiced or were they socialized to be prejudiced? This question turned the attention of psychologists to the racial attitudes of children.

In 1929, in *Race Attitudes in Children*, sociologist Bruno

Lasker "dogmatically" asserted that "race prejudice" was not an "inborn trait, and that all the observed responses are the results of acquired habits." Even so, he found that children could develop racist ideas about members of "outgroups" as early as five years old. Lasker's work inspired Eugene and Ruth Horowitz to develop tests to assess the racial attitudes of children. The Horowitzes in turn inspired Mamie and Kenneth Clark.

In 1940, the Clarks assembled 253 Black children from three to seven years old, some of whom attended segregated nursery schools in Arkansas and others an integrated school in Massachusetts. The children were shown two dolls with yellow hair and white skin, and two with black hair and dark brown skin. "Give me the doll you like to play with," the Clarks asked the children. Most of the Black children gave them a White doll.

These are the results of the original doll test that juddered through generations of parents of Black children. Including me. I couldn't help but think of the doll test when Imani kept clinging to the White doll. Did Imani prefer playing with the White doll, too? And why?

The Clarks gathered some clues to why so many of the Black children seemed to prefer the White doll. When they prompted the children to "Give me the doll you like the best" or the doll that's "nice" or that has a "nice color," the children mostly gave them the White doll. When the Clarks then asked a child in rural Arkansas which doll resembled him the most, the child smiled, pointed to the Black doll, and said, "That's a nigger. I'm a nigger." In Massachusetts, some children refused to answer which doll resembled them. Other children burst into tears and stormed out of the room. As Chicago Blues legend Big Bill Broonzy immortalized in song in the 1940s:

They say if you's white, should be all right,
If you's brown, stick around,
But if you's black, well, brothers, get back, get back, get back.

In 1950, Kenneth Clark presented the available research on the negative effect of segregation on Black *and* White children at the Mid-century White House Conference on Children and Youth. When the U.S. Supreme Court agreed to hear *Brown v. Board of Education of Topeka,* NAACP lawyers asked Clark to submit a similar report. Thirty-five of the era's leading anthropologists, educators, psychiatrists, psychologists, and sociologists cosigned Clark's conclusion: "Segregation, prejudices and discriminations, and their social concomitants potentially damage the personality of all children." White children "gain personal status in an unrealistic and non-adaptive way," the experts stated. "When comparing themselves to members of the minority group, they are not required to evaluate themselves in terms of the major basic standards of actual personal ability and achievement."

On May 17, 1954, Chief Justice Earl Warren issued a unanimous decision in the *Brown* case. As much as the Clarks rejoiced over the landmark *Brown* decision striking down "separate but equal" as unconstitutional, they were dismayed. "Segregation of white and colored children in public schools has a detrimental effect upon the colored children," Warren wrote. It tends to delay their "education and mental development" and deprive "them of some of the benefits they would receive in a racial[ly] integrated school system." While acknowledging the effects of segregation on "colored children," the court dismissed the detrimental effects of segregated White schools on *White* children. Then and now, segregated White schools tend to delay White children's educational and mental development and deprive them of the benefits they would receive in racially integrated schools.

The court struck down segregated schools but did not strike down the racist idea that the Whiter the school, the better. The proposal that White students could have integrated formerly all-Black schools *and benefited* was lost on the justices. Desegregation largely became a one-way affair, with a handful of Black students going to formerly all-White schools and ostensibly benefiting. After *Brown,* the Black threat who had to be segregated increasingly became the Black savage who had to be assimilated. And to be assimilated meant to be civilized. And to be civilized meant to become White. Blacks and Whites are "being drawn closer" together, facilitating Black "assimilation of . . . the more formal aspects of white civilization," sociologist E. Franklin Frazier had already favorably concluded in *The Negro Family in the United States* (1939).

It didn't quite work out that way. In the 1940s and 1950s, Italians, Jews, Irish, and Eastern Europeans had been assimilated or were assimilating into the broader racial category of White. Black people, too, were expected to assimilate into this White identity, especially in the wake of the desegregation rulings. After all, Black people were "White men with Black skins," as historian Kenneth Stampp wrote in 1956. But the new White American identity that made room for previously excluded ethnic groups still had no room for Blackness.

You can follow this history through the evolution of American toys. The myth of American homogeneity, based on a White norm, emerged as America's superpower after World War II. Toy makers followed suit, largely stopping production of toys ridiculing purported ethnic and racial differences. Popular board games like "Chutes and Ladders" and "Candyland" presented exclusively White children on their boxes and boards. In 1959, Mattel introduced the exclusively White Barbie doll at the American International Toy Fair in New York as a "Teen-age Fashion Model."

Toys went color-blind. Which is to say major toy makers assimilated nearly all toys into Whiteness. Images of Black people were largely excluded from toys in the postwar era. But stereotypical portrayals of Native Americans, the other perennial outlier from Whiteness, continued. Toy makers could not stop making sacred cultural materials into playthings for non-Native children, or stop encouraging non-Native children to dress up and play "Cowboys vs. Indians," simulating genocide.

But by the late 1960s, Black people and other people of color started resisting assimilationism en masse. They had been inspired by Malcolm X, who in 1962 asked a capacity audience of Black people in Los Angeles: "Who taught you to hate the texture of your hair? Who taught you to hate the color of your skin? To such extent you bleach, to get like the White man? Who taught you to hate the shape of your nose and the shape of your lips? Who taught you to hate yourself from the top of your head to the soles of your feet? Who taught you to hate your own kind? Who taught you to hate the race that you belong to?" By 1968, James Brown was singing the anthem of a new anti-assimilationist consciousness: "Say it loud, I'm Black and I'm proud." Black had become beautiful during the Black Power movement, which inspired the Red Power, Brown Power, and Yellow Power movements in the late 1960s and 1970s.

These anti-assimilationist movements compelled some toy companies to produce a more diverse assortment of toys. Remco's line of Black dolls appeared in 1968. Black, Asian, and Latinx Barbies and Black and Asian G.I. Joe figurines appeared by the 1980s (Hasbro did not introduce the first ex- plicitly Latinx G.I. Joe figurine until 2001).

In 2015, the "Fashionista" line of Barbies appeared with a variety of skin tones and hair textures. A new Ken arrived in the marketplace in new body sizes, skin tones, and hair tex- tures in 2017. The first Barbie to wear a hijab debuted in 2017. Mattel introduced "the world's first gender-neutral doll" in 2019, the same year it produced a line of dolls with wheelchairs and prosthetic limbs. In 2019, 55 percent of all dolls sold were underrepresented in some way, either by race, ethnicity, religion, gender expression, or body variance, com- pared with 36 percent in 2016.

This has been a helpful development, even as some toys re- mained carriers of racist and ethnocentric ideas. For example, in 1985, Nintendo's Mario character played on the old stereo- type of "jovial Italians—short and round, with big dark mous- taches and wide smiles," not to mention all the racist caricatures of Black, Native, Middle Eastern, Asian, and Latinx people and cultures in Halloween costumes in recent years.

To raise an antiracist child is to seek out toys and games that reflect our child's complexion and culture, but also reflect the complexions and cultures of others. One of the most im- portant forms of childproofing the environment is ensuring the child's toy box reflects the multiracial, multiethnic, multi- cultural world.

Even if we childproof the toy box, we still must watch our kids at play. To raise an antiracist child is to reflect on the po- sitions our child assumes in games, particularly with children of other races (and classes and genders and sexual orienta- tions). Is the White male child routinely assuming the posi- tion of leader during imaginative play with his Black female friend? Is the Native child routinely assuming the position of

follower in the game with her Asian friend? We should encourage all children to play the follower as much as the leader.
I want my daughter to learn how to lead *and* to follow people
of all races and backgrounds. But a democratic leader and an
authoritarian ruler are different. To raise an antiracist child is
to discourage tyrannical games with rulers and servants, good
cops and bad robbers, bad people and good people. Which is
hard. But it's vital that we teach our kids, even in play, that
there aren't bad or good people; just people who do bad or
good things.

In 2010, CNN commissioned child psychologist Margaret
Beale Spencer to design an updated version of Mamie Clark's
doll test. She tested 133 Black and White kids, aged four to
five or nine to ten, hailing from both integrated and highly
segregated schools in New York City and Georgia. The Clarks
did not test White children, but Spencer's findings with Black
children resembled what the Clarks found seventy years prior.
Black children generally displayed what researchers called
White bias, identifying their skin color with negative attributes
and White skin color with positive attributes. But Black children displayed White bias far less than White children. The
reason, Spencer suggested, is that Black parents are more likely
than White parents to protect their children from that bias.

But did I? Was I protecting Imani from that bias?

Whether Imani valued the *White* doll or the White *doll*
didn't matter. Whether she had already learned to devalue
Black things didn't matter. What mattered was that I had not
actively sought to protect her from that possibility. I had not
actively raised her to be antiracist.

But I had been deliberately teaching her numbers for
months. We'd play counting games on the car rides to and
from the daycare. "One Imani! Two Imani! Three Imani!"
She'd count back: "One Daddy! Two Daddy! Three Daddy!"

We counted into the teens and twenties before the game bored her.

In between the counting games, I'd sing the ABC song and remix the last line:

Now I know my ABCs
wiilllllllllll EEEEE-mani siiiiiiinnnnnggggg with
meeeeeeeeeeeeeeeeeeeeeeeeee

She'd respond "No!" and chuckle. Or grimace. Sometimes she'd be so amused that she'd say "Yes," and we'd sing the ABC song again and again.

In addition to numbers and letters, I taught her words. Carefully sounding them out. Defining them. Using words in sentences. Sadiqa and I were actively urging Imani to use her words instead of her whines and tears. When she had to wait for what she wanted, we taught her patience. Yes, the dreaded "P word"! When she finally got what she'd been waiting for, we'd encourage her to be grateful and share.

Imani at age one did not understand most of the numbers and letters and words we were teaching her. She did not fully comprehend the behaviors of communication, of patience, of gratefulness, of self-sacrifice. But that did not stop us. We assumed she'd grow in her understanding.

Why don't caregivers think the same way about the behavior of being antiracist? Being antiracist *is* a behavior, not unlike the behaviors of impatience and patience, ingratitude and gratefulness, selfishness and self-sacrifice. We can teach these behaviors at a young age and babies can learn them. Babies can also reason about the mental lives and intentions of others; they can intuitively comprehend what approximates addition and subtraction; they understand cause and effect; and they are sensitive to the statistical probability of events, according to a report by the Board on Children, Youth, and Families at the National Academies of Sciences, Engineering, and Medicine. "What is going on in babies' and young children's minds is much more complex and sophisticated than their outward behavior reveals," the report explained. "Early learning occurs on two levels: the growth of knowledge that is visible and apparent—language learning, for example, and learning about how objects work—and the growth of implicit learning, which is harder to observe." Perhaps the earlier we explicitly teach our children to be antiracist, the earlier they will implicitly begin to learn this humane behavior.

But shamefully, I did not see the urgency when Imani was a one-year-old. I saw the urgency for adults, which is what drove me to start writing *How to Be an Antiracist* in 2017 when Imani was a year old. I charted the long and difficult steps adults must take to be antiracist by charting the steps I took. These steps, for me, began in childhood. But my tunnel vision remained on adults. By not seeing how all of this applied to my role as a caregiver, I betrayed my daughter, my story, my training, my research, and the antiracist world I envisioned; the one that our children will inherit or build. I did not turn my focus onto children until Imani's doll incident, which turned out to be *my* doll test.

At one year old, our children are seeing the different skin colors—in humans, in dolls. We can impress upon them the equality of dark and light colors, and the equality of difference. At this age, books are again a key tool—not just for them to notice the human variety in the characters but to explicitly call it out for them to see. We can impress upon them the equality of differently shaped eyes, like Joanna Ho's majestic picture book *Eyes That Kiss in the Corners*. We can impress upon them the loveliness of different hair textures, as Matthew A. Cherry did in Imani's favorite picture book, *Hair*

Love. I can put all this equality of difference together through reciting the verses of Grace Byers's picture book *I Am Enough:* "I know that we don't look the same: our skin, our eyes, our hair, our frame. But that does not dictate our worth; we both have places here on earth." I can bring Imani to large and diverse crowds and adoringly point out to her all the skin colors and eye colors and hair textures and body frames that all have places here on earth. I can use dolls. Dolls are one of the ultimate nurturing instruments. We can use dolls to circumvent racist notions of the lighter, the better. We can use dolls to discuss the racist experiences faced by different groups. A diverse assortment of toys in general "open[s] dialogue around prejudice and enable[s] discussion and empathy," explained psychologist Sian Jones. "If such toys are not there, the opportunity for this discussion is lost." It wasn't enough that we put Imani in diverse environments and modeled antiracist behavior. Just like we taught her to use her words when confronted with difficult situations, we as caregivers needed to learn to use our words, and make our antiracist beliefs explicit.

In the end, we did not know what to make of Imani clinging to the White doll. On day 5, Sadiqa and I arrived at the daycare together. Imani loved both of us picking her up. When we walked in, Imani saw us come in together, tossed the White doll aside, and ran to hug us.

"Group hug!" Sadiqa shouted, widening her arms as I did the same.

Imani buried her face between our inner legs. Sadiqa and I made eye contact, probably thinking in unison that on the fifth day, the doll had finally lost.

Doll 4, Parents 1.

Imani released her grip. I walked around the daycare and found the large toy chests. I rummaged through the toys and did not come across a single Asian doll, Native doll, Latinx doll, Middle Eastern doll, or Black doll. Every single doll I saw looked White!

Rage overtook me. Not at the daycare owner. At myself. Imani had been going here for several weeks, and not once did I examine the toy chests. Not once.

We had Imani all wrong all week long. Imani did not choose to play with the White doll over dolls of color. Imani did not have another option.

We told the owner about the dolls before leaving. Changes came. But I had failed the doll test. Soon, I'd fail another test—the test of my life.

CHAPTER 5

Empathetic Toddler

Weeks after the doll test, my body sent warnings. It was the fall of 2017. Weight loss. Fatigue. Trips to the bathroom only for nothing to come out. I ignored it all.

After Thanksgiving, I could not ignore the blood clots I passed into toilets. Upon Sadiqa's urging, I got checked out after we returned home from a New Year's vacation. I discovered the worst. I had colon cancer. Stage 4. Only 14 percent of people diagnosed with Stage 4 colon cancer are still living five years later. I was thirty-five years old. In the middle of writing *How to Be an Antiracist,* I determined to finish it before I died.

I endured six grueling months of chemotherapy. On August 28, 2018, I had reached the summit: surgery.

After an all-day surgery, I lay in the intensive care unit, or ICU. When the anesthesia wore off, I awoke to see Sadiqa seated next to my hospital bed. "The surgeons couldn't find any cancer left," she said. "So it took longer than expected.

They took out less than expected. But everything is good. Like really good."

Sadiqa reached over and hugged me as pain immobilized me on the hospital bed. I felt the presence of a miracle, a chance for renewed life. I wanted to hug Imani now.

The next day, before dawn, nurses moved me out of my hospital bed; placed me upright. I had asked Sadiqa to hand me Jesmyn Ward's novel *Salvage the Bones*. I started reading. A few hours later, my parents and brother, if I remember correctly, walked Imani into my intensive care room. Two years old now, Imani had become terribly inquisitive. The *whys* started eclipsing the cries in quantity, and my parents delighted in the payback for my own childhood interrogations.

Imani slowly walked to my reclining chair, where I was seated in some discomfort. Pain shooting from surgical wounds. Pain cutting from wounds inside my body where the surgeons removed parts of organs. Discomfort flowing from the tubes draining the excess fluid, and the catheter assisting my bathroom use. Pain medicine doing so much and so little.

"Hi, missy," I said, smiling. No pain control is better than a toddler's presence.

"Hiiii," she responded.

Standing before me now, Imani examined all the tubes and lines coming out of my hospital gown like her mom examines a new patient. I noticed all the empathic (or empathetic) concern coming out of her.

Imani's ability to show empathy increased in her second year of life (as it normally does for toddlers). Between fourteen months and two and a half years, toddlers can be observed examining their own fingers when they see someone else hurt their fingers—they are learning to distinguish the pain of others from their own. By two and a half years, toddlers recognize that difference, and usually try to comfort the harmed person. Imani entered my hospital room a month shy of two and a half years.

Beginning around three years and nine months and increasingly thereafter, children develop the foundation for sustained empathetic action: what researchers term "mental-state understanding." Which is to say preschoolers begin understanding someone's else perspective *and* experience and take action accordingly. Which is to say preschoolers have the foundation to begin to understand the perspectives and experiences of Asian Americans facing heightened racist violence during the COVID-19 pandemic and take antiracist action. And yet do *we* understand what the kids can understand? Are we teaching the perspectives and experiences of people being harmed by racism? Are we using dolls or real people to nurture their empathy? Because childproofing our racial environment is futile if we aren't nurturing the child's empathy, if we aren't encouraging the child to take action, and if we aren't modeling that action taking. As Brené Brown wrote, "Dare to be the adults we want our children to be."

By age eight, children can completely empathize with another person's "overall life situation." They can be aware that someone has a life-threatening illness even if all seems well in the moment. By age eight, children can also probably empathize with another racial group's "overall life situation" even if all seems well.

I wonder if seeing her father recovering from life-giving surgery caused Imani to skip a year or two ahead in terms of her empathetic development. Not long after she arrived, the resident returned to pull out a few drains from my surgical sites. Imani insisted on holding my hands.

Our brains have been "hardwired" for empathy. When we

cringe at the sight of someone crashing their bike into a tree, the same areas of our brains are stimulated as if we crashed our own bike into the tree. When Imani watched me cringe from the pain of my surgical wounds, she cringed. Sadiqa cringed. My parents and brother cringed. As much as I wanted to be, I was not alone in my pain. Empathy is like a hug.

Though these hugs of empathy come naturally, "empathy is a mutable trait, it can be taught," explained psychiatrist Helen Riess. "We're all born with a certain endowment, but it can be dramatically up-regulated or down-regulated depending upon environmental factors." We can up-regulate by how we care for the child in the home, in school, and in our larger society. We should avoid dismissing our children's questions or feelings or issuing judgments. "Don't ask that. That's wrong. That's bad to feel that way." Because when we dismiss their feelings, judge their feelings, or are hostile to their feelings, we are hardly raising them to be empathetic. When our child seems afraid of an animal, let's not say, "Don't worry. She won't bite you." Let's ask, "Are you afraid? Why are you afraid?" When the child says, "I don't like Richard. I don't want to play with him," instead of declaring it's wrong to not like Richard and ordering our child to play with Richard, we can ask, "Why do you feel that way?" In that way both the caregiver and the child will learn something: The caregiver will learn how the child feels; the child will learn to respond to others with similar curiosity, wonder, and empathy.

One of the most important jobs of caregivers is to teach and model empathetic action and invite children to participate. But that hasn't been happening of late. Over the last forty years, studies show, young people have been leaving high schools and homes for college with markedly less empathy, with the most significant drop occurring after 2000.

In 1980, psychologist Mark H. Davis introduced a "multi-dimensional" concept of empathy. This model of empathy has four dimensions: *fantasy, perspective taking, empathic concern,* and *personal distress.* Fantasy is "the tendency to identify with characters in movies, novels, plays and other fictional situations." Since our little ones will identify with characters in fictional situations, it is critical to childproof the movies, shows, books, plays, and dolls our children are exposed to. I suspect the ability to identify with a diverse set of fictional characters and see them as equals aids the child in identifying with a diverse set of real-life characters, and treating these peoples as equals. And so we can suspect that fantasy goes hand in hand with the three non-fictional dimensions of empathy. *Perspective taking* refers to "spontaneous attempts to adopt the perspectives of other people and see things from their point of view." *Empathic concern* describes "feelings of warmth, compassion, and concern for others." *Personal distress* is characterized by "personal feelings of anxiety and discomfort that result from observing another's negative experience."

Empathy leads to altruism. "Higher empathy countries," as researchers termed them, "have higher levels of collectivism, agreeableness, conscientiousness, self-esteem, emotionality, subjective well-being," and altruistic behaviors like donating money, volunteering, and helping strangers in need. Adults who have higher levels of empathy, especially empathic concern and perspective taking, reported higher rates of regular (rather than episodic) volunteerism. Elementary-school-aged children with higher levels of empathy tend to be more altruistic.

Children and adolescents who defend peers against bullies have "enhanced levels" of cognitive and affective empathy. While cognitive empathy is the "ability to *comprehend* another person's emotions," affective empathy is the "capacity to *experience* another person's emotions." Bullies generally have less cognitive empathy, and even less affective empathy.

Bullies are bred, not born—just as racists are bred, not born. We can guard against raising bullies by cultivating empathy. We can teach children to understand that "I can hurt others with my words, my actions, and even my silence," to quote Susan Verde's picture book *I Am Human*. Empathy can be taught in classrooms alongside literacy skills. Problem-solving games, storytelling, group discussions, and role-playing can all teach empathic skills. Schools and teachers can prioritize social and emotional learning over the standardized tests of eugenicists.

But if we are truly committed to raising empathic kids and not bullies, then parents and teachers must first look in the mirror. Do we bully children in ways we don't realize? How do we discipline? Do we actualize in our classrooms and homes the same mindset as what abolitionist Mariame Kaba calls the "criminal punishment system"? Or what psychologists call "power-assertive discipline"? When kids misbehave, do we immediately punish them, or threaten to punish them? I admit that I have acted reflexively in this way at times. I am trying to change. I don't want to wield power over Imani in this way, like the institution of policing. Because when I do, I am modeling a bully. I am raising a bully.

As an alternative, caregivers can practice "inductive discipline." When kids misbehave, we prompt the child to consider how their action impacted another and what they can do for redress. Not: "Don't do that. That was bad. Now take a time-out." Instead: "How does Jeff feel right now? What can we do to make him feel better?"

Inductive questions unlock the child's mind to empathy, which can allow her to think twice before hitting someone else again—and make Jeff feel better, too. Restorative justice for children and adults is based in empathy, and it is radically different from our criminal punishment system, which is based in bullying. The empathy of inductive discipline isn't just more humane, it is more effective at preventing harm and building community.

Yearlong suspension rates were cut in half when middle school teachers practiced inductive discipline as opposed to punitive discipline. Their inductive discipline involved speaking privately with the student and assessing whether the student's needs were being met rather than threatening the student with punishment or involving school administrators.

Adults with low levels of empathy and orientations to social dominance—defined as a preference for social inequality partly conditioned during the socialization process—consistently supported anti-Black racism, chauvinism, "law-and-order" policies, and military funding, while opposing social welfare programs, antiracist policies, women's rights, LGBTQ+ rights, environmental causes, and interracial marriage. Adults with high levels of empathy and feelings of connectedness to others, on the other hand, endorsed antiracism.

Raising a child on empathy involves more than raising them on its four dimensions. Empathy most powerfully expresses itself when it draws on the even deeper "principle of care," the ingrained belief that one should help others in need. Mere empathic concern for others is more likely to lead to "spontaneous, short-term helping," like allowing a stranger to go ahead in line. But a moral principle of care is more likely to lead to "planned, long-term helping" behaviors, like joining a local antiracist organization that's striving to free a community of color from environmental hazards.

But is our empathy absolute or is it conditional? For some people, empathy motivates charitable giving, but only if the recipients are not perceived as "responsible" for their condition. In these kinds of situations—when we put conditions on our empathy—the principle of care is trumped by the *undeserving principle:* People who are responsible for their plight are undeserving of care. Empathy, thereby, becomes transactional and conditional, like a tip we give someone for good service, or a favorable court ruling for seeming "respectable." We are the jury and those seeking our empathy must prove they are worthy of our assistance. This idea can bleed into how we view antiracism.

Late afternoon came the day after my surgery. Hours had passed since my lines came out. I was still reading *Salvage the Bones*. Dad and my brother had already taken Imani back to the hotel. Her empathy, though, the empathy of my family, had already shot me up with valor.

A nurse arrived with a wheelchair. I was being transferred from the ICU to a regular bed on the other side of the hospital.

"I can walk," I said.

The nurse objected. Sadiqa objected. The nurse told me how far my new room was.

"I can walk," I insisted. "I'll be fine. Just help me."

A woman constantly pushing herself to the limit, Ma looked proud if not amused. Sadiqa and the nurse looked at each other puzzled. Sadiqa and the nurse knew no one walks out of the ICU the day after a major surgery. I didn't know that. All I knew was that I had done a lap around the unit that morning, holding on to Sadiqa's shoulder for dear life. And what the doctor said earlier that morning kept ringing in my head: The more I move my body, the faster it will heal; the faster it heals, the faster I can go home. I wanted to go home.

The nurse and Sadiqa realized they weren't changing my

mind. Ma wanted to see if I could do it. Ma took hold of the empty wheelchair as I took Sadiqa's shoulder and slowly ambled out of the room, with the nurse at my other shoulder ready for me to collapse. When other ICU providers noticed what was happening, they looked at me like I was a creature from outer space. Or at least that's what Sadiqa told me afterward. I didn't see anyone as I walked. I focused my eyes down on my steps. Every step was hard. I was glad when we reached the elevator so I could rest. I made it to my new room without collapsing.

On this walk and subsequent walks through the hospital, moving slowly, clothed in a hospital gown, holding on to Sadiqa for dear life, flanked by monitoring machines, I could feel the empathy of the people around me, patients, visitors, and hospital staff alike. I imagine that many people felt I deserved their empathy—I was sick and hospitalized and clearly trying my best to get better. But it struck me how alien that feeling was, the feeling that people around me were spontaneously granting me empathy. As a Black man in America, I don't know if that has ever happened to me before or since.

Racist ideas convince us that people—namely people of color—are responsible for their own plight and are undeserving of our empathy. Racist ideas—as well as classist, homophobic, transphobic, sexist, xenophobic, and ableist ideas—are baked into public distinctions of the deserving and undeserving. The idea of who is "deserving" or "undeserving" drives support for (or opposition to) government assistance programs. Low-income White widows were considered deserving of welfare in the 1950s, but low-income Black mothers were considered undeserving of welfare in the 1960s and thereafter. While Black people addicted to crack cocaine were framed as undeserving of treatment in 1986, White people addicted to opioids were considered deserving of treatment in

2016. All the while, wealthy people (who are disproportionately White) are deserving of the government assistance of land seizures, of tax cuts, of public subsidies, of public funding for their institutions, of government purchases of their goods and services, of capitalist policy that makes it cheap to be rich (and expensive to be poor).

Are we indirectly teaching our children to have a moral compulsion to help only people who look like them? Or are we openly and aggressively encouraging them to help people who don't look like them, don't live like them, and don't live near them—all the people being framed as undeserving? Who are we raising our kids to care about?

Empathy is not necessarily color-blind or race neutral. *Racist empathy* is when someone exudes concern, takes the perspectives, or feels personally distressed for the racial group on the higher end of racial disparity and injustice, but not people of lesser status. Racist empathy has fueled the politics of White grievances for decades, if not centuries. When elected officials dog-whistle to White parents that critical race theory is harming White children, they're relying on a deep well of racist empathy to make it pay off. When a White girl goes missing there's overwhelming concern in the media—as there should be—but less concern in that same media about the ungodly levels of missing Native girls or Asian Americans facing hate attacks. As such, racist empathy leads to racist apathy toward the struggles of groups considered unworthy.

"Individuals tend to have the most empathy for others who look or act like them, for others who have suffered in a similar way, or for those who share a common goal," psychiatrist Helen Riess added. But our emotional empathy can be moderated or controlled, by reason, by perspective taking, "by executive functions in the prefrontal cortex," Riess explained.

Racist empathy can be controlled by *antiracist empathy,* which is displaying concern, taking the perspectives of, or feeling personally distressed for the groups at the lower end of racial disparity and injustice. When health equity activists pointed out the racist policies and practices behind Black, Brown, and Native people dying at the highest rates from COVID-19, they relied on a well of empathy for those people to activate policy changes.

"Black Lives Matter" is a term of antiracist empathy, emerging as a movement by 2014 in response to racist empathy. But even this statement of empathy is often derided. Empathy requires some imagination—so imagine the situation was even more intimate: Your relatives are dying from police violence at much higher rates than my relatives. How would you feel if every time you expressed empathetic concern about your relatives being murdered, I showed indifference? Or I blamed your relatives for their own deaths and turned the conversation to the *living* officers who claimed they feared for their lives? Or if I asked, "Don't blue lives matter?" and then turned the conversation around to my family: "Don't all lives matter?" Perhaps this exercise helps make clear how common it is for many of us to evade true empathy.

But it also makes the point that antiracist empathy isn't just about equality. Let me explain: When two racial groups are in equal situations and they are being harmed at similar levels, antiracist empathy involves engaging in similar empathetic feelings and actions for these similarly harmed racial groups. That's *equality* of action, and it is needed in equitable situations to maintain equity. But when one racial group is being harmed much more than another racial group, engaging in similar empathetic actions for the two groups maintains the inequity. In inequitable situations, antiracist empathy involves engaging in *more* empathetic actions for the racial group being harmed *more*. Whether that's Black women dying in pregnancy, Latinx men being deported, Asian women being objectified, Middle Eastern men being terrorized, Native women being abducted, or White men dying by suicide, they need our empathetic action more than their peers being harmed at lower rates. That's *equity* of action, and it is needed in inequitable situations to create equity. That is the kind of empathy we need to be antiracist.

After a week, the doctors discharged me from the hospital. We returned home at dusk. Imani joined Sadiqa in going through the accumulated mail. One package contained *The Day You Begin,* a picture book by Jacqueline Woodson. Imani's eyes widened as she took in Rafael López's stunning cover illustration of a Brown girl opening the classroom door holding a book. *The Day You Begin* conveys how we feel alone until we begin to share our stories (and the more children share their stories, the more connected they feel to other children; the more connected different children are to each other, the more empathetic they can be to each other).

Upon Imani's urging, Sadiqa read Woodson's words then and there. Imani flipped the pages before Sadiqa could finish.

The next day, after Imani got home from daycare, she saw me lying on the couch. I had covered my legs with a blue blanket. I had on a blue robe that opened at my chest. She came over to the couch and examined my large bandages. She cried.

"What's wrong? What's wrong?" I asked as her tears fell on the couch, as I struggled to reach over to hug her. Her stare remained locked on the bandages on my belly. Did they scare her? Did she think I was still in pain?

"I'm okay. I'm okay," I kept saying. As her wails slowly tapered into sniffles, I had a thought for her empathy.

"Do you want to put on some bandages like Daddy?" I asked. Her eyes lit up as if she was seeing *The Day You Begin* again for the first time. "Yes!" she blurted out.

Sadiqa had been standing over both of us the whole time. She left and came back with two large Band-Aids and a very large bandage to resemble mine. She placed them on and around Imani's belly button. Imani smiled, staring at my belly and hers.

Over the next few days and weeks, Imani added new Band-Aids and bandages to her belly and arms and legs. No gift pleased her more than a box of Band-Aids. She became attached to Band-Aids like other kids were attached to dolls. As I healed, Imani allowed herself to heal symbolically, too.

I had to heal. I had people to love. I had a book to finish. I had a new antiracist research center to get off the ground. I knew recurrence was most likely in the first year. I dreaded the cancer coming back. Because in a year, I wanted to be there for what I hadn't thought I'd be there for. I wanted to be there for the day Imani began.

CHAPTER 6

Preschooler's Race

Imani wore a blue denim shirt, sleeveless, fastened with three pink buttons below her neck. The tail of the shirt hung over her light pink jeans. The cuffs of her jeans tumbled over her peach sneakers. Her hair lay down flat in two big cornrows, parted in the middle.

Three years old now, Imani was already selective about her outfits. Her grandmothers tended to buy her clothes, and Sadiqa tended to pick out what she would wear each day. I picked out her pajamas when I put her down, but only with her consultation. She was even particular about her sleepwear!

I couldn't complain to Ma. "That's what you get for requesting the red coat instead of the blue coat, or the blue coat instead of the red coat," she'd tell me. Let her tell it: At three years old, I'd oppose whatever she picked out.

On this morning, Imani didn't oppose what Sadiqa picked out. She seemed genuinely happy to go to her first day of preschool on August 30, 2019. The normally fraught process of getting her up and ready and fed and seated in her car seat had gone without a hiccup. That is, until I pulled out of our driveway and opened my mouth to sing, "AAAA—B—C—DDDDD . . ."

"Daddy, noooo!" she shouted. "I do *not* want to sing."

"Why not?" I asked.

"I'm a big girl now. Going to big school!"

I saw her smile in my rearview mirror as she shut me up. Ordinarily, I'd shut up, delighted in her using her words. Sometimes, I'd feel miffed about her asserting her power. I had yet to leave behind power-assertive discipline and fully adopt inductive discipline. I toggled between the two disciplines like Americans toggle between punishing (those other people) and empathy (for our own people).

Imani clung to me far less than she did to Sadiqa. That's why we decided that I'd drop off Imani on her first day, and Sadiqa would pick her up.

I parked down the street from Imani's school. My mixed emotions were already mixing me up. The car shading us, I snapped some pictures of the schoolgirl on a strip of grass separating the curb from the sidewalk. Imani gave an easy smile. I smiled much harder, joyful to be alive for Imani's first day of school. A year prior I was in the hospital healing from surgery. The cancer had not returned.

Imani and I held hands as we walked up the street. She tugged me over to walk up the accessibility ramp. Within days, she'd be running up the ramp when we arrived for school and racing me down it whenever I picked her up. She always, of course, won. She hated to lose, like her mom, and beat me repeatedly, like her mom.

Thinking back, I never took the time to tell Imani why the ramp was there. I never took the time to say: "Do you remember the other day when we saw that person in a wheelchair? She may not be able to walk up the steps like you. But she is just like you because she loves using the ramp, too. The ramp makes her experience better and yours, too! The ramp is called an *accommodation*. Say ac-com-mo-da-tion."

We could have talked about accommodations. But I did not. Going and coming, I needed to remember to slow down my life when I was with Imani to really see what she was liking and seeing. Because the things she was liking were the things she was probably open to learning about, like the ramp. The things she was seeing were the things she was probably trying to understand. "Why do people have different skin colors? Why are there steps AND a ramp? Why doesn't this building have a ramp, too?"

Imani's preschool classroom was on the first floor near the building's entrance. With every step we took toward the room, our smiles started to fade as a fear of the unknown started to settle on us. We finally arrived at the open door of the correct classroom. Imani froze in the doorframe. She grabbed my leg, suddenly quiet and looking around the room intensely, curiously fearful.

Gazing inside, I liked her first classroom. I had already made it a point to see if the toys, games, and books were childproofed to prevent racial harm. I wasn't going to fail another doll test. But I didn't think Imani was looking at all that stuff. She was studying the kids.

Imani's teacher noticed us and began walking over. In our orientation session, she seemed poised and unflappable. A clear communicator. Assertive rather than reactive. Youthful and affable around adults, but displaying a mature confidence around the kids, as if she'd already raised generations of children. This teacher appeared to be everything we tried to be as parents. There may be no greater human being than a great teacher. And on the day our children enter preschool, the teacher becomes as important a caregiver as anyone.

The teacher grasped Imani's hand and led her around the corner to the locker area. She showed Imani her open wooden locker. I handed Imani her bookbag. She looked at the teacher and the teacher looked at her locker. Imani set her bag inside. The teacher took Imani's hand again and led her back around the corner into the classroom. A few steps inside the classroom, Imani froze. She looked back at me in the doorframe. "I'll stand here for a few minutes," I said, smiling. "Go play."

My voice cracked. I wanted to hug her. I wanted to say goodbye. I wanted a send-off moment. But what was best for Imani was for me to just allow her to settle into her new classroom. What I wanted in that moment was not what was best for Imani.

Sadiqa and I aimed to be child-centered: What's best for the child trumps the adult's personal feelings, philosophies, discomforts, and baggage. It wasn't always easy and we didn't always achieve it, and I know we were not alone in our occasional failures—and there are so many ways to fail. It's a process that takes constant self-interrogation: Do we sometimes put our personal desires over what's best for our child? How often do we convince ourselves something is best for our child when it is really just what's best for us? How often do we *not* do what's best for our child because it is uncomfortable for us? Like not actively teaching our child to be antiracist. Like not choosing diverse neighborhoods and schools. Like not checking our nonverbal racist messages. Like not admitting how much the environment shapes our child. Like not childproofing the environment. Like not nurturing the child's empathy.

.   .   .

"Bye, Daddy," Imani said, waving twice. She turned and her teacher walked her onto a large blue rug in the middle of the classroom. Two Black girls and a White girl sat in a semicircle playing. Imani completed the human circle. I watched from the doorframe.

Now *I* was frozen. I wanted to stand there for more than a few minutes. Framed in fear, I didn't want to leave.

Looking into the door of the American preschool classroom, I didn't see a safe space for my three-year-old Black daughter. I looked past Imani's teacher and thought about the unregulated and unacknowledged fear of precious little Black girls and boys in schools across the land. Parents are taught to fear their kid going to school with too many Black children. Teachers are taught to fear a classroom with too many Black children. All this fear made me fear for my daughter. The fear of Black schoolchildren makes the school dangerous for Black children.

Especially those schools with school resource officers. An incredible 91 percent of these law enforcement officers are armed as they patrol hallways with children. In more racially diverse schools, school resource officers are more likely to see students as a threat. And Black students tend to feel less safe around school resource officers. "People who often know little to nothing about child or adolescent development, and who often lack the appropriate awareness and training for the school environments they patrol, are responding to behaviors that were previously managed by skilled teachers, counselors, principals, and other professionals," explained Monique W. Morris, who cofounded the National Black Women's Justice Institute.

Some skilled teachers aren't much better. Among Black and White preschool teachers, one study found that teachers of both races, but more often Black teachers, are primed to expect "challenging behavior" from Black preschool children, particularly Black boys. In 2020, Black girls comprised 19 percent of the female preschool enrollment, but accounted for 53 percent of female suspensions. Black boys made up 18 percent of the male preschool enrollment but 41 percent of the male suspensions. The school-to-prison pipeline begins in preschool. I feared dropping my daughter into this pipeline.

This punitive and punishing state of American schools collaterally damages White schoolchildren, too. Suspensions and expulsions lead to lost learning time and deprive preschoolers of the opportunity to overcome early academic and social challenges, particularly those children with disabilities. In 2014, the Obama administration issued a policy statement that called for an end to preschool exclusionary punishment. Since that year, at least nineteen states have limited exclusionary punishments in preschools and almost every state has seen at least modest executive action to remedy the issue in childcare settings. The overall rate of suspension and expulsions fell sharply thereafter—but the racial disparities remained stark. Meaning there had been two problems: (1) the number of preschool children of all races being suspended; and (2) the disproportionate number of Black preschool children being suspended. But policy solutions addressed only the former; the latter remained neglected.

At some point, teachers, parents, and all caregivers must start holding policies and practices accountable. At some point, they must stop blaming children—*children*—when they struggle. What if we stopped that cold turkey? What if we realized the absurdity of blaming a bored child for misbehaving in class? What if we realized the inhumanity of blaming a child for being unable to articulate her emotions? What if we realized the error of blaming a learner for not knowing? This kind of shift in perspective is incredibly hard. I've failed at it constantly myself. But we must stop problematizing children and start problematizing power and policy—and ourselves. We can parent better. We can teach better. We can care for the child better. But there are limits to what we can do as caregivers, especially when resources are lacking, when kids are irritable from hunger, when parents and teachers keep getting evicted from homes or buildings, or because the state, through its policies, is imposing a racist curriculum onto parents and teachers.

I want to live in a society where adults see all children *as children.* As people new to the world and worthy of our patience. Children are bound to make mistakes in this new world they are trying to understand. If children can't routinely make mistakes *and learn from them,* then how will humanity grow? I wanted Imani to be a kid. I didn't want her fearing the stalker of Black people: punishment. I was ready to battle the stalker. Is that why I didn't want to leave the doorframe? Did I feel I needed to protect her?

Imani flapped her hands over her head, a gesture signaling her excitement. I had stood there for a few moments watching her play. Now I turned away from the door to go. Imani's excitement at being in the company of the other girls unfroze me. Their innocence, her innocence. She was three years old. They were around three years old.

At least this is what I convinced myself to get myself to go home. I told myself what I wanted to hear—not what I had learned. I had already learned better from the scientific literature on the racial attitudes of toddlers. But what I had learned had yet to become what I knew. Fear stopped my learning from becoming my knowing, as it often does for so many of us.

I didn't want to believe what I'd learned about the development of three-year-olds. I wanted to believe that when it comes to race, toddlers are harmless and naïve. I wanted to believe that they resided outside the racialized world adults are navigating. I wanted to believe Imani had nothing to worry about around her new classmates. I wanted to believe her new classmates had nothing to worry about around Imani. But I should have *known* better. I'd already learned better.

By age three, children associate negative traits like anger with *other* racial groups—and these perceptions don't change much thereafter with age. One study found that most White preschool children "choose a Black person as looking 'bad,' having negative qualities or as being the least preferred playmate." By age three, kids usually think "race is fixed-at-birth and governed by biological processes like growth and inheritance" and "that race determines whether or not one is honest, smart, or clean," found Lawrence A. Hirschfeld, the director of the New School's Center for Research with Infants and Toddlers. "Even 3-year-olds' grasp of race is markedly adult-like," Hirschfeld added.

Adult-like, but preschoolers aren't adults. Preschoolers confuse race and ethnicity (as many adults do). Preschoolers are still learning the nonsensical groupings of extremely light- and dark-skinned people from Africa, Asia, and Latin America into the same supposed biological races. But many have already learned bias—and even the racial slurs of adults.

Sadiqa grew up in Albany, a relatively big town in rural southwest Georgia. She lived on a mixed block—mixed racially and mixed with houses and apartments. As Sadiqa grew up, her block became increasingly Black.

One day, when she was fourteen or fifteen, her family dog, Dela, ran away. Sadiqa walked up and down her street but couldn't find her. In the past, the runt sometimes ran out of the backyard of Sadiqa's house and down the alleyway to another house she liked. Remembering this, Sadiqa turned to walk back toward her house down the alleyway. As she walked along this dirt road, she saw something out of the corner of her eye. She looked over in the direction of a duplex apartment building. There she saw a three- or four-year-old White boy standing alone on a second-floor balcony, glaring at her.

"Nig-ger!" the boy shouted.

The boy didn't yell anything else. Or if he did, Sadiqa didn't hear it. She kept walking. She didn't respond. What do you say to a White preschooler who calls you a "nigger"? Anger boxed her confusion: White adults tossed slurs, teens her age, too; even kids—but Sadiqa never expected to be called the N-word by a preschooler. It remains the only time she remembers being singled out with this verbal assault. Nearly three decades later, she is still returning to that moment when she was walking home, seething and trying to figure out what just happened to her—*and* that child.

What happened is that by three years old, human beings can already be infected with racist ideas. The boy could have learned the N-word from a caregiver or another three-year-old. The age shouldn't be surprising. Three-year-olds are rapidly learning their worlds, including their racialized worlds. At two years old, a child's brain is learning at a faster pace than at any other time of life, and this critical period of development lasts until around age seven. Caregivers need to ask: What is this young brain quickly learning about race? Antiracist or racist ideas?

I support early childhood education advocates who call for making preschool free and universally available for all these rapidly learning three-year-olds. Preschools effectively build a desire to learn and generate positive self-worth, trust in other children and adults, discipline and structure, and literacy skills.

Research shows that, compared with kids who do not attend preschool, kids who attend preschool are more likely to graduate from high school, attend a four-year college, and earn a higher income.

But universal preschool education can be beneficial for another, less talked about reason. Preschools can systemically impart what young adult and middle-grade novelist Jason Reynolds calls the *antibodies* of antiracist education. These antibodies are necessary for kids who, by the time they start preschool, are already exposed and vulnerable to the virus of racist ideas. These ideas can then show up in racist action, even at that young age: A White child might not desire to play with a Black boy because he's Black, for instance. Or maybe they just launch racial slurs from their balconies. Of course, not all kids are engaging in racist actions. Far from it. But the antibodies of antiracist education can protect all of our children from getting the disease, or ensure it doesn't get worse but heals. An antiracist preschool education can set our kids on a path to live healthy racial lives.

When we choose not to talk to kids about race as they enter preschool, is it for their benefit or ours? The majority of Black and White parents do not discuss race with their three-year-olds. White parents engaging in color-blind socialization are concerned about pointing out racial differences that their children "hadn't noticed before." They obviously don't know—or don't want to know—that three-year-olds "notice physical differences such as skin color, hair texture, and the shape of one's facial features," as Beverly Daniel Tatum explained. Black parents express less reluctance than White parents. But they are more likely to justify their neglect as I did: thinking their three-year-olds are too young to be exposed to this toxic truth.

Do preschool teachers have similar views? Because every

preschool teacher should also be offering the antibodies of antiracist education. Every preschool teacher should be actively teaching students that skin color is as irrelevant as eye and hair color; and the colors of our bodies don't mean anything more than the colors kids are learning like orange, brown, and white. They should be teaching kids not to judge a human being by their skin covers; that below the covers we all look the same. When kids point out differences in skin color and hair texture and culture, teachers and parents and caregivers should not silence them. Those moments are opportunities to teach, to acknowledge the differences, to appreciate the differences, to convey that though people may be different, they are equals.

But we should take the conversation a step further and talk about bad rules making life harder for dark-skinned people—and how those rules are wrong and racist. Whatever racial inequity our children see, we can engage them on it. Preschool children have a powerful sense of right and wrong, fairness and unfairness. If there's any group of people who can learn and understand how racism is wrong and unfair, then it is preschoolers.

Sometimes we won't be able to teach. But we should admit to our child when we don't know. We can research the answers with children and discover them together and apply them together. We can model the genius of recognizing when we don't know and then aggressively striving to know.

We must also show preschoolers our outrage with the unfairness of racism. We must show them it is outrageous to mistreat someone because of their skin color. Or, just as powerfully, to be antiracist is to admit the times we are being racist. This admission of the teacher or parent is profoundly instructive for our kids. They learn how they could be wrong for mistreating a person because of their skin color—just as we were wrong. They can make amends as they see us make amends.

Many Black and White preschoolers, ages three to five, said they'd like to have interracial friendships, but they thought their mothers would be sad or angry, a research team found. White three-year-olds (86 percent) are far more likely than Black three-year-olds (32 percent) to select same-race friends. Maybe not because their mothers directly told them to stay away from interracial friendships. But perhaps because their mothers did not model interracial friendships. The "racial attitudes" of White four- and five-year-olds are more closely related to the *number* of interracial friendships of their mothers than the racial attitudes of their mothers.

The racial makeup of parental friendship circles is nonverbal communication. Researchers have found a direct correlation between a White child's positive attitudes toward Black people and their White caregiver's positive nonverbal behavior toward Black people. Preschoolers learn what racial groups adults are emphasizing, privileging, or normalizing even in the complete absence of explicitly judgmental messages about racial groups. And in these observations, preschoolers are learning from us how to be antiracist or racist.

And what they learn is what they know. That's what is beautiful about kids. They are open to new facts. Children don't have an ideological filter catching anything that challenges their worldview. They aren't allowing the Bonnie and Clyde of beliefs and opinion to rob their minds of facts and science. In that sense, kids are more intellectually honest than adults. Preschoolers are establishing an intellectual foundation for their lives. Preschools can help create an antiracist foundation as part of that process.

Imani's preschool seemed to be providing that foundation. She came to adore her first "big school." Sadiqa and Imani's grandparents came to adore it, too. Her teacher continued to impress us with her creativity and sensitivity. Imani developed close friendships. We didn't see any red flags of racism. And yet I remained leery those first few months. Reflecting now, my wariness was not totally about coming to terms with how racism affects preschoolers. Maybe there was more to my freezing in the doorframe. Maybe something I had long forgotten returned to my subconscious. Maybe what happened when I entered my first big school still haunted me.

CHAPTER 7

Critical Kindergartener

For kindergarten, I attended Winchester Public School 18, a predominantly White school at the edge of Queens and Long Island, New York. It was my introduction to school, *my* first "big school," in the fall of 1987.

I don't remember my first day all those years ago as vividly as I remember Imani's first day. But I do remember that two or three weeks after school started, my first teacher sent home a note in my bookbag. My parents read it with surprise. I had not received a single note of bad behavior during the previous two years in daycare and preschool. But the first note from my first elementary school teacher said I was misbehaving in class.

Days later, the teacher sent a second note about me being disruptive. Ma called the teacher, a young White woman with ash-brown hair. Ma tried to figure out what was going on. Didn't receive a clear answer. After the third note sometime later, Ma took action. She wanted to investigate. Was her five-year-old Black boy misbehaving or was the White woman teacher misbehaving? Or both?

Ma arranged with the principal to spend a day in my class. She wanted to observe me (and the teacher). Fortunately, she had the type of job where she could take a day off.

Getting that job years earlier wasn't easy. She had just returned from a rural Liberian village outside Monrovia where she taught for nine months as a Christian missionary in 1974. But her foreign teaching and missionary experiences and her new college degree in elementary education were all for naught. Hiring for teachers had all but ceased. New York City was laying off teachers during the U.S. recession of 1973–75.

Ma landed a job as a bank teller at Dime Savings Bank in Valley Stream, near John F. Kennedy International Airport in Queens, New York. Soon, she transferred to the department training employees. She worked her way up to manager of Dime's training department by the time she gave birth to my brother in 1980.

Ma's employer and the government did not provide her with paid maternity leave. Nearly forty years later, it remained the same for Sadiqa. Ma had to request three months' leave without pay, thirteen years before President Bill Clinton signed the Family and Medical Leave Act in 1993 providing her that right. Ma's supervisor denied her request. She demanded Ma return to work three weeks after giving birth. Ma successfully appealed to the bank's president.

Ma also received three months without pay after I was born, on August 13, 1982. Ma and Dad brought me to a single-family house in Queens Village, not far from the Belmont racetrack, home of the third leg of the Triple Crown of Thoroughbred racing. Our neighborhood: mostly Black. But the school I'd attend for kindergarten resided in a mostly

White neighborhood. I had been going to that White neighborhood for years to attend preschool at the Cross Island YMCA. Had my White classmates been coming to my Black neighborhood for years?

Not long after I started kindergarten, a group of White children aged three, four, and five were asked by researchers to create neighborhoods. They were given drawings of people from different racial and ethnic backgrounds along with neighborhood structures, like homes, schools, churches, playgrounds, and stores. The children re-created the very neighborhoods that the structures of racism had largely made for them. White children routinely created neighborhoods that integrated White, Chinese, Puerto Rican, and Crow Indian children, while separating out Black children into different neighborhoods. White five-year-olds were the most likely to separate out Black children. By contrast, the Black, Crow Indian, Chinese, and Puerto Rican children created neighborhoods that integrated children of all races and ethnicities.

My parents became first-time homeowners in 1981, the year before my birth. The house of three bedrooms and two baths was slightly more than a thousand square feet. Plants covered much of that space, at least in my memory. They occupied the large bay window on the main level: a monster plant, a philodendron, a praying hands plant, and a fern gifted to my parents at their wedding in 1976.

I had the middle bedroom upstairs, between my parents' room and my older brother's room. Of course, a towering plant took up too much space and blocked the only window. The plant always seemed to be staring at me. Did it function as Ma's kid monitor?

Black homeowners were also being monitored. A racist assumption goes that Black people do not take care of their homes. That would have been news to me as a child. Because our house appealed beautifully from the curb. Its beige siding hung with green trim.

There was a long bed of flowers to the right of the concrete steps to my house. Green shrubs were encircled by a yellow rosebush, purple and red petunias, white and pink lilies, red and yellow daylilies, orange and purple azaleas, and black-eyed Susans. At the top of the first flight of stairs, a long platform hugged a bed of grass that could not have been cleaner or greener. My father—and eventually I—had to keep the grass cut so it never disturbed or distracted from my mother's flowers in front of it and behind it. The platform led to the second flight of stairs up to the front door that overlooked all these red, yellow, and purple blossoms, and all sorts of chrysanthemums.

My mother took care of all these outside flowers and inside plants like they were her adopted children. She made it as clear as a summer day to her biological children that if we ever injured any of her adopted children, we would be next. What would have happened if we *killed* one of them? I can imagine Ma acting on that old Negro spiritual: "I brought you in this world, and I'll take you out."

I was growing conceptually. And a growing mind is a questioning mind. Apparently, I asked questions constantly, like so many children, including questions my parents couldn't answer, like: "Who was before God?" "Why is the sky blue?" And then there were my questions of defiance: "Why do I have to go to church again?" "Why do I have to get out of the tub?"

Ma had finished giving my two-year-old body a bath. The water and soap and dirt had drained out. She dried me off.

"Time to get out of the tub."

Leaving my left leg in the tub, I pulled out my right leg, touched the cold bathroom floor, and looked up.

"I'm out of the tub," I said, smiling, showing my teeth and power.

"Boy, if you don't get out of that tub," she snapped, showing her teeth and power.

Starting kindergarten three years later, I did not respond well to adult assertions of power. When Ma or Dad or another adult asked me to do something unreasonable, I asked "Why?" No response battered my feelings more than "Because I said so." I was like Imani: I resisted when adults expected me to do as they said without question. When people explained things to me, I'd be fine, like Imani whenever I explained to her that someone was coming in or departing from the front door. Most times, my parents explained things to me. My preschool teachers did. Apparently, my first kindergarten teacher did not.

My parents liked to debate where my defiance, this onslaught of questions, came from. Sometimes they conceded the obvious: What they did rubbed off on me. I defied because I saw them defying, especially my father. I asked because I saw them asking, especially my mother. Caregivers must model a critical home, a critical classroom, a critical community for kids to defy and question everything that's questionable. Easier said than done, as every teacher and parent and grandparent and daycare provider knows.

Then again, not everything is questionable. Facts are not questionable. Not all racial questions are antiracist. Our questions should be premised on the basic fact of our common humanity. To be racist is to assume that racial groups are not, or may not be, equals. This racist assumption ignores the nearly six centuries of power constructing the races and failing to prove that these racialized groups are anything but equals. To be antiracist is to assume that racial groups are equals. These different assumptions lead to different questions. Racist: What is wrong with those people? Antiracist: What is wrong with these racist policies? Different questions lead to different solutions. Racist: changing people. Antiracist: changing policy. The question—if wielded in antiracist fashion—is the most powerful sentence. The question is the seed to knowing. This process of persistent questioning is the key to critical thinking. To raise an antiracist is to raise a critical thinker.

And to raise a critical thinker is to raise an antiracist. Next to ensuring that all children have lodging, food, health, safety, empathy, and childproofed environments, perhaps the most important job of societal caregivers is to ensure that all children are being raised to be critical thinkers. Not uncritical believers in secular mythology. From preschool to college, the best policies and the best teachers are those focused on raising critical thinkers. Literacy is not an end. Literacy should be taught as a means to critical thinking. Knowledge isn't an end. Knowledge is a means to critical thinking. The smartest student is not the student who is the most literate, or who knows the most. The smartest student has the greatest desire *to* know—to know all the facts and perspectives of human life and of the world. As educator and philosopher Paulo Freire states, "Knowledge emerges only through invention and reinvention, through the restless, impatient, continuing, hopeful inquiry human beings pursue in the world, with the world, and with each other." The more our children know, the stronger their foundation to question injustice and unfairness, and to protect their own minds from propagandistic lies. Few lies about human life are more dangerous than racist ideas.

Psychologist Debbie Walsh did not mince words: "Thinking critically is the antithesis of prejudicial thinking." According to the American Philosophical Society, one of the many critical-thinking "skills and dispositions" is "flexibility in considering biases, prejudices, stereotypes, egocentric or sociocentric tendencies." To be a critical thinker is to be inquisitive on a range of issues, to trust the reasoning process of questioning and investigating and discovering and complicating, to be open to different thoughts and informed opinions, to be able to understand those differing opinions, to be honest about one's own worldview, to be capable of suspending or changing one's own thinking on a topic. Critical thinking is the "willingness to reconsider and revise views where honest reflection suggests that change is warranted," as the American Philosophical Society explained.

Critical thinkers are not confined by what psychologists call *confirmation bias,* or how people tend to "seek and find confirmations" of their own views and "disregard disconfirmations" of their views. Confirmation bias is the opposite of critical thinking, of the self-critical journey of being antiracist. But confirmation bias is already happening with our children. Research has shown that White children better remember stories that reinforced racist ideas about Black Americans as mean, dirty, or lazy than stories with the same racist ideas about White people.

Most teachers—and likely parents—say they value critical thinking. In reality, there exists "a gap between teachers' values and their practices," as Concordia University researchers find. What did my first teacher value? What was her practice?

When Ma returned to work in November 1982, my paternal grandmother took care of me. After a while, Grandma got sick, physically—which required an operation—and cognitively, with dementia. My parents had to solve the chronic problem for working parents of young children in the United States: childcare. Universal free childcare for kids under three remains as essential as universal free preschool for three- and four-year-olds. It can prevent what has happened to millions of working women over the years, what happened to Ma. She had to quit her hard-earned managerial job to stay home with me in 1983. Meanwhile, Dad continued working, advancing his career.

Our stint at home together lasted almost two years. In 1985, Ma landed a job as a trainer at Electronic Data Systems (EDS), where she worked for thirty years until she retired (Hewlett Packard acquired EDS in 2008). I went to daycare for a few months until I turned three, and on to a preschool at the Cross Island YMCA, which was around the block from my first big school.

Ma's day of observing my kindergarten class arrived. It must have been toward the end of September in 1987.

We arrived at the school earlier than normal and I ran into the schoolyard to play as Ma found somewhere to wait. As the day's starting time approached, the teachers came into the yard. Students lined up with their classmates. The lines filed out of the schoolyard into the hallways and into our classrooms. When I walked into my classroom, I saw Ma seated at the back.

Among my parents, Dad is the talker; Ma, the listener. She listens deeply and observes keenly, traits I learned from her. I'm most at peace when I'm listening and observing, studying. Perhaps that's why I grew into a researcher. I enjoy quiet work. As they did for me, Ma's listening and observing and studying were ultimately to prepare her *to teach*. But I'm also a writer and speaker like Dad. Once upon a time, Dad yearned to be a poet.

Perhaps Ma was thinking about her dashed plans to be an elementary school teacher as my teacher began class. Maybe any regrets came and went as soon as she started to observe. Ma saw a group of kindergarteners at vastly different developmental levels. What a challenge for any teacher, let alone one who Ma suspected was inexperienced. The teacher divided the students into groups based on developmental levels. Tried to teach us that way. Ma even jumped in and worked with one group of kids.

When my group finished our work early, Ma observed the teacher instructing us to sit at our seats, do nothing, be quiet, be still, and wait until *all* our classmates finished. She never explained why. Didn't make sense. In those days kids were considered disruptive when they thought for themselves. The same is true today, depending on the class and race and gender and sexual orientation and ability of the child, depending on whether the child is transgender or gender nonconforming.

I wasn't learning critical thinking. My first teacher did not organize her lessons or units around the three instructional methods most effective in teaching critical-thinking skills to kids of all ages: dialogue, exposure to problems to solve, and direct mentoring. Dialogue is particularly effective when teachers pose questions, and there are teacher-led discussions or teacher-led group discussions. Facilitating student problem-solving and role-playing are also impactful methods. But it goes deeper if critical-thinking instruction is tailored to cultivating children to be antiracist. When age appropriate, a wide variety of data and information on race and racist ideas must be paired with a variety of critical-thinking activities. Teachers must draw clear connections between what students are learning in the classroom and what students are learning in the world.

A recent study in Sweden found that high school students

attending classes where critical thinking was systematically taught reported lower levels of anti-immigrant attitudes than students in classes where instruction in critical thinking was scant. These sociologists defined instruction in critical thinking as promoting "initiative and independent judgement as well as problem solving and conflict resolution." In the end, the researchers concluded "that developing critical thinking skills better equips students to overcome stereotypical thinking."

Perhaps the best way to develop critical-thinking skills with preschoolers and kindergarteners is with the question. Kids are asking their caregivers tons of questions. Why can't caregivers return the favor with questions when opportunities arise? We are walking to the store and see a Latinx homeless man: "Why do you think he's homeless?" We are watching coverage of police violence: "Why do you think that cop kept his knee on that man's neck for so long?" We are at the library: "Why do you think there aren't more picture books with dark people on the covers?" We are headed to see an incarcerated relative: "Why do you think they keep caging so many Black and Brown people?" Even if they don't know, we should not stop asking. We should not stop them from critically thinking about racism.

In other ways, we raise a critical thinker in much the same way we raise an antiracist. Asking, not telling. Modeling, not lecturing. Radically changing the environment and ourselves. "Research suggests that direct teaching of prejudice-reduction techniques may be ineffective, whereas indirect teaching of the skills and dispositions needed to combat prejudice is effective," psychologist Debbie Walsh explained. "This simply means that merely telling students they should not be prejudiced is ineffectual."

·   ·   ·

On that kindergarten day, I kept finishing my assignments earlier than my peers and then I'd sit there and do nothing, being quiet and still while I waited. My other classmates did the same as they finished their assignments. But not for long. Soon we'd start shifting in our seats. We'd start talking. We'd leave our seats to go and play with something or bring the plaything back to our seats.

The teacher saw us as unruly, but the truth is: How can you expect five-year-olds to *not* do their own thing when they aren't engaged? And I don't know if she saw *us* as unruly. I don't know how she saw my White classmates. I don't know if she sent notes home to their parents, too. Whatever my first teacher saw didn't matter as much as what Ma saw: a White teacher singling out her Black boy as unruly.

Did my introduction to a big school end up being my introduction to racist harm? Is that why I was so scared for Imani on her first day of school? Is that why I didn't want to leave the doorframe?

What likely happened to me as a five-year-old happens to many Black children. White teachers disproportionately target and discipline Black male students for minor infractions. This targeting has a *teaching* effect, nurturing the racist perceptions of the children who witness this disparate treatment. By age six, most White children "show significant degrees of pro-White, anti-Black bias," psychologists Phyllis A. Katz and Jennifer A. Kofkin found. One study of White kindergarteners found 85 percent held racist ideas about Black people. Another examination found at least two-thirds of White children between the ages of five and seven described Asian, Black, or Native people as "bad or disliked."

The racist influence teachers have on White students is even more widespread. Teachers, in general, have the highest expectations for Asian students. Teachers have higher expectations for White students than Latinx and Black students. Teachers tend to make more referrals for gifted programs and fewer referrals for special education and punishment for White students than for Latinx and Black students. All this is teaching classrooms of kids racist ideas in nonverbal ways, while also failing to see individual students for who they really are and what they really need.

Aside from my mother's observations and instincts, the research suggests that it is unlikely my first teacher sent notes home to all the students doing their own thing after finishing early. It is likely she sent notes home to the students she thought were misbehaving the worst. Can Black boys escape being perceived as the worst?

Back in September 1987, Ma observed me in fear. "I knew as a Black boy if you started out school getting notes home then it would be downhill from there," she told me recently. Prison or death awaited me at the bottom of the hill, with racism pushing me on down and blaming me for falling.

Lunchtime came. Ma didn't go to the lunchroom. She bade me and my first teacher goodbye, walked out of the classroom, down the hall, and out of the school's front door. She stopped as the door closed behind her. She exhaled deeply. She lowered her head almost as if to pray. "Lord, I have to get him out of there," she said to herself.

The Lord seemed to answer. A solution popped into Ma's head. A friend had told her about an early-childhood magnet school that served kindergarten through second grade off Springfield Boulevard in southern Queens. Fifteen minutes later, Ma was walking into P.S. 251, asking to speak with the principal. They met. Ma toured the school. Met the kindergarten teacher. Observed her engaged students. Pictured me there blossoming. Apparently, Ma had talked me up and impressed everyone. The principal informed Ma that a spot had just opened up in kindergarten. Ma enrolled me on the spot.

In this new school, my second teacher in kindergarten was going to be Black. It's a sad fact, but having a same-race teacher "significantly increased the math and reading achievement of both black and white students." The effects of same-race teachers on student achievement are most significant among "lower-performing black and white students." Assigning a Black teacher to a Black male student, especially to the most economically deprived Black male students, in third, fourth, and fifth grades significantly reduces the likelihood he drops out of high school. (I had Black teachers in the fourth and fifth grades. Shout-out to Mrs. Miles and Mr. Henry!) Research on the impact of same-race teachers focuses on Black teachers-students because such a pairing is exceptional compared with White teachers-students. In fact, *The Washington Post* reported in 2019 that "99.7 percent of white students attended a district where the faculty was as white as the student body."

The reason for the success of Black teacher-student pairings is simple: higher expectations. Black teachers tend to have higher expectations for the same Black student than White teachers. This trend seems to apply to same-race teachers and students across the board. Black, White, Asian, and Latinx teachers generally give more favorable assessments to the abilities of their same-race students. Higher expectations from teachers that students will finish high school and college translate into greater high school and collegiate completion rates. To be an antiracist teacher is to have the same high expectations for all students no matter their identity.

When Dad got home, Ma told him about the observations and the opportunity. He trusted her judgment. Together, they told me before bed. "We found another school for you," Ma said. "I don't feel that teacher can teach you anything."

The next morning, Ma drove me to P.S. 251 for my second first day of elementary school. I'd be there until second grade. None of my Black teachers there ever sent a note home about me misbehaving.

But I still wish I didn't leave my first big school in that way. Ma did not share with me her observations of racist mistreatment, her fears of me going downhill if I stayed there. I probably knew something was wrong. I probably knew my first teacher was targeting me. I didn't resist leaving.

I probably didn't know how to express what I was experiencing. No one was teaching me how to handle racist mistreatment. But I needed to know, to protect myself and others. I had a run-in with my second White teacher. This time, in the third grade.

CHAPTER 8

Aware Kid

M aybe the day was May 5, 1990, a Saturday. With intense work schedules on weekdays and church activities on Sundays, my parents shopped only on Saturdays. They did not go to the shopping district on Jamaica Avenue anymore. It was no longer the shopping hub of southern Queens and western Long Island. The anchor stores departed as the White shoppers did. Macy's closed in 1978, Gertz in 1980, and Mays in 1988. Small businesses remained for Black, Asian, and Latinx shoppers, low-income shoppers, and young people looking for the hottest new gear. It would soon be my home away from home.

Not for my parents. Instead of the short ride to Jamaica Ave., my parents took the longer drive to Green Acres Mall in Valley Stream, Long Island, just outside Queens. The Green Acres Mall opened in 1956 to cater to White Americans who fled the city to newly built housing in the Long Island suburbs. White shoppers traveled to the mall on the same parkways that urban planner Robert Moses designed to halt poor people and people of color in the city from traveling to Long Island. Low-clearance bridges blocked public buses from the city. Public buses were the way to get around Queens. Not the way to get to Long Island.

But now Green Acres had started to attract more and more Black shoppers in southern Queens alongside the White shoppers in western Long Island. Ma, my brother, and I were shopping at Green Acres that day for birthday presents for Dad. His thirty-ninth birthday approached (my very age as I write these words). I was seven years old at the time; my brother, nine.

Ma is a serious shopper. Frugal and meticulous, she hunted for the best sales in stores. She wouldn't step foot in a store if sales hadn't wooed her inside. She scrutinized sales sheets in Sunday newspapers like her life depended on it. In many ways, it did. Our middle-income family stood two lost jobs away from falling into destitution, like many low- and middle-income families without personal safety nets in the 1980s, when the Reagan administration was assaulting the community's safety net.

A&S wooed Ma on this day. Ma pointed us toward sales in the men's department. I noticed a salesclerk watching us. She did not approach us and ask if we needed help. She kept her distance. As we moved from looking at the dress socks to picking out a tie, she followed us. From the ties to the dress shirts, she followed us. From the dress shirts to the suits, she followed us. I kept eyeing her. She kept eyeing us.

By age six, children have acquired the cultural and social-cognitive skills that allow them to independently identify racism and other forms of oppression. With each passing year, these perceptions sharpen. It is during elementary school that children move from being relatively unaware of the racist ideas of others, to being able to infer them, to an awareness of broadly held racist ideas—and forms of racist discrimination.

"Why is that person watching us?" I asked Ma as she examined marked-down trench coats. Tall and slender, Dad loved trench coats.

Ma glanced at the White woman as she pretended to organize some coats nearby. Ma knew exactly where she was.

"She wants to make sure we ain't trying to steal anything," Ma said.

Ma's eyes locked back on Dad's potential gift. Ma did not explain why the clerk thought *we* might steal something—as opposed to any of the White families the woman passed while following us. And yet the times when children ask questions are the most important learning opportunities. Ma could have answered:

"What she's doing is called *racial profiling.* That is when people follow Black people around because they think Black people are criminals. Do you think Black people should be followed like we are criminals? Do you think what she's doing is wrong?"

Not explaining racism to children in their moments of recognition leaves children having to explain it to themselves. So how did I explain what I saw to myself? Did I think there was something wrong with my family? With Black people? Did I think she followed Black people more because Black people stole more? Did I explain it to myself with racist ideas?

Probably so. But there's a chance I did not. Maybe Ma's socializing me to be a critical thinker already allowed me to ask some of those questions myself, even without Ma's prompts. And maybe, just maybe it helped that Ma had already conveyed to my brother and me nonverbally that "No matter how many say so, my sons, you are not a problem." She made us feel as African American Studies scholar Imani Perry wrote in a literary letter to her sons: "Mothering you is not a problem. It is a gift. A vast one. A breathtaking one, beautiful."

Was I developing a greater awareness of racism at this time, like other kids? Black and Latinx children "show earlier and greater awareness of broadly held stereotypes" than White and Asian children. These children often bear "stereotype threat," a vicious cycle by which their worry about validating racist stereotypes (while taking a test, for example) hinders their performance. But how does that awareness of stereotypes come? How can this awareness come for all children?

I wonder if one of the White kids in the store noticed this clerk following my family. I wonder if any of them asked their parent, "Why is she following those people? Is it because they are Black?" How would their parent have responded? Explained the racial profiling? Or closed a newly opened mind with: "No, don't say that. It's not a racial thing. Let's go."

If studies show White parents are the most likely to totally deny racism, then Black parents might be the most likely to totally accept it. A total denial *or* a total acceptance has the same effect. No reason to address it. No reason to critically think. Ma was used to being racially profiled. "I accepted it and moved on," she recalled. She expected the same from me at seven years old.

My grandparents expected the same from Ma at seven years old. Her father complained bitterly about White racism. But he didn't talk to his six kids about it. It did cause him to join the Great Migration and flee Georgia for New York City after serving in the Second World War.

Almost as soon as he left, Granddad's brothers urged him to come back home to Guyton, about thirty miles northwest of Savannah. They claimed the stranglehold of White supremacy had eased. He and Grandma obliged, moving back from NYC in 1957 when Ma was six. Ma enrolled in an all-Black elementary school three years *after* the *Brown* decision. Her parents didn't get on the voting rolls. Grandma went back to laboring in the White-owned fields in Effingham County, picking fruits and vegetables, and stringing tobacco. She had heatstroke once. Almost died. After Grandma recovered, she returned to the scorching fields to earn a living that risked a dying. It was the old song of racial capitalism.

Granddad went back to pressing clothes in downtown Guyton on the White side of town. When they walked the miles to visit their father at work, Ma and her siblings were told: "Once you cross into the White section, do not talk to anybody, do not look at anyone, do not go in any yards, do not stop or shop. Just walk there and come back."

For many caregivers of Black, Brown, and Native children, the fear today is less about encountering the line of segregation— it's about encountering the police. Black, Brown, and Native parents give talks to their children today about how to remain safe from the racist violence of cops and wannabe cops. After wannabe cop George Zimmerman chased and killed seventeen-year-old Trayvon Martin on February 26, 2012, counseling psychologists Anita J. Thomas and Sha'Kema M. Blackmon asked 104 Black parents how they described the murder to their children aged six to eighteen. Nearly 30 percent provided "behavioral guidelines" for children, "including what to wear, the need to walk with others, and how to respond to authority figures and strangers." In addition, 14.7 percent of Black parents explained Zimmerman's act as a "reflection of racist beliefs and attitudes"; 13.1 percent described the death as "an individual act of violence"; and about 10 percent did not discuss Martin's death with their children.

Around the time Ferguson police officer Darren Wilson fatally shot Michael Brown on August 9, 2014—sparking demonstrations and news coverage across the United States—sociologist Megan R. Underhill surveyed a small group of middle-income White parents in Cincinnati, Ohio. Of the twenty-nine participants interviewed after Brown's death, twelve reported discussing it with their children. But ten out of the twelve adopted a "neutral or a defensive colour-blind frame." Only two of the study's participants openly acknowledged and discussed racism past and present. Underhill concluded that these White parents were attempting to curate a "worry-free" racial life for their White children.

The most "worry-free" racial life is to thoughtlessly support racist policies, express racist ideas, and deny when one is being racist, and to hardly worry about the harm one has wrought on others. What's worry-free for the perpetrator is worry-full for the victims. If other parents worry about their children being aware of racism, then I worry about my child *not* being aware. Because unaware children of all races are more likely to harm themselves and others.

Weeks after my family was racially profiled in the department store, I graduated from P.S. 251. My parents put me in a new private Lutheran school for third grade. Almost all my classmates were Black. A handful of Asian and Latinx kids. Three White kids, two girls and a boy, who all sat at the front of the class. I noticed the teacher favoring them almost immediately. Overlooking hands of color and calling on White hands. Punishing students of color for minor infractions she didn't punish the White students for.

I also noticed that these three White kids often kept to themselves. We often ask: Why are the Black kids or the Asian kids sitting together in the predominantly White school? But we rarely ask: Why are the White kids hanging together in the predominantly Black school? White children with higher levels of racial prejudice tend to have fewer "cross-race" companions and tend to rate companions of color lower in friendship quality than White friends. Black and White elementary schoolers both indicated that same-race friends provided more intimacy, and those friendships were more stable and lasting, according to psychologists Frances E. Aboud, Morton J. Mendelson, and Kelly T. Purdy. But that comes at a cost.

With White children the most likely to live in predominantly homogeneous racial environments, it becomes more incumbent on their parents to usher them into diverse spaces where they can meet kids of other races. But parents tend to defer the responsibility for widening their child's social life to their school—which is also likely predominantly White. And research shows that teachers in such schools defer this responsibility to their students. My third-grade teacher did. I can't remember her ever ushering one of those White kids to play with the rest of us.

During Black History Month in February 1991, the third-grade teacher asked us to give presentations on Black leaders. I pulled from my stack of Junior Black Americans of Achievement books, an acclaimed series promoted by Coretta Scott King. Dad bought me dozens of these biographies. Martin Luther King, Jr. Ida B. Wells. Frederick Douglass. Mary

McLeod Bethune. Richard Allen. To Dad, this was an ideal age for me to learn about African American history and culture. Maybe because I had started asking questions about race.

I chose the MLK biography and worked hard on the presentation. Not because I wanted a good grade. Not because I wanted to satisfy this teacher. Months before, the teacher had posed a question in class. A Black classmate had raised her hand first and instead of calling on her, the teacher had called on a White girl. I'd had enough. Chapel service had come next. I'd refused to leave after the service ended. I wouldn't end my one-boy sit-in until the principal arrived and heard my very first lecture on racism.

After my sit-in, the teacher and I functioned like co-workers who avoided and despised each other, while looking for any signs of misbehavior we could use to get our enemy in trouble.

When my turn came to give my presentation during Black History Month, I walked to the front of the classroom. I did not look in my teacher's direction. I took a long pause before beginning. I would start when *I* wanted to start. I looked down at my speech, all written out.

I began. I told the story of King's life. Going to Morehouse College. Attending Boston University, where I now teach. Studying the nonviolent philosophy of Gandhi. Boycotting segregated buses. Battling Bull Connor. Fighting the suppression of Black votes all over the South. Proclaiming his dream that one day anti-Black racism would be no more.

"What this all means is King fought for the lives of *Black* people," I loudly proclaimed.

"No, Ibram. King fought for the lives of all people," the teacher interjected, startling me. My teacher had all-lives-matter-ed me before that phrase entered common parlance. She had not interrupted any other student during any other presentation. Why me? Why did she interrupt my talk?

Some studies suggest the racist attitudes of W
declining between ages six and nine. But th
an illusion, a behavior learned from caregiv
blind" and avoid any outward acknowledgm
private opinion is examined, White children aged six to
harbor more racist ideas than their older peers in middle
school and high school—they just don't express them aloud
when they know adults are listening. In other words, kids
aged six to eight are "externally motivated" to hide their racist
ideas. Older children aged ten to sixteen become "internally
motivated" to hide their racist ideas.

What this all means is that in third grade—at around eight
years old—I was not alone. Children are likely being pressured
by caregivers not to talk about racism. Even during Black History Month! For a teacher to dismiss that King fought for
Black people is for a teacher to dismiss talk of anti-Black racism.

By ten years old, the external pressure is no longer needed.
Many White children become more or less like their teachers
and parents: not talking about racism, ignorant of racist power
and policy, reasoning away racial inequity with racist ideas, and
in denial about their society and their own place in it. "A
consequence of increased understanding of norms pertaining
to race," one team of psychologists concluded, "is the tendency to avoid acknowledging race altogether."

This isn't by happenstance. Pre-seven-year-old children do
not simply adopt their parents' racial attitudes and often have
stronger racist attitudes than their parents. Post-seven-year-old
children are more likely to be influenced by the racial attitudes of their parents. At the very age children are more influenced by the racial attitudes of parents—and presumably
teachers—caregivers are abrogating that influence.

Therein lies the tragedy. As six- and seven- and especially

ght-year-olds become more racially aware, they start observing more about race and racism. But the more they try to talk about it, the more their caregivers shut down that talk. The first lesson American children usually receive on racism is that it is unmentionable.

Caregivers must stop putting children back to sleep when they start waking up to racism. Because as they grow, their sleep will only deepen. When they become adults, they will go about putting another generation to sleep. But to raise an antiracist is to break this cycle.

What if kids were instead more systematically taught about racism at the moment they are starting to see it themselves? What if we started by teaching third-graders about the racial inequities that they are already starting to notice—or that affect their lives? What if we taught these racial inequities as the problems that society needs to fix?

Kids can learn that it is a problem that the average non-White school district receives $2,226 less per student than the average White school district. They can be taught the problem of poor White school districts receiving about $1,500 *more* per student than poor non-White school districts. Kids can discover that it is a problem that Black families are up to 4.6 times more likely than White and Latinx families to live in areas of concentrated poverty.

In 2010, an estimated five thousand people of color died prematurely from exposure to polluting cars, trucks, and power plants. This is a problem kids can learn. They can also be taught that Puerto Rican children (17 percent) and Black children (14.3 percent) are much more likely to be diagnosed with asthma than White children (5.6 percent). Pediatricians and pediatric nurses can discuss with children the problem of how the high cost of healthy food in Black and Latinx communities contributes to chronic diseases among children.

By age seven, White children associate White people with superiority and wealth. Seven-year-olds can be living in an area where White people predominate on the wealthier side of town, and people of color predominate on the poorer side of town. Kids can see White people usually in leadership positions, like doctor and principal, while seeing people of color usually in service positions, like maid or waitress. If no one is telling our kids otherwise, then they will think this is normal; that White people have more because they are more; because they are superior. But seven-year-olds can learn that these disparities are a problem. They can learn the basic elements of the racial wealth gap. They can learn about inheritance: When people die they leave their money to their loved ones. They can learn that Black families are much less likely than White families to receive an inheritance, and when they do it is about a third of the value of White inheritances. And when they ask why—*because we know they are going to ask why*—we can then teach an age-appropriate history of structural racism. We can strive to teach the basic elements of slavery, of sharecropping, of Jim Crow segregation, of redlining, of standardized testing, of mass incarceration, of tax laws, of predatory lending—and how these structures have contributed to the racial wealth gap.

What if our elementary schools began teaching the elements of racism? What if the instruction became more advanced as students progressed to middle school and high school? What if while learning about racial inequities students were learning that though groups may look different and practice different cultures, under our skins and cultures the different racial groups are equals? It'd be so enlightening. Students seeing bad rules as the racial problem—not bad people. Students learning about people of all races across time and space, fighting these bad rules.

What if teachers learned about racism as they prepared to be teachers? To raise antiracist humans we must raise an antiracist teaching force. But the training of teachers remains grossly inadequate, like their salaries. Most teacher education programs provide teachers with only one or two courses on "multicultural education, culturally responsive pedagogy, teaching English language learners, or social justice teaching," found educational researcher Christine E. Sleeter. Among the multicultural education courses that are taught to prospective teachers and working teachers, the majority (58 percent) celebrated "difference and self-awareness." But they "failed to consider systemic inequities in education," let alone society. Less than a third (29 percent) of these courses prompted participants to explore "power relationships, oppression in society and schools, and the ways in which educators reify or dismantle inequity." Nearly a fifth (16 percent) of the multicultural courses for teachers conveyed racist ideas, particularly "assimilationist terminology and often included 'othering' language when referring to non-dominant groups."

The problems most visible to teachers trained in this way are likely the ones tied to student behavior, while the deeper structural problems are harder to name and see. Take a recent study of public school teachers in the U.S. Southwest, where about 40 percent of the teachers and 80 percent of their students were people of color. When asked to explain the academic struggles of their students, the teachers blamed the students: attendance and participation (81 percent), student motivation (66 percent), families and communities (52 percent), and home language (30 percent). Teachers were less likely to blame structural factors like inadequate resources (48 percent), institutional structure (24 percent), and administration and leadership (18 percent). Teachers were less likely to point to cultural mismatch (33 percent).

If teachers are not systematically taught about other cultures, then how can they even begin to connect with the other cultures of their students? If teachers are not clinically taught about power and structures, then how can they instruct their students on something they barely grasp? It's easy to blame the teachers. It's not teachers' unions that are the problem. It's the union of teaching preparatory programs and professional development courses that leave teachers ill-equipped to enter real classrooms and prepare students to enter the real world.

In the real world, there are multiple cultures. In the real world, there is difference *and* sameness. In the real world, there is racial inequality and inequity. In the real world, there is racist power reinforcing structures that maintain inequity. In the real world, children are making sense (*or nonsense*) of the real world of inequity. To educate a child is to prepare a child for the real world.

When my third-grade teacher stopped me with her comment about Martin Luther King, Jr., fighting for *all* people, I turned to her for the first time since I walked to the front of the classroom.

"NO! King fought for the lives of BLACK PEOPLE!"

I glared at her. We locked eyes like horns. Moments felt like minutes. She looked away.

I turned back to the class, and shouted, "KING FOUGHT FOR THE LIVES OF, UM, BLACK PEOPLE!"

I trembled. I looked down at my words. I couldn't find my place in the script. I could not finish.

"Thank you," I said, eyes down.

Into the awkward silence, I paced back to my seat. But I was not looking for applause. I was upset. I was thinking. Was I right or wrong? I planned to ask my parents.

That night as we were finishing dinner, I sat at the kitchen table with my brother, who was still eating. My brother always had the best appetite in our family. My father left the table to take the garbage out and my mother stood washing the dishes. I was trying to assemble the courage to tell Ma about what happened in school. As I started talking, Dad returned to the kitchen. He heard most of the story.

I finished the story. "So, Ma. Who was right?"

"I think the teacher was right," she said rather matter-of-factly as she washed. "King did fight for the rights of all people."

"But . . ." Dad cut off my opening argument, standing by the door to the basement.

"I think Ibram is right, too."

Ma stopped washing the pot. She looked out the window over the sink. Dad continued. "King did fight for the rights of Black people. But the movement transcended Black people."

"What do you mean by transcended?" I asked, curious.

"The civil rights movement helped many groups of people: Asian Americans, Hispanic Americans, even many White people. But you were right, son, King did specifically fight for the rights of Black people."

"You are right, Larry," Ma chimed in, bringing on my smile.

I didn't smile too wide. I still had to go to school tomorrow, where I wished I could have this conversation in the classroom. But my teacher had not developed what English teacher Matthew R. Kay called the *ecosystem* that "successful race conversations depend on." The elements are healthy classroom relationships, sound conversational structures, and honest interpersonal skills. And "without clear methods of establishing purpose," Kay added, "students will rarely decide to invest enough mental, spiritual, and emotional energy to move any race conversation from light to fire."

Sometimes caregivers avoid discussions about race with their kids because they don't know the right answer. But oftentimes the right answer is simply to have the discussion in the first place, even when caregivers and their kids don't arrive at the right answer. Having the discussion creates an intellectual space for critical thinking and reflection. I grew up watching my parents regularly discuss matters, learn together, and change their minds as they got further information, or more time for reflection. Don't get me wrong. They were human. They were not always open to learning. They were not always changing their minds.

· Ma seemed to be more openminded in the moment of discussion than my father. Dad normally sat with feedback and came back in an hour or the next day with a changed mind.

My parents went back and forth some more on King and the movement. It was as if they were giving their own Black History Month speeches. Much better than mine. It turned out I was wrong and right. Ma changed her mind. I could, too. I was becoming aware.

After the school year ended, my parents plucked me out of that school and placed me in another: my fourth elementary school to start fourth grade. I was privileged, whether I knew it or not. My struggles in school, with racist discrimination, paled in comparison with the struggles of my brother.

CHAPTER 9

Preteen Disability

The phone rang. It rang. It rang.

My brother and I kept on playing between bites. Ma nodded off from the grueling day. Dad rose up from the dinner table to answer the phone.

My brother's fourth-grade teacher was calling. Notes home for me had become calls home for my brother three years later. He struggled with his fourth-grade teacher during the same school year I battled my third-grade teacher. Which isn't surprising to researchers. Black boys entering the fourth grade have "the lowest reading levels; the lowest expectations from teachers; and the highest suspension, expulsion, and special education referral rates of any racial group of children in the United States," human development scholar Hakim M. Rashid explained years ago. This is not because there's something wrong with Black boys but rather because of the cumulative effects of a policy structure of racism that has already failed them as they reach their tenth year of life.

The calls started coming early in the school year. Probably

before my solo sit-in. Likely in October 1990, three months after the passage of the Americans with Disabilities Act (ADA), which prohibited ableist discrimination against people with disabilities in all sectors of public life.

"There's something wrong with your son. He's not talking," the teacher began to Dad.

The teacher drew the wrong parent that night. Not Diplomat Ma who recognized that her boys could do wrong. If she'd gotten the call, she would've gone into investigation mode, like when I was in kindergarten. Nope, the teacher drew General Dad. My brother and I loved whenever Dad came up to school. A six-foot-three-inch, 180-pound, dark-skinned man with an Afro, trench coat, business suit, and a way with words. Calling Dad up to school (or on the phone) was like calling him into battle. Dad's boys were his country. He defended us no matter what. He was serious.

When my parents met in 1970, and again when they reconnected and started dating in 1973, Ma's first impression of Dad was his seriousness. He didn't smile much in public. He took his relationships seriously. He took his job seriously. He took laughter seriously! He took every single conversation seriously (something that rubbed off on me). He struggled to let things go as I do now. He's gotten better at it. I'm still working on it.

Dad can't stop smiling now when he jests with Imani. But back when he was a young man, Dad had an awful lot to prove. He grew up a low-income dark-skinned boy in public housing in Queens with people around telling him he wasn't going to amount to anything. Is that why he needed only the slightest impetus to jump to the defense of his sons? Because he didn't have generals of his own to defend him when he was a kid? His father wasn't around. His mother worked a low-wage factory job. Coming up to school to defend him meant lost wages.

Did Dad's seriousness come from this pain? Ma had been closer to the pain of Black folks in the segregated South. Dad had been closer to the pain of dilapidated housing, food insecurity, police violence, economic exploitation, and job scarcity that strangled low-income Black urban communities in the North and West in the 1950s and 1960s.

My brother said something to me. He's a loud talker when excited. Probably joked on me for some reason. He's a jokester, too, when excited.

"Oh, I didn't know he could talk," the teacher said, overhearing my brother.

"Yeah, he can talk!" Dad damn near shouted. "What the heck are you talking about?"

Ma woke up.

"Um, well, okay," the teacher said. "Can you ask him to talk more in class?"

At the time, my older brother was ten years old, the age when kids increasingly experience or witness racism. The age when kids usually don't have the ability or vocabulary to talk about it, especially kids with cognitive disabilities.

When my brother was two and a half years old, he wasn't talking in phrases. He'd smile. He'd sweetly say, "Hello." But at times he couldn't tell my parents what he wanted, prompting cries from him and distress all around. I was eight months old at the time, hardly making it easier on my parents. It was a challenging time.

In April 1983, my parents visited our pediatrician, a friendly middle-aged White doctor. He recommended that my brother be evaluated at Long Island Jewish Medical Center, considered the best hospital around. Weeks later, my brother was diagnosed with a speech impairment and a learning disability.

A disability is "any mental or physical impairment that impacts activities of daily life," explained Rebecca Cokley, a disability rights activist. This definition encompasses everyone from my brother to the children of Flint, Michigan, who acquired learning disabilities from drinking the city's polluted water; to civil rights activist Fannie Lou Hamer, who was involuntarily sterilized; to the countless people of all races facing long-haul COVID; to the youth (and adults) acquiring a disability during the trauma of incarceration. A learning disability is a form of disability.

I always wondered if my brother would have been diagnosed differently if he had been a White child. Being evaluated at the best hospital around, being in a middle-income, two-parent household, does not insulate Black boys from being misdiagnosed. Decades after my brother's diagnosis, researchers found that Black boys who attended school districts with houses valued in the ninetieth percentile ($192,027) were "dramatically" being *over*diagnosed with a learning disability. On the other hand, poverty could be a factor, but it is not *the* factor. White students who lived in poverty were *less* likely to be labeled with a learning disability, with deeper poverty correlating to fewer diagnoses.

School districts with large populations of students of color usually protect Black and Latinx students from the overdiagnoses of learning disability. In school districts with the largest populations of Limited English Proficient students, Latinx students are diagnosed at about the same rate as White students.

The racist problem of *over*diagnosing Black and Latinx students also bleeds into the racist problem of *under*diagnosing

White students with a disability. White students attending predominantly White schools have lower odds of disability diagnosis and special education receipt. Yet when White students attend diverse schools, they are more likely to receive disability diagnoses.

The ableist ideas of there being something wrong with kids with *disabilities* intersecting with the racist ideas of there being nothing wrong with *White* kids can prevent teachers, particularly White teachers, from referring a White child for testing. White kids with disabilities end up suffering from White ableist racism by not receiving the services and accommodations they need.

What's more, Asian kids with learning disabilities suffer from the racist stereotype of Asian students as high-achieving "model minorities." Asian kids have the lowest odds overall of being diagnosed with a learning disability, possibly a collateral effect of high academic expectations. Educators often overlook the vast economic and ethnic diversity of the Asian American Pacific Islander (AAPI) community and fail to acknowledge that children of recent AAPI immigrants facing financial hardship have different needs than children of American-born AAPI parents with more economic security. Additionally, scholar Kim Fong Poon-McBrayer explains, "linguistic barriers, cultural differences, and economic pressures" inhibit many Asian parents' ability to advocate for their children against these racist assumptions.

Complicating the problem further, along with racist ideas, sometimes the inability to access advanced diagnostic tools can prevent Black, Latinx, and Native kids from being diagnosed with a disability. Racist ideas of Black kids as intellectually inferior can cause some adults to *not* suspect a learning disability. *The Black girl is not learning as efficiently as other kids not because she has a learning disability, but because she's Black.*

That's the irony: Black kids end up being overdiagnosed in certain circumstances and underdiagnosed in other circumstances. Overdiagnosing and underdiagnosing are both problematic; if inequity in one direction is bad, then inequity in both directions is doubly bad.

One proven remedy for students: teachers of color. "White students experience the most consistent increases in special education receipt from increases in proportion of teachers of color," sociologist Rachel Fish found. Black and Asian children, too. The type of special education referral matters. More teachers of color decrease the likelihood that Black students will be referred to special education for "emotional disturbance," a subjective category that often relies on racist ideas about Black youth. More teachers of color decrease Latinx students being referred to special education classes, likely because teachers of color are referring them to English as a second language services instead of diagnosing them with a speech or language impairment. Though the number of teachers of color is on the rise, only 7 percent of teachers are Black, compared with 15 percent of students; 9 percent of teachers are Latinx, compared with 27 percent of students; 2 percent of teachers are Asian, compared with 5 percent of students; and 1 percent of teachers and students are Native (79 percent of teachers are White, compared with 47 percent of students).

This is not essentially about the race of the teachers. This is about ableist racism—the intersection of racism and ableism. Researchers find that White middle-class women—who make up the bulk of the teaching force—especially struggle with recognizing structural bigotry, like racism and ableism. Disability rights organizers Talila Lewis and Dustin Gibson define ableism as a "system that places value on people's bodies and minds based on societally constructed ideas of normality, intelligence, excellence, desirability, and productivity." The system of ableism creates, re-creates, and codifies institutions, structures, social expectations, and cultural customs that accommodate and normalize the needs of able-bodied people to pursue their daily activities while disregarding or marginalizing the daily needs of people with disabilities.

Ableism is 83 percent of polling places not being fully accessible, suppressing the votes of people with disabilities. It is people who receive Supplemental Security Income being effectively barred from marriage in order to maintain access to income and health insurance. Ableism is reflected in people with disabilities facing unemployment rates nearly double the rate of people without disabilities. Ableism contributes to the high school graduation rate for people with disabilities being nearly 20 percentage points lower than the rate for all students (67 compared with 85 percent)—and the intersection of ableism and racism leads to Black students with disabilities being 1.5 times more likely to drop out than their White peers. Ableism is why at least 38 percent of the people populating American prisons—compared with 26 percent of the U.S. general population—have some type of disability. Ableist racism is why between one-third and one-half of the people being killed by police have a disability—with Black disabled people dying at high rates. More than half (55 percent) of all Black Americans with disabilities have been arrested by their twenty-eighth birthday.

To be anti-ableist is to be antiracist. To be antiracist (and anti-ableist) is to challenge these effects of ableist racism. It is to ensure people with disabilities are at the table of power. It is to believe people when they disclose a disability, listen to people when they request an accommodation, incorporate accessibility into building plans, event plans, website plans. It shows up in our language, too. Anti-ableism means using words like *unreal* (not insane); *unbelievable* (not crazy); *jerk* (not psycho); *awful* (not stupid); *bad* (not dumb); *moody* (not bipolar); *ridiculous* (not retarded); *eccentric* (not mental case); *dismantled* (not crippled); *organized* (not OCD); and *accessible* (not handicap-accessible). To be antiracist (and anti-ableist) is to value and extend worthiness to every human being no matter their personal appearance, no matter their ability to produce, reproduce, or behave in societally prescribed ways. Just as humans look different, humans have different abilities. To be antiracist (and anti-ableist) is to equate—not rank—human difference. It is to ensure that our policies and practices systematically accommodate and normalize all people.

White teachers should make sure their high expectations for all students don't stop them from recognizing when a child of any race may have a disability—in other words, stereotypes about a child's race should not affect the teacher's analysis of the likelihood that they have a disability. At the same time, teachers of color should not assume that they don't need to be antiracist and anti-ableist, too. All teachers must be antiracist for all our kids.

Teachers and pediatricians accurately referring the right students for testing is only the beginning. Teachers, parents, and all caregivers must teach kids of different abilities that kids with disabilities are not inferior and abnormal. I had just turned eight years old when my brother's teacher called home. Kids as young as one and a half or two start asking questions about physical disabilities. Did I? Did my caregivers help me make sense of the one in four people around me with disabilities? Did they teach me that just as people look different and talk differently, people have different ways of moving, learning, and experiencing the world? Did they share with me the importance of accommodations; that "as long as the tools are in place that they need," people with disabilities "lead ordinary lives," as explained by disability and media expert Kristen Parisi? Or when I asked about my peers, or brother with a disability, did they shush me like some caregivers do when kids ask about different skin colors?

After my brother's diagnosis at two and a half years old, Ma and Dad planned to put him in an intensive language-enriched program where he could make up ground in his speech. Several programs refused to take him, claiming he needed to be potty-trained. All these years later, Dad remains angry. The General is still warring over it. His suspicions of racist discrimination may have been correct. White children are overrepresented in the receipt of services for speech or language impairments (SLIs) by the time they reach kindergarten (a critical developmental window when children most need these services), possibly because SLIs are not among the most clearly stigmatized forms of disability. In 1986, three years after my parents' search, White students accounted for 87 percent of students enrolled in New York's speech enrichment programs (even as they accounted for 68 percent of the total school enrollment and likely a smaller percentage of students with disabilities).

My parents found a rarity: a diverse speech enrichment program in Far Rockaway, Queens, thirty minutes away from our home. "He's not potty-trained because he can't tell you when he has to go," the program administrator told my parents.

My brother was like Imani on her first day of preschool. When the small yellow school bus arrived on my brother's first day, he walked out of our house. Didn't say goodbye. Didn't look back at Ma walking behind him. Or me, in her arms.

In the months since my brother's diagnosis, Ma had become very protective of him in a way she'd never become of me. It made sense. Parents of Black children can be ultraprotective, knowing they are raising their children within the dangerous smog of racism. Parents of children with disabilities can be very protective, knowing they are raising their children within the dangerous smog of ableism. Now imagine the level of protectiveness for parents of children of color with a disability, knowing they are raising them within the doubly thick smog of racism and ableism.

My brother settled onto the bus. It pulled away. Ma walked over to her silver Oldsmobile Cutlass. She strapped me into the shotgun seat (car seats were not commonly used back then). She pulled out. Caught up to the bus. Followed it. From pickup to pickup all the way to my brother's school. It could have taken hours. Ma didn't mind. When the bus and her car arrived at the school, she parked. She scoped out her firstborn son getting off the bus and walking into the school-like building that contained several programs for young children.

Ma waited a long while as my brother settled into his class. An internal alarm clock sounded. She jumped out of the car. Came around and grabbed me. Hurried into the school and up to the second floor and over to his classroom of about a dozen students. Holding me in her arms, she froze in the doorframe, thirty-six years before I did the same.

My brother sat at a table. He seemed satisfied, almost content, proud of himself. But Ma, like me, had a difficult time leaving her child behind. Within a week, my brother started speaking more.

My brother remained in this intensive speech program for two years. Before he could enroll in a public preschool, NYC's

Department of Education tested him again in 1985. Diagnosed him again as a person with a learning disability. Placed him in a separate special education classroom.

In recent years, Native Hawaiian and other Pacific Islander students, Asian students, Black students, and Latinx students—were "[more] often segregated in self-contained classrooms or in separate schools" than White and Native students. In other words, AAPI students seem to be the least likely to be diagnosed with a disability, but when they are, they are among the most likely to be grouped with other kids with a disability. During the 2005–2006 school year, White students with disabilities (59.1 percent) were the most likely and Black students with disabilities (43.9 percent) were the least likely to be placed in general education classrooms for at least 80 percent of the time. A decade later, the proportion of students with disabilities of all races in general education classrooms has grown, but White students (65.5 percent) remained the most likely to be integrated.

In 2016, the U.S. Justice Department sued the Georgia Network for Educational and Therapeutic Support for violating the ADA. The DOJ argued that the students in the program—the majority of whom were Black—received low-quality instruction, lacked access to electives and extracurricular activities, and often had their classes in inferior buildings that housed segregated Black schools during Jim Crow.

School districts can no longer openly segregate students by race. But they can segregate students by ability and economic class. Yet ability and race are conjoined—as class and race are conjoined. To segregate by class is to segregate by race. To segregate by ability is to segregate by race. Racist policies have changed sneakers. But they are still running our kids toward racial segregation.

.   .   .

My brother attended P.S. 138 in Rosedale from third to sixth grades. At the edge of southeast Queens, bordering Nassau County and near Green Acres Mall, Rosedale was an "all-White middle-class area" around 1970. White Rosedale residents organized an advocacy group named Restore Our American Rights (ROAR) to maintain their American right to segregate. These White segregationists roared at the sight of new Black and Latinx residents throughout the 1970s and 1980s, threatening, demonstrating, even firebombing a Black home.

On the Fourth of July in 1989, weeks before my brother's first day of school in Rosedale, eight Black youth were playing and setting off firecrackers in a playground about ten blocks from the school. A group of White kids approached. "This is our park," one said, setting off a fight. Outnumbered as a mob of thirty White youth formed, the Black kids ran home. The White mob chased them and surrounded the house. The White kids pounded on the door for a while before leaving. The police later arrested five of them, including the son of an assistant district attorney in Queens.

My family lived five miles away from Rosedale, which was equivalent to living fifty miles away in other places. New York City is one of the most densely populated cities in the world. Neighborhoods are like counties. It can take fifty minutes to drive five miles in Queens. Perhaps that's why my parents were unaware of the White racist resentment in Rosedale. They hoped P.S. 138 would be a good school for my brother since it was in an affluent neighborhood. They didn't hear about the Fourth of July attack. But everybody heard about the Central Park Five case, when five Black and Latinx teenagers were falsely accused of assaulting and raping a White woman in Manhattan's Central Park on April 19, 1989. Real estate magnate Donald Trump called for the return of the death penalty in a full-page newspaper advertisement in May 1989. Black and Latinx youth were the perceived menace to the city. Not White youth in Rosedale or nearby Howard Beach, where in 1986 they murdered a young Black man for being in their neighborhood.

White youth were hardly in my brother's special education classes in Rosedale. There appeared to be an Indian American girl, a White boy, and ten Black boys in his third-grade class during the 1989–1990 school year. All eleven of his classmates in his sixth-grade class during the 1992–1993 school year were Black: four girls and seven boys.

Between 1988 and 1990, educator Jonathan Kozol visited schools in about thirty neighborhoods across the country. The former fourth-grade teacher visited P.S. 24, an elementary school in the Riverdale section of the Bronx that resembled the school my brother attended in Queens at the time. Kozol counted about 700 "mainstream" and "gifted" students, almost all of whom were White or Asian. He counted about 130 students—most of whom were poor, Latinx, or Black—assigned to the twelve special education classrooms that were half the size of the "mainstream" classrooms. Walking into one with the principal, Kozol saw eleven Black children and one White child. "Placement of these kids," the principal explained to Kozol, "can usually be traced to neurological damage." Kozol asked himself in his notes, "How could so many of these children be brain-damaged?"

Meanwhile, the so-called "gifted classrooms" were overwhelmingly White at P.S. 24. In one "gifted" class, he counted nine White students and one Asian student. At the time, Kozol noted, Black children were three times as likely as White students to be placed in special education classes nationwide "but only half as likely to be placed in classes for the gifted: a well-known statistic that should long since have aroused a sense of utter shame in our society."

"What did you say?" Dad asked in a fighting tone.

"Can you ask your son to talk more in class?"

Perhaps my brother's silence signified a depressive symptom brought on by the Rosedale teacher's racist discrimination. The majority of Black preteens between ten and twelve years old report experiencing racist discrimination, and that their close friends have endured the same. Black and Latinx fifth-graders who reported experiencing racist discrimination were more likely to have symptoms of depression. Children who face racist discrimination sometimes become withdrawn and struggle to pay attention, which likely brings on more racist bigotry and more depression.

Sometime later in the school year, the school support team called my parents up to school to share my brother's latest evaluation. My brother was now eleven years old. Every year since his first evaluation, when he was two and a half years old, my brother had been diagnosed as having a learning disability. But this team from his school—no doubt influenced by this fourth-grade teacher—changed my brother's diagnosis to an intellectual disability. While a learning disability conveyed that my brother learned differently from his peers, an intellectual disability conveyed that he was incapable of learning like his peers. *Intellectual disability,* which used to be termed *mental retardation,* is more serious and stigmatizing than *learning disability.*

Recently, the U.S. Department of Education found that Black students ages six through twenty-one are twice as likely as non-Black students to be assigned to the category of intellectual disability. White students are more likely than Black students to be diagnosed with autism. The suspension risk of students with emotional, learning, and intellectual disabilities is much higher than the suspension risk of students with autism. Black students with disabilities, on average, lose seventy-seven more days of instruction from suspensions than White students with disabilities. Losing instructional time is a fact of Black student life, with or without disabilities. When all else is equal—same household income and education, presence of a second caregiver, ratings of child's behavior at home, utilization of special educational services—Black and multiracial Black children are at least three times more likely than their White peers to receive detention or suspension.

Misdiagnosing a Black student—or student of any race—with a more stigmatizing disability is more than a misdiagnosis. It leads the person deeper into the oppressive clutches of ableism. My parents knew the stakes. They closely reviewed the school assessment. Realized the tests were inconclusive. Appealed to the school district and won their appeal. My brother kept the designation of learning disability for the rest of his schooling.

After leaving his fourth-grade teacher behind, my parents made sure school officials and teachers knew the General and the Diplomat were watching. My brother entered his teen-aged years as the delightful child of the family. He did well at school. Rarely caused trouble there or anywhere. Not like racism and ableism. Not like me.

CHAPTER 10

Feared Middle Schooler

The drive into Manhattan always awed. We'd approach from Queens on the elevated highway. The Empire State Building stood tall in the middle of the skyline. Towering monuments stood for towering wealth. I didn't see either in southern Queens. The buildings there were as low as the wealth of the mostly low- and middle-income Black, Latinx, and Asian families who lived there.

By now, Ma and Dad both commuted on the subway to Manhattan each weekday. The only time they brought my brother and me to the island was to visit Ma's younger sister, her Puerto Rican husband, and my two multiracial cousins.

The drive took around forty minutes. But on this day in 1995, the traffic in the Midtown Tunnel prolonged the trip to more than an hour. I was thirteen years old. My brother was fifteen. My aunt's family was making plans to migrate to northern Virginia the next year, around the time many Black people had been leaving northern cities for the South in what has been called the *reverse* Great Migration. Perhaps our visit was to see them off.

Guests had to be buzzed into the apartment buildings at Stuyvesant Town–Peter Cooper Village (StuyTown for short), so when we arrived, we always had to call up to my aunt's apartment on the outside intercom. Sometimes she didn't answer right away and we'd have to wait a long while until she heard our buzzing. In the dead of winter or summer, the wait felt deadly. Ma grumbled as we waited, and grumbled some more as my aunt finally let us into the building, as we rode up the elevator, and as we walked over to her unit. When my aunt opened her door, she'd deflect Ma's irritation as only younger siblings know how to do. My aunt's exuberance and humor always seemed to swallow her older sister's grumbles whole. She always had Ma smiling a few steps into her home.

On this day, someone was entering the building ahead of us. He happened to be a White man. But StuyTown did not just *happen* to be predominantly White in 1995. Back when it opened in 1947, the developer, MetLife, intended the eighty brick apartment buildings to all be occupied by White tenants. "Negroes and whites don't mix," said Frederick H. Ecker, the president of MetLife at the time. "If we brought [Negroes] into this development, it would be to the detriment of the city, too, because it would depress all the surrounding property."

City officials agreed with this disproved racist idea that substantiated MetLife's racist policy. Civil rights and labor organizations tried but could not stop city officials from approving this segregated development, which was specifically marketed to White veterans returning from World War II. Black veterans, like my grandfather, served their country but were not served by their country in this case, in the many segregated and redlined neighborhoods and housing developments across the country. In 1949, the New York Supreme

Court upheld MetLife's "right" as a private entity to segregate, the same right Jim Crow segregationists were claiming in my grandfather's home state of Georgia, the same right ROAR would claim years later in Rosedale. Appeals failed. The U.S. Supreme Court declined to review the case.

Many of the first tenants of StuyTown were Jewish veterans who opposed MetLife's racist policy. They organized the Town and Village Tenants Committee to End Discrimination in Stuyvesant Town. By 1950, MetLife retaliated by moving to evict the tenant leaders, but the protests met with moderate success: Three Black families successfully desegregated the new development. After NYC's city council made StuyTown's segregationist policy illegal in 1951, many Black families were aware of the development's racist origins and stayed away because they didn't feel welcome.

By the time my aunt moved to StuyTown in 1986, my father, ironically, worked at MetLife. Dad started working in their accounting division in 1969, one of two Black people. In time, he swapped this full-time job for a part-time one while he completed his bachelor's in accounting at Baruch College in Manhattan. His take-home pay of $22 per week barely covered living expenses for him and his out-of-work mother, who had acquired a physical disability caused by a work-related injury. During those years he snuck into MetLife's cafeteria to eat the free lunch reserved for full-time staff. Had to wear the same clothes and shoes for years. When he learned about the racist policies of StuyTown, he didn't consider leaving the company. He wanted to leave his working poverty as a student. When Dad graduated from Baruch in 1972, he took a full-time position at MetLife. He worked there for the next twenty-five years.

·   ·   ·

The White man in StuyTown looked back at us as he hurried to enter the building. We tried to enter the building behind him, to catch the door he opened. Keeping a hand on the open door, he turned around, stopping us in our tracks.

He glared at Ma. Looked livid.

"Where are you going?" he asked, his voice as stern as a cop's.

"My sister lives here," she said. "We're visiting her."

The White man looked past Ma. He glared at my brother and me flanking her like wings. Fearful of his fear, we tried to hide our Black bodies behind Ma. To no avail.

The stranger looked us up and down as if he knew us. What did he see? An innocent thirteen-year-old and fifteen-year-old who could be his grandsons or sons or nephews or mentees? He almost certainly did not. If the two boys before him happened to be White, would he have seen his kids? Would he have seen *kids*?

In one study, White Americans "prematurely" perceived Black boys aged ten to thirteen as equally or less innocent than White boys aged fourteen to seventeen, while perceiving Black boys aged fourteen to seventeen to be as innocent as White boys aged eighteen to twenty-one. Respondents rated Black boys as less in need of protection and care, and more likely to be a danger to themselves and to others. When psychologists repeated the study with police officers, they found that officers overestimated the ages of Black felony suspects by an average of about 4.6 years. The more officers dehumanized Black children by implicitly associating them with apes and overestimating their ages, the more often they used force on Black children. Not to mention that White Americans, who disproportionately serve on American juries, generally view Black juvenile offenders as "more similar to adults" than White juvenile offenders, and thereby recommend stronger sentences.

When I was thirteen years old, I was no longer a child to racist America. I was no longer cute when I misbehaved or even behaved. I was no longer like a pet for racist America to play with. For Black children, adolescence is when neglectful policies that deprive them of support as young children turn into helicopter laws and policies that patrol and surveil them with suspicion. Patronizing smiles transform into irrational fears. In racist eyes, I became a man. A Black man, and therefore dangerous, a threat to fear and cage.

The most dangerous racist idea is the idea of the dangerous Black person. The adult criminal. The misbehaving child. When teachers assume Black kids misbehave more than other kids, they keep an eye on Black kids for misbehavior. Wherever teachers are looking for misbehavior, they are more likely to find it. They therefore see more misbehavior among Black kids, which reinforces their racist ideas that Black kids misbehave more. As Black people age, the teacher ages into the cop. The perception of Black people as criminals leads to more suspicions and more cops patrolling Black people. More suspicions and more cops lead to more Black people being arrested. More arrests and jailing of Black people codify the racist belief that Black people commit more crimes, which leads to even more suspicions and even more cops.

In the end, racist ideas lead to Black adults being treated like children who need to be watched and punished, and Black children being treated like adults who need to be feared and restrained. But it goes beyond that. Researchers find that the "adultification" of Black girls is especially pernicious between the ages of five and fourteen. People view adultified Black girls as "less innocent and more adult-like" than their same-age White peers. Stripping them of their childhood innocence, adults imagine that Black girls need "less nurturing," less support, "less protection," less comforting than White girls. No wonder that Black girls are six times more likely to be expelled, four times more likely to be arrested, and three times more likely to be suspended than White girls in school.

Adults impose these racist fears onto their kids, many times without saying a word. They might visit a predominantly Latinx school for an event and their kids see the flash of fear across their parent's face. The kids might overhear them touting tough-on-crime policies as they stare at a Black girl's perp walk on the screen. They freeze up on the street when a Middle Eastern boy asks for directions, when their kid knows they remained calm when a lost White girl asked to be directed a week prior. They worry about the Asian boyfriend in ways they did not worry about the previous White boyfriend. When something goes missing after a Black friend visited, they voice suspicions about the friend to their child. They don't express outrage at the police officers who killed twelve-year-old Tamir Rice in Cleveland and twelve-year-old Adam Toledo in Chicago, but direct it instead at the child who "resisted arrest." They express outrage when young people destroy property after a police murder but show no interest in the murder itself. In other words, they raise their kids in fear. But the real danger is what they are saying to their children, through words and actions, about teens of color.

To raise an antiracist is to convey to kids that kids of color, just like White kids, are not dangerous. That a thirteen-year-old Black boy is as innocent as a thirteen-year-old White girl. That a Native boy is a child just like a Muslim girl and her brother. That all "children" should be receiving support or treatment—not handcuffs. Caregivers should approach the lost Middle Eastern boy on the street and ask him if he needs help. They should express delight when their child is dating someone different, which allows her to learn firsthand about the ways we are all the same—while also not fetishizing that difference. Caregivers should ask their child if their Black friend lost anything, too, when things went missing. They should rage when they learn that the compliant boy was shot dead by police; or say to their child that even if he wasn't compliant, that *child* should be alive. They should explain every chance they get about racial capitalism; that even when communities erupt and property is damaged or destroyed, these same communities have long been victimized by even more destructive plunder, often officially sanctioned, that has kept the people poor. Our children deserve to understand the world around them in all its complexity.

I want caregivers to raise their children to see children of color the way my fourth-grade teacher saw me. I feel a survivor's guilt about fourth grade. My brother's worst grade happened to be my best grade, which delayed my adultification. For fourth through sixth grades, I went to an Episcopalian private school near our home in Queens Village. In fourth grade, the age when Americans started to see my Black boy body as older, less innocent, academically deficient, and a more "appropriate target for police violence," Mrs. Miles saw me as . . . a child. I remember her warming my juvenile coldness. I remember her learning who I am (not what I am). I remember her captivating lessons. I remember her marathons of encouragement when I made mistakes. I remember her teacher's green thumb, cultivating my potential. I remember her sky-high expectations. I remember pushing myself to meet her expectations. I remember receiving 100s on *all* my final exams and the joy that filled me because of the joy that filled Mrs. Miles that day. I remember we embraced, our joy flowing like her ocean into my river.

I went to another school for seventh and eighth grades, a Lutheran school where nearly all the teachers were White and nearly all the students were Black. I remember the coldness of my seventh-grade teacher. It was like kindergarten all over again. I felt this aching boredom. When I tried to free myself of the boredom, my teacher didn't see a bored kid. Like my kindergarten teacher, she saw a misbehaving kid. Don't get me wrong. It is hard to keep middle school students engaged. It is hard to be a middle school teacher. But this is what makes teachers great—and great teachers. Teachers do hard work for a living. And the stakes are high. Like pediatricians and pediatric nurses, when teachers do their jobs right, a child is healed. When they mess up, a child often gets hurt. When teachers fail their students, they really fail their students, just as schools and societies fail teachers by not supporting and training them adequately.

Middle school teachers in one survey perceived Black *and White* adolescents with African American "culture-related movements"—or swagger—as aggressive. They lowered their academic expectations for these students and anticipated they would need special education services. What does an eighth-grader's strut have to do with an eighth-grader's academic potential? Why are teachers "more troubled" by the second infraction of a Black middle school student than a White middle school student? Why are teachers far more likely to recommend "more severe" punishment for the Black students? Why are they more likely to view a Black student's behavior as "indicative of a pattern"? And when Black students resist these racist attitudes and practices, their resistance reinforces the teachers' racist attitudes and practices. They become like the undocumented Latinx person brutalized *by* the police for resisting the racial profiling *of* the police. It's an ever-reinforcing cycle of racist policies and ideas and practices.

Cycles for girls of color often bring together racism and sexism—and sometimes classism. In a school primarily populated by kids of color, teachers perceived the "assertive" behavior of seventh- and eighth-grade Black girls "as challenging to authority, loud, and not ladylike." Sociologist Edward Morris found that Black women teachers were the most likely to police "ladylike" behavior among Black girls. When these girls came from low-income families or had mother-headed households, these misperceptions were worse. Perhaps these teachers intuitively knew that one of the oldest racist ideas about Black women is they aren't ladylike. But the antiracist answer is not policing and punishing and pushing out Black girls who aren't being "ladylike." The answer is to think more deeply about how we are raising our children. Are we—and our institutions—policing how Black girls dress, how they speak, who they love? The antiracist answer for caregivers is teaching and speaking out against the racist idea of the unladylike Black woman. The antiracist answer is encouraging cisgender and transgender Black girls to assert themselves and be themselves, no matter what, no matter their class, no matter the makeup of their families.

But generations of policymakers have built and rebuilt a policed state for youth. Generations of teachers and cops, long before they were teachers and cops, were raised to police the behavior of youth. Societal caregivers are doing this raising. Everyday Americans are raised to see two unknown Black teenagers approaching their building as suspects.

The man kept staring. Likely for a few moments. Felt to me like a long while. He shook his head. He lunged forward with his free arm and shoved Ma, pushing her back into my arms. Then he turned and walked through the door and slammed it shut. He didn't look back.

I raged looking at his back. Not because of the racist discrimination. But because he pushed Ma.

By middle school, I'd grown used to racist discrimination like Ma had. Black youth report more than five incidences of racist discrimination *per day*. Some call these *microaggressions*. I call it all *racist abuse*. Because like abuse, these incidents compound themselves like debt onto our minds, hearts, and bodies, bringing on depression.

If my brother became more withdrawn because of the racist discrimination he faced, then I became more outspoken and oppositional. Some Black youth adopt an oppositional social identity—embracing styles of clothing, speech, and music that White people and our parents demean—as a form of protective resistance. And if there was ever a decade in American history when Black youth needed to protect themselves, it was the 1990s, the decade of my own Black youth. This was the decade when Black teenagers like me were projected as *the* American problem. We weren't children. We were super-predators. "For as long as their youthful energies hold out, they will do what comes 'naturally': murder, rape, rob, assault, burglarize, deal deadly drugs, and get high," political scientist John DiIulio wrote in 1995. Generational shaming, a prison-industrial complex, law-and-order policymaking, broken windows (and bodies) policing, and mass incarcerating and prosecuting were all unleashed on Black youth to protect the American people from the "super-predator." The line of a father figure to two Black male teens in the 1993 film *Menace II Society* says it all: "The hunt is on, and you're the prey."

How does it feel to be preyed upon while being considered the predator? Native youth could have given an answer in 1802. Irish youth could have given an answer in 1853. Asian youth could have given an answer in 1885. Jewish youth could have given an answer in 1902. I could have given an answer in 1995. Middle Eastern youth could have given an answer in 2002. Latinx youth can give an answer today.

White suburban and rural males predominantly perpetrated the school shootings that led to a rapid expansion of "zero tolerance" policies in schools in the 1990s. But urban kids of color felt the brunt of these policies through policed schools, suspensions, and expulsions. Initially these policies focused on so-called "objective criminal activities" like possessing a weapon, but they expanded by the end of the 1990s to "subjectively defined behaviors that have little impact on school safety," like disrespect, insubordination, and disruption.

Racist ideas, unlike economic prosperity, had a trickle-down effect. While police officers and new crime laws harassed us in the streets, my classmates and I sometimes hurled our own racist insults in the classroom. We were kids after all, even if trapped in adultified bodies.

Eighth grade was my funniest school year. I clamored for joy in a school environment I increasingly hated. I developed a thick skin and even thicker sense of humor. Almost all my classmates were jokesters. Almost everyone got joked on for something. Our White teacher allowed it. I remember her fondly for functioning more like an instructor than a cop. She didn't break up banter like it was a fight. She treated us Black kids like the kids we were, while also not letting us get too carried away in our jokes. They joked on my "big ass head." My classmates called me Bonk after the character in a Game Boy game that attacked with his incredibly large head, blaring a rhythmic "Bonk. Bonk." My big head was a big target for big head jokes all year long. But I always had a comeback, clowning my classmates right back every chance I got.

One day, I was sitting alone for some reason in my eighth-grade classroom. I could hear something softly, then louder, then "Bonk. Bonk. Bonk." The door to the classroom flung open. My classmates started piling in, holding their bookbags on their heads, swaying their heads back and forth to the beat of their "Bonk. Bonk. Bonk" chant. One after another came in doing this, grinning. They lined up along the walls of the classroom, encircling me. "Bonk. Bonk. Bonk." Their book-bagged heads flapped in bigness. I sat at my desk stone-faced and staring. My shock turned to embarrassment. My embarrassment turned to anger. My anger turned to amusement by the time my last classmate filed in. They stopped chanting for a moment and stared at the door. They started back again. My White teacher walked in, red-faced, with a bookbag on her head, chanting, "Bonk. Bonk. Bonk." The class burst out laughing. All I could do was join them, thoroughly humbled and thinking, *Damn, they got me. There is no way I could ever top that.*

But Lord knows I tried. We called one boy Speedo. So uptight with no *swag* (as it is termed today). He was, in our lingo, a *herb* (the opposite of cool). Another boy endured camel jokes for the divot on the top of his head. We clowned one girl's tallness, another girl's shortness, another boy's obesity, another girl's appearance, another boy's thick glasses.

Our jokes shot out bigotry. We had internalized so much, including the racist ideology of colorism. We certainly thought there was something wrong or inferior about dark skins or light skins. Medium-toned, I roasted the dark-skinned and light-skinned kids whenever I had the chance.

I starred on my school's basketball team along with the darkest kid in our class. Eighth grade was the pinnacle of my basketball "career." My jump shot was pure when I was thirteen. I aggressively defended. Loved to throw the no-look pass.

One game, I must have scored close to thirty points, draining three-pointer after three-pointer in the second half. I led the team all the way back after being down big early. But my light-skinned teammate blew the game by missing a foul shot at the end. And then *he* got the pretty girl's number! I sneered at his light skin as I watched him talk to the pretty girl after the game.

Light-skinned children and biracial children can often be targeted for racist jokes, and sometimes don't feel a sense of belonging anywhere. At the same time, dark-skinned kids are more likely than light-skinned kids to be suspended in school. Light-skinned kids are more likely to be told they aren't really Black or White. Teachers, parents, and caregivers must be conscious of colorism, actively encourage their child to embrace their skin color—no matter how dark or light. Actively guide the child through their own complicated ethnic ancestry. Encourage them to see lighter or darker skin color as not better or worse—but different.

I was just hating on our teammate and using racist ideas that disparaged light skins to do it. He was tall, attractive, built like a football player, and had more game (with girls, not basketball) than any of us. I had yet to hit my growth spurt and was skinnier than skinny.

Skinnier than skinny—but still dangerous? Our individuality as Black teens didn't matter. Racist America didn't treat us as boys, girls, and nonconforming youth, as kids learning, having fun, making large and small mistakes, and finding our way to adulthood. All the surveilling, policing, and punishment took a toll. It all forced me to go my own way. Toward some of the most ill-advised decisions of my life.

CHAPTER 11

Confined High Schooler

I was accepted into St. Francis Preparatory School, one of the premier private high schools in Queens. But I opposed going. Opposed, even, going to church. Rarely went. I gave up baseball and the piano after playing both for eight years. I was on the cusp of learning to play the piano by ear. These were ill-advised decisions. But I was desperate to escape anything that felt confining. Don't ask me why baseball and the piano felt confining. Psychoanalyzing oneself—or one's teenager—has its limits.

As I turned fourteen in 1996, I somehow convinced my parents to let me attend John Bowne High School in Flushing, Queens, a stone's throw from Queens College. Maybe they were just delighted I wanted to go to *a* school.

John Bowne, my new school's namesake, embodied the contradictions of America's founding. Bowne immigrated to Boston from England in 1649 and ended up in Dutch New York, or contemporary Queens. In 1662, director-general Peter Stuyvesant arrested and deported Bowne for holding

Quaker meetings in his home. Bowne traveled to the Netherlands, where he successfully lobbied the Dutch West India Company to overrule Stuyvesant and enforce the 1645 Flushing charter of religious freedom. While Bowne's name is etched into school façades for his role in securing religious liberty in New York, his enslaving is largely forgotten. Bowne enslaved at least two people to work in the fields surrounding his home in Flushing in the seventeenth century.

My good friend Gil also attended this overcrowded public school of more than three thousand students. I don't remember any White students at John Bowne. White teens had their own predominantly White schools out in the suburbs. I assumed the world was out to get me. Many of my White peers assumed the world was in harmony with them. White teens are likely to assume their friends share their racial beliefs. Which makes sense. They learn from caregivers not to critically discuss racism. Assumptions fill in the blanks when the voice of communication is absent.

If caregivers of White teens are not talking to them about race, then how will caregivers discover the red flags? How will they know if their teenagers are internalizing racist ideas—or worse, if extremists are recruiting them to join White supremacist organizations? White supremacist recruitment on college campuses is increasing. But the typical age range of most extremist recruits is eleven to fifteen years old, a critical stage of development when adolescents are seeking belonging and purpose. In 1987, Christian Picciolini was fourteen years old and smoking a joint in an alley when a bald man in a muscle car pulled up to him to begin his recruitment. Two years later, Picciolini became the leader of the Chicago Area Skinheads. Picciolini has since left the movement and now supports parents of teens and young adults who need help breaking their child free of White supremacy.

These days, the recruitment is more likely to happen on-line, particularly on platforms popular with kids like YouTube, iFunny, Instagram, Reddit, and multiplayer video games. Ten percent of the teens between the ages of thirteen and seventeen who play popular online multiplayer games—an estimated 2.3 million children—recently reported that they had been exposed to the racist idea that "white people are superior to people of other races and that white people should be in charge." But the most common threat (17 percent) of exposure to racist ideas among thirteen- to seventeen-year-olds occurs on social media.

The founder and editor of the neo-Nazi website Daily Stormer has stated his site targets White children beginning at age eleven. Editor and parenting writer Joanna Schroeder watched her boys' online behavior and noticed how racist propagandists strive to turn impressionable White teens into White supremacists. Schroeder observed that the White teens, often from progressive or centrist families, are "inundated by memes featuring subtly racist, sexist, homophobic, anti-Semitic jokes." According to the Western States Center's Lindsay Schubiner, who co-authored a tool kit for caregivers facing online recruitment: "White-nationalist and alt-right groups use jokes and memes as a way to normalize bigotry while still maintaining plausible deniability, and it works very well as a recruitment strategy for young people." Not seeing the nuance, young people share and repeat the jokes. But then get in trouble for doing so at school and online and feel ashamed. Meanwhile, they're consuming propaganda that "people are too sensitive" and "you can't say anything any-more," causing them to believe they are "getting in trouble for nothing," Schroeder added. Their shame is replaced with White male supremacist anger and hate toward women, people of color, Jews, and queer folks. "These boys are being set up," Schroeder said. "They're placed like baseballs on a tee and hit right out of the park. And NOBODY seems to notice this happening." When Schroeder noticed, she intervened. She showed her boys how "these people are trying to pull the wool over your eyes—they're trying to trick you" and "get you to believe something that, if you think about it, you really don't believe." That discussion really connected.

Caregivers must initiate these discussions to protect White teenagers. Discussions, not lectures. Discussions, not accusations and judgments. Open discussions, so the child feels valued and taken seriously, which is the best approach in these situations, according to Harvard psychologist Gil Noam. When White teenagers do embark on discussions on race with antiracist caregivers, they become more tolerant and willing to interrogate internalized racist ideas. From infants to teenagers, the research on White youth remains the same: The more caregivers engage them about racism, the more they're able to protect themselves from racist messages; the more likely they'll enter adulthood being antiracist.

Because at around "age thirteen, kids have a big developmental shift, cognitively," says Alice LoCicero, a clinical psychologist and cofounder of the Society for Terrorism Research. "There's a sense of idealism and altruism and wanting to make a difference in the world. It's an age where a sense of justice becomes really important, and that can be misconstrued and manipulated." What is the sense of justice for our teens? Is making a difference to them stopping the supposed scourge of Jews, Muslims, women, and people of color, like many mass shooters? Is their altruism ridding the discourse of discussion of race and racism, since they've been led to believe talking about race and racism is unjust and racist? Or is their sense of idealism about ridding their world of the long-standing injustice of racial disparities? For me: I strove to help

Black people by encouraging Black people to be better and do better (as if Black people were the problem).

I did think racism existed, but primarily at an interpersonal level. I wasn't alone then or now. In a recent study of African American, Latinx, Asian and Pacific Islander, multiracial, Native, and White teens, researchers found that 78.9 percent of them consider racism to be an interpersonal rather than a structural phenomenon.

I wasn't striving to be antiracist when I entered high school. I was striving for freedom, a different type of freedom from John Bowne. Freedom to rock my baggy button-down shirts over my Carhartt jeans over my Air Force 1s. Freedom to hang out on Jamaica Avenue where my parents only went to hop on the subway to Manhattan. Freedom to skip school or class.

I usually skipped class during the school's multiple lunch periods. I'd play spades in the lunchroom throughout my extended lunch period each day.

One day, my spades partner paused a hand to go to the bathroom (or so he said). Ten minutes later, he still hadn't come back. Time was ticking until the next bell.

I left to find him, asking a friend to watch the other team so they didn't cheat. When I reached the hallway, I heard a commotion. Walked over to it. I pushed to the front of the circle. I saw my spades partner fighting somebody. All I could think was *Damn, that's the end of that game.*

I walked back into the lunchroom, sat down at the table, and started telling the other kids what I saw. We were at the main spades table that always drew the crowd. Of course, I had to talk trash. "He out here whoopin' somebody's ass and I'm trying to whoop y'all ass right here." Before I could finish, my partner sat back down, not completely composed.

"My bad for the wait, gaad," he faintly said, still gathering himself.

Since he was back, the fight probably wasn't that serious. Then again, whenever Black teens fought, it was serious, at least to everyone else. Their futures could be ruined. When White boys fought, they were just being teenagers. Let's not ruin their futures.

"You aight, son?" I replied.

"Of course, motherfucker!"

My partner remembered: It was his turn. He remembered we had won all the books so far. He snapped back into himself. He slammed a little joker onto the table. Started back trash-talking like nothing happened. And oh, that boy could trash-talk!

Teachers were there in John Bowne's classrooms but they might as well have not been. I only remember one Latinx math teacher trying to get to know me, an exception among teachers who mostly treated us students as faceless problems. How could they teach me if they did not know me? How could they know me if they did not know my community? As teacher educator Christopher Emdin explains, "Teaching more effectively requires embedding oneself in the contexts where the students are from." Meaning teachers must immerse themselves in the communities of their students, fully engaging with and learning about the communities, and then making connections in the classroom between what they observed and the content they are charged to deliver.

But instead, teachers avoided or punished me. And I avoided them right back, like I avoided cops outside school. Teachers have been found to be regular sources of racist abuse for Black teenaged males, treating them in "collective deficit terms." Which is to say they assume that Black students are intellectually and culturally inferior and characterize them as "being mischievous, having problematic behaviors, and disengaged from the educational process." Some White teachers don't realize how they are contributing to, if not causing, the behaviors they perceive or see. As teacher-educator Bree Picower explains, "White teachers are often entering the profession with a lifetime of hegemonic reinforcement to see students of color and their communities as dangerous and at fault for the educational challenges they face." This kind of "deficit thinking," teacher-education scholars Marilyn Cochran-Smith and Curt Dudley-Marling say, "pathologizes individual students, their families, their languages and cultures, and the communities from which they come" instead of accounting for the social and institutional factors that might be affecting a student's class performance. In other words, racist, sexist, and classist ideas might lead a teacher to see misbehavior where there is none, because they don't understand the source of or context for a child's behavior. When their racist ideas are challenged, some teachers lash out emotionally: "Stop trying to make me feel guilty!" Or ideologically: "Now that things are equal," racism "is individual not structural." Or they perform: "I just want to help them."

The louder I talked and dressed, the louder I blasted Mobb Deep in my earphones, the louder I hated their school. My teachers at John Bowne were miles away from Mrs. Miles. I was miles away from fourth grade. Close to dropping out. I experienced what education scholar Lisa Delpit calls the "deadly fog" that forms "when the cold mist of bias and ignorance meets the warm reality of children of color in many of our schools."

In 2018, Native (9.5 percent), Pacific Islander (8.1 percent), Latinx (8 percent), and Black (6.4 percent) high school students had the highest dropout rates. These rates were an improvement from 2006, when the dropout rates of Latinx (21 percent), Native (15.1 percent), and Black (11.5 percent) students doubled or tripled the White (6.4 percent) rate, which was twice as high as the Asian (3.1 percent) rate. Pacific Islander high school students were the exception to the declining dropout rate; their dropout rate increased between 2006 (7.4 percent) and 2018 (8.1 percent).

The only thing keeping me in school in 1996 was the wrath of my parents. Ma would have taken me out if I dropped out. Really. And Dad wasn't defending me on this one. The only thing keeping me on the passing side of my classes was wanting to remain on John Bowne's junior varsity basketball team. They called me E Wap. Wap rhymes with "stop." We'd shout "Waaaap" whenever someone swished a jump shot. And I didn't miss many swishes. I had many dreams to swish jumpers in the NBA.

Perhaps being on the basketball team saved me from the harm of being expelled or suspended. Students between the ages of fourteen and seventeen who were suspended or expelled were twice as likely to be arrested *that same month*. Twelve years later, suspended youth were less likely than non-suspended youth to have finished high school and earned a bachelor's degree—and more likely to have been arrested and on probation.

My parents almost certainly noticed that's where I was being pushed. They also noticed the less frenetic and more affordable life in northern Virginia, where my aunt from StuyTown had relocated in 1996. Almost as soon as my aunt left, my parents started to consider following her on the reverse Great Migration. Another aunt had fled for Texas. Other relatives were fixing to move to Texas, too. But uprooting was difficult. Ma had lived thirty-eight of her forty-five years in NYC. Dad had lived all of his forty-eight years in NYC. My brother and I lived our whole lives in Queens.

Perhaps I made the decision easier for my parents. Maybe my parents looked into my future if I remained in NYC. Potential buried. Who knows how much potential racism has buried?

When my freshman year grades came as spring ended in 1997, I was proud of them. Three Cs and two Ds. Enough to remain on the basketball team. My parents were horrified, enough to propel their decision to move to Virginia. They were surprised when I agreed it was time. But I was ready to go, too. My whole environment had become confining. Like those White teens being into White supremacist organizations, I didn't feel like I belonged.

My brother and I lived with my aunt for a few months as my parents looked for jobs and a home in 1997. We attended Centreville High School in Virginia. My parents found a home in the next town, Manassas. We transferred after the Christmas break to Stonewall Jackson High School, a predominantly White school named after the enslaver of six people and a general in the Confederate States Army. In 1861, Confederate vice president Alexander Stephens declared "our new government" rested "upon the great truth that the negro is not equal to the white man; that slavery—subordination to the superior race—is his natural and normal condition." Nonetheless, in 1962, White community leaders branded the school with Jackson's name like a middle finger to the civil rights movement. In 1972, the Prince William County school board voted six to one to continue Jackson's commemoration when the school moved to a newly constructed building. The school's name did not change until 2020.

My parents managed to enroll me in Stonewall Jackson's International Baccalaureate (IB) program, a set of rigorous college preparatory classes that are akin to Advanced Placement (AP) classes. I don't remember John Bowne having IB or AP classes for its students of color. For the class of 2011, the College Board found that 79.7 percent of Black high school students *who would have done well* on an AP course did not take one. Qualified Native (73.7 percent) and Latinx (70.4 percent) high school students were also far more likely to be left out of these courses than White students—even as the number of White students left out of these courses is also incredibly high (61.6 percent). With such vast racial disparities, how is performance on these college prep courses a "race neutral" college admissions factor? How is the SAT exam a "race neutral" admissions factor when its creator, Carl Brigham, was an avowed eugenicist and producer of racist ideas? In 1923, Brigham declared, "The intellectual superiority of our Nordic group over the Alpine, Mediterranean, and negro groups has been demonstrated," with standardized tests providing the proof. Beyond its racist origins, how is the SAT exam a "race neutral" admissions factor when the scores don't necessarily correlate with success in college but do correlate with the wealth of the parents of the test takers—and White people have nearly ten times more wealth than Black people? How is grade point average (GPA) a "race neutral" admissions factor when students taking IB classes get their GPAs artificially boosted? When I was in my high school's IB program, a B counted for 4 points, A for 5 points—more than their respective 3 and 4 points for other students—allowing some Stonewall IB students to graduate with 4.8 GPAs.

Instead of calling these IB and AP courses "gifted" classes, I call them *privileged* classes. The students in the classes are privileged. Colleges give preferential treatment to students who take these classes. These classes are not offered at all or in full in some schools. Others have a full slate of IB or AP classes. Many IB programs require letters of recommendation, allowing eligibility to hinge on teachers' assumptions and expectations of students. Depending on their race, students aren't just steered away from them; they are also steered toward them.

Despite a sizable Black student population at Stonewall, I was typically the only Black student or one of two Black students in my IB classes, where White and Asian kids predominated. I was often alone in the room, but had lots of company among Black kids who are isolated in privileged classes. During the 2013–2014 school year, Black public school students (4.3 percent) were the least likely of any racial or ethnic group to be enrolled in privileged classes, followed by Pacific Islander students (4.4 percent), Latinx students (4.9 percent), and Native students (5.2 percent). Asian students—the group of students with the highest teacher expectations—were the most likely (13.3 percent) to be enrolled in privileged classes, followed by White students (7.7 percent).

When I wasn't told I was an impostor in these privileged classes, I was told I was privileged. To be a student in these classes is to be constantly told you are better than the students not in these classes. It is to be told you are gifted and hardworking—not like those other kids. For a teenager— whether White or Black or Asian or any other race—to be constantly told you are better is to start believing it. How else are you going to explain why so many kids like you or not like you are in—or are not in—these privileged classes? People like you are there because people like you are smart. People like you are not there because people like you are not as smart *as you.* You are extraordinary—not like those ordinary and imprudent other people of your race.

If I didn't have a big head in eighth grade, then I certainly grew one at Stonewall Jackson. Two years removed from hating high school and getting poor grades and nearly dropping out, and now they were telling me I was extraordinary? I hung out with the Black and White kids in the *deprived* classes who were as capable as me, and I was extraordinary? Black students in privileged classes routinely express racist ideas about Black kids in deprived classes, identifying them as lazy, unwilling to work as hard as them. And they complain about being accused of "acting White," without thinking that might refer to them looking down on their fellow Black students, an action too many White people engage in.

As much as I imagined myself as better than the Black and Latinx kids from outside the privileged classes, I imagined myself as less than the White and Asian kids inside the privileged classes. I thought less of myself because I quantified my intelligence, as if that's possible, and saw it lacking. I got lower grades on assignments, and so I thought I must be lower. I had a sub-3.0 GPA, so I thought I must be subpar. I scored lower on the SAT than my peers in IB classes, so I thought my intelligence must be lesser.

My White and Asian classmates in privileged classes were not hostile toward me. They ignored me, made me Ellison's invisible teen, made me feel self-conscious because they didn't want to know me; they didn't want to work with me in groups; they didn't want to study with me outside classes. They avoided me like something was wrong with me.

I didn't mind that my classmates didn't try to befriend me. I didn't want to befriend them. I didn't want them to see my futility and discover I was an impostor. Then again, I wasn't an impostor when I hung out with my friends from outside the privileged classes. I didn't know about the racism (and classism) keeping my friends out of these classes. I just consumed the ideas that I was there because I was better. The more I believed there was something better about me, the better I felt.

I was conflicted, I know. I thought better of myself and worse of myself. But this *conceited insecurity* is the way of being racist.

To be racist is to be conceited *and* insecure. To be conceited is to have an exaggerated sense of self, to think you are better than you really are, to think others are worse than they really are, to think you, and people "like" you in your racial group, sit at the top of an imagined racial hierarchy. To be insecure is to undervalue the self, to think you are worse than you really are, to think others are better than they really are, to think you, and people "like" you in your racial group, sit at the bottom of an imagined racial hierarchy. Conceit and insecurity are the twin children of being racist. Every racist idea is a conceited idea or an insecure idea. Every racist idea proclaims the proficiencies or deficiencies of a racial group. Racist ideas are red meat for ravenous egos and insecurities.

And it's not just students who face this dichotomy—parents also suffer from these twin manifestations of racist thinking. There are parents who think better of their kids based on what their words say, but think worse of their kids based on what their policies say. These parents *say* their kids are smarter and harder working than those other kids but these same parents resist equalizing educational opportunities between their kids and those other kids. They resist efforts to ensure all schools are highly and equally funded, all school facilities are renovated and up-to-date and up to code, all teachers are highly trained and supported, all school materials in all schools are high quality, all students have the amount of support to meet their unique needs. Instead, these parents defend a rigged educational system where high-priced test prep courses artificially boost their kids' test scores; where their large donations, legacy hookups, and high-cost sports activities get their kids admitted to selective colleges; where the race and class of their kids matter in terms of expectations of teachers, tracking, and punishment; where their kids have access to extraordinarily experienced teachers and a full slate of privileged courses at extraordinarily funded schools through extraordinarily high local property taxes and extraordinarily racist and classist state "performance" measures. Their defense of a rigged educational system conveys maybe they don't think their child is smart after all; that they don't believe their kids could rise above the pack if their kids were not privileged. It is the conceit of parents who claim their kids are excelling solely because they are smarter or harder working. It is the insecurity of parents who resist changing the structure to one that better benefits all children, including their child. This is an allegory for racism. The very racial groups at the top of the racial hierarchy claim they are there due to their superiority at the same time they resist antiracist efforts to create a fair and equitable society where they could actually show they are superior. Parents defending their first-class public schools, all fearful that an educational revolution would send their kids back into coach with those Black kids, don't realize they are defending a system that stops their kids—all our kids—from receiving the private jet education now accessible only to the super-rich. To be racist is to have misplaced fear. To be racist is to flaunt a huge ego and hide a deep insecurity.

That was me in those privileged classes. Wholly and unjustly confined. Merely surviving. Needing Bettina Love's abolitionist teaching to set me free; that "drawing on the imagination, creativity, refusal, (re)membering, visionary thinking, healing, rebellious spirt, boldness, determination, and subversiveness of abolitionists to eradicate injustice in and outside of schools."

I had a long way to go to discover an understanding of my position that didn't elevate me because of my place in the structure, or degrade people like me. I had a long way to go to the way of being antiracist by adopting a *humble confidence.* A humble confidence is appreciating racial groups in all their imperfections, and not rendering racial groups, including your own, inferior or superior to other racial groups. It is to consider Black people beautiful—and ugly, too, but not any more beautiful or ugly than non-Black people. It is a loving acceptance of Asian people not based on any hating disregard for non-Asian people. It is a loving acceptance of White people not based on any hating disregard for people of color.

The journey to being antiracist is the journey of coming down from the ladder of conceit or coming up from the burial of insecurity to the solid ground of humble self-confidence. To be antiracist is to remain grounded, looking over at people in all their familiar and unfamiliar diversity. Ironically, to raise an antiracist is not to raise your child at all. It is to keep them grounded.

My egotistical insecurity fit in these privileged classes. But on the other hand, I did not fit because coming from Queens, I had lived most of my life in Black spaces, socialized in African American culture. Children socialized in White American culture are more likely to be selected for the privileged classes. Teachers also ridicule Black kids for teasing Black kids in privileged classes for "acting White," which is to say, treating their Black peers with the same contempt as racist society. But some of those very teachers think more highly of Black kids who are, at least culturally, "acting White."

In the racist worldview, I was "acting Black" when I struggled in my IB English II course senior year. I hated the literature of Shakespeare. I could not relate—and frankly, I did not want to. My parents bought me CliffsNotes to keep up. It didn't matter: Sometime during my senior year, I was tossed out of the IB English course. I was glad to leave all that reading behind. I hated reading. Or so I thought. "There's no such thing as a kid who hates reading," author James Patterson once wrote. "There are kids who love reading, and kids who are reading the wrong books." Shakespeare's plays were the wrong books for me.

In my English classes in high school, I don't remember reading any Black authors. In my science classes, I didn't learn about eugenics and the soon-to-be-completed Human Genome Project. In my arts classes, I was not exposed to any Native artists. In my math classes, I didn't examine racial disparity data. Even in my social studies classes, my high school teachers rarely discussed racist policy—except to teach us that it's interpersonal or past tense.

I was set to leave the nest functionally illiterate about racist policy and unknowingly fluent in racist ideas. To be illiterate about racist policy in a nation of widespread racial inequity is like being illiterate in German in a German-speaking book club. But year after year, caregivers send their young people off into society unprepared to read their world. Our children find it hard to articulate or understand what's even going on around them—and to them, and through them. Victims seem like they are the victimizers. Victimizers seem like they are the victims. Racist policies appear to be neutral. Rhetoric on equity matters more than the outcome of equity. Racist power projects its force as benefacting. Racial inequities are routine. Racial violence is justified as self-defense. The structure of racism hides in plain view. Racist ideas hide the structure.

Ordinary people are manipulated to be angry about all those other people rather than all this racism. All this racism appearing to be nothing at all.

How could my caregivers send me off into this world, in this way? Why didn't they protect me from harming myself and others?

But how could they protect me if they didn't know I needed protection? How could they raise me to be antiracist if they didn't know they needed to actively raise me to be antiracist?

I did not leave the nest antiracist. I want different for my child. I want different for your child. That's why I wrote this book.

Afterword:
Leaving the Nest

"**M**an Dies After Medical Incident During Police Interaction"—went the title of the first official police account. The man was stopped by police on May 25, 2020, Memorial Day, suspected of "forgery." When "two officers arrived" on the scene, they ordered the man "to step from his car," the police account alleged. After he got out, he "physically resisted officers." As officers handcuffed the man, "he appeared to be suffering medical distress," the account stated, and officers "called for an ambulance." He was "transported" to the hospital "by ambulance where he died a short time later."

But a cellphone video by seventeen-year-old Darnella Frazier captured George Floyd handcuffed, facedown, and Minneapolis police officer Derek Chauvin kneeling on his neck for nearly ten minutes as Floyd cried out "I can't breathe," cried out for his mother, and eventually lost consciousness. Frazier's video was uploaded to Facebook. In three weeks, nearly eight out of ten Americans had seen some or all of the recording. By the summer's end, between 15 and 26 million Americans in all fifty states took to the streets in the largest series of demonstrations in American history.

The original police account became a Memorial Day for America's official fabrications about racism. It was all denials and victim-blaming, reflective of what the nation teaches us.

Frazier's video became the Memorial Day of truth about racism. Racist power hardly flinching and letting up as it suffocates the life of its victims. What the nation is too ashamed to teach.

In 2020, Memorial Day provided the ultimate lesson of racism's ferociousness and the normality of covering it up. Frazier's video uncovered so much for so many and began what some started calling the *racial reckoning*. A nation reckoning with what it had been, what it was, and what it no longer wants to be.

Many parents were unprepared for this so-called reckoning. It's not that there weren't resources: Parents of younger children could have used the picture book *Something Happened in Our Town*. Parents of teens could have used Angie Thomas's *The Hate U Give* or *All American Boys* by Jason Reynolds and Brendan Kiely. After Floyd's murder, just 34 percent of White parents of children ages six to eleven had conversations "on occasion" with their children about "the need for racial equality." Teachers were as unprepared as parents. Only 14 percent of teachers said that year they had the training and resources to offer their students an antiracist education.

With state standards found to be inadequate, the textbooks used to meet those standards were also inadequate. One popular textbook, *The American Pageant,* labeled enslaved people as "immigrants." A Florida middle school textbook, *Discovering*

Our Past, details Thomas Jefferson's life without mentioning he was an enslaver. U.S. history curricula often "center on the white experience," as the Southern Poverty Law Center discovered prior to Floyd's murder. As education scholar Gloria Ladson-Billings once wrote, "All instruction is culturally responsive. The question is: to which culture is it currently oriented."

Since 2010, a majority of states have adopted the Common Core standards, with its canon of classic works primarily authored by White people. Even the authors presented in the curriculum materials in the New York City public school system—whose student population is only 15 percent White—remained overwhelmingly White. All of this during our current renaissance of middle-grade and young adult authors of color, including Nic Stone, Darcie Little Badger, Elizabeth Acevedo, Vashti Harrison, Thanhhà Lai, Renée Watson, Erika L. Sánchez, Cherie Dimaline, B. B. Alston, Paula Yoo, Jasmine Warga, and Tomi Adeyemi.

What students are not learning—the absences in their education—can be more harmful than what they are learning. Educators teach when they don't teach. The duality of hardly teaching about racism *and* about the lives of people of color standardizes an education of racist ideas. When students don't learn the racist policy behind the racial inequity in their communities, it can lead them to believe that White people have more because they are more. These racist ideas are reinforced when students see White people *more* in their curricula.

Students across the United States organized against this education of racist ideas during the summer of 2020. Petitions circulated around communities, like the roughly seventeen hundred students across two hundred school districts who signed up to be organizers for Diversify Our Narrative. Students organized numerous demonstrations like one in mid-

June 2020 with about a thousand young people at the Baltimore School for the Arts. "We don't know the truth," said Kayah Calhoun, a rising senior, speaking for her generation. Eleven-year-old Makayla Downs, who attended with her twelve-year-old sister and their mom, said she wants to learn about "not just the Greek gods, but the African gods." An eighteen-year-old White organizer named Quinn Fireside bristled, "Everything is told through a white perspective."

Educators tried to respond to the racial reckoning. Gladwyne Elementary School in suburban Philadelphia decided to teach age-appropriate lessons about racism, privilege, and justice during the last week of classes in June 2020. But parent Elana Yaron Fishbein ripped off a letter to the school superintendent. Fishbein omitted the roughly one-quarter of students of color at the school, complaining about "reprehensible resources designed to inoculate Caucasian children with feelings of guilt for the color of their skin and the 'sins' of their forefathers." These new lessons plan "to indoctrinate the children into the 'woke' culture," she wrote.

And the old lessons? Were they indoctrination?

When the teacher primarily imparts the literature and history of White people in a multiracial society, to be racist is to call that *education*. When the teacher refuses to instruct young people about racism in a society of widespread racial inequity, to be racist is to call that *education*. When the teacher strives to impart the literature and history of multiple racial groups in a multiracial society, to be racist is to call that *indoctrination*. When the teacher instructs young people about racism in a society of widespread racial inequity, to be racist is to call that *indoctrination*. By this illogic, in a society of widespread racial inequity, *racism exists* is a doctrine and *racism doesn't exist* is not a doctrine. By this illogic, teaching the literatures of multiple racial groups in a multiracial society is brainwashing children while primarily teaching the literatures of White people in a multiracial society is not.

Trained in social work with no expertise in curriculum design, Fishbein thought what was helpful for her child was harmful. She launched a campaign against a barely budding antiracist education movement and named her group No Left Turn in Education. In no time, Fishbein's group was also advocating against teaching about sex and climate change in schools.

By the summer's end, Fishbein's group had organized a handful of chapters and fewer than two hundred Facebook followers. But in September 2020, she appeared on Tucker Carlson's prime-time Fox News show. She "was totally taken by the harsh criticism" of her letter to the school superintendent. "And in fact," she said to Carlson, "in some places I told them that they are like lynching me." In fact, people who were lynched, like George Floyd, don't live to tell Tucker Carlson they were being lynched.

Fishbein "questioned the validity of this teaching" because "in fact this teaching turns Martin Luther King's teaching upside down." In fact, Fishbein turned MLK's teaching upside down. In a speech titled "Where Do We Go from Here?" on August 16, 1967, King talked about the ways teachers are "forced to teach the Negro . . . to despise himself, and thereby perpetuate his false sense of inferiority, and the white child . . . to adore himself, and thereby perpetuate his false sense of superiority."

In addition to Fishbein, Tucker Carlson provided a platform on his show for Christopher Rufo in September 2020. Rufo had spent much of his twenties and early thirties producing documentaries, mostly abroad. He made touristic films like *Diamond in the Dunes,* about a baseball team in China. He also made a film on houselessness that blamed poor people for their own poverty. Rufo had about as much expertise in critical race theory and anti-bias trainings as Fishbein had on lynchings and King's teachings. But while quarantining from COVID-19 in Seattle in 2020, Rufo became outraged looking at the anti-bias trainings for his city's employees.

On Carlson's show in early September 2020, Rufo's opposition to trainings in the Seattle government had expanded to the federal government. Rufo's comments on Carlson's show caught the notice of Trump, who banned these trainings on September 4. Less than two weeks later, on September 17, Trump announced the creation of the 1776 Commission to promote a "pro-American curriculum that celebrates the truth," the latest Republican rebuttal in a series of rebuttals of *The New York Times Magazine*'s 1619 Project, created by Nikole Hannah-Jones. This award-winning project reframed our understanding of American history by placing slavery and its ongoing legacy at the center of the American narrative. But many Americans weren't interested in this antiracist reframing. Weeks prior, U.S. senator Tom Cotton introduced legislation to ban schools from using the 1619 Project while calling slavery "a necessary evil."

Cotton and Trump were allergic to historical truth. And they wanted American kids to be, too. Trump said a "patriotic" curriculum was needed because the summer's antiracist demonstrations—which ended up being peaceful 96.3 percent of the time—were "left-wing rioting and mayhem" and "the direct result of decades of left-wing indoctrination in our schools."

The manufactured problem of "left-wing indoctrination in our schools" went dormant in the final months of 2020. The actual mayhem came in the New Year. After losing the 2020 presidential election by 74 electoral votes and more than 7 million popular votes, Trump indoctrinated his supporters with the Great Lie that the election had been stolen from him—and therefore *them*. Trump and his GOP operatives lied constantly that "illegal votes" in cities with large Black and Brown populations—namely Atlanta, Philadelphia, Milwaukee, Detroit, Las Vegas, and Phoenix—had stolen the election from (White) patriots who voted legally. On January 6, 2021, a mob of Trump's supporters violently stormed the United States Capitol to stop Congress from certifying Trump's electoral defeat to President-elect Joe Biden. The insurrectionists ransacked offices. They left graffiti on walls. They destroyed or damaged historic items. They left democracy's floors littered with their feces and the broken glass from the countless windows they smashed. They brutalized police officers who stood in their way. Five people died. Many more were wounded, including more than one hundred police officers, four of whom later died by suicide.

It was the most devastating assault on the Capitol since the British burned Washington in 1814 during the War of 1812. One of the insurrectionists flew a Confederate battle flag inside the Capitol for the first time in history. The Union Army held off the Confederate rebels from seizing the Capitol during the Civil War. But the rebels could not be held off on January 6. History rhymed as Republicans and Democrats, including President-elect Joe Biden, issued the same calls for "unity" and "healing" that deflated the Reconstruction era's initial promises of justice and equality.

For all their talk of truth, of patriotism, of America First, of making America great again, Trump Republicans labored hard in the aftermath of the attack on America's structural heart to change the subject. *To change the existential racial threat.* A reversal was made—the existential threat was no longer the racism uncovered in Trump's presidency and again in Floyd's murder and again on January 6. Now the existential threat was "critical race theory," as garbled in GOP disinformation.

One of the founders of CRT, law professor Kimberlé Crenshaw, defined CRT as "a way of looking at the law's role platforming, facilitating, producing, and even insulating racial inequality in our country." But Trump Republicans made up their own definition of CRT and condemned it. "Critical race theory says every white person is a racist," Senator Ted Cruz said. "Critical race theory says America is fundamentally and irredeemably racist. Critical race theory seeks to turn us against each other and, if someone has different colored skin, seeks to make us hate that person."

Drumming up outrage against what they defined as CRT were Republican think tanks and periodicals. They drove countless White parents to speak out against CRT at school board meetings in 2021. "[My daughter] is one of the most innocent little girls in the whole world, and she has friends, Black and white kids in her classroom, and she doesn't see any difference," a blond-haired White mother said at a school district meeting in Eureka, Missouri (a clip of her speech went viral). "Just because I don't want critical race theory taught to my children at school doesn't make me a racist, dammit."

"The aggrieved white parent is perhaps the most potent reactionary figure in this country," writer Esther Wang explained at the time. And the force driving these reactionary figures: "the need to protect (and save) White children."

Trump Republicans proclaimed antiracism, not racism, as dangerous to children. It was like saying a virus that had been clearly harming the American people wasn't the existential threat to children; the threat was the effort to protect the children from the virus. Ironically, this idea actually arose at around the same time, in the form of disinformation about

COVID vaccines: Vaccines were dangerous, not COVID-19. How many parents would spend 2021 resisting antiracism, vaccines, and mask mandates in the name of protecting their children? How many children were harmed?

After mentioning "critical race theory" 132 times in 2020, Fox News mentioned it 51 times in February of 2021, 139 times in March, 314 times in April, 589 times in May, and 737 times in the first three weeks of June 2021. Fishbein's No Left Turn in Education expanded rapidly in 2021 to thirty chapters in twenty-three states. At least 165 local and national groups sprang up, like the Educational Liberty Alliance and Critical Race Training in Education, organizing parents to confront school administrators to ensure schools were conserving a Eurocentric education that rarely examines racism (not to mention sexism, homophobia, transphobia, ableism, or classism). In 2021, Rich Lowry, the editor of the *National Review*, urged the opponents of antiracist education to take "control of the K-12 schools in a swath of America." Education, he wrote, "is too important to be left to educators."

"Families did not ask for this divisive nonsense," Mitch McConnell, the Senate minority leader, wrote in a letter to Secretary of Education Miguel Cardona. "Voters did not vote for it. Americans never decided our children should be taught that our country is inherently evil."

The attack on antiracist education as divisive repackaged the attack on desegregation. The *Brown* decision outlawing segregated schools "has planted hatred and suspicion where there has been heretofore friendship and understanding," stated 101 members of Congress in the Southern Manifesto of 1956. And those Jim Crow segregationists were only repackaging the attacks of enslavers. In response to the proliferation of

abolitionist literature, proslavery state legislators passed a series
of bans and censorship laws in the 1830s. Enslavers even railed
against Webster's dictionary for its accurate definition of
"slave" as "a person subject to the will of another, a drudge."
Recognizing how much this campaign led by the plantation
class had succeeded, Maine-born traveler John Abbott observed in 1860, "There is not another spot on the globe where
the censorship of speech, and of the press, is so rigorous as it
is now in the slaveholding States."

The maintenance of racism has required the public's ignorance of racism. The public's ignorance of racism requires a
perpetual undermining of public education. Enslavers resisted
the establishment of free public schools for poor White south-
erners and made it illegal to teach enslaved Black people to
read and write prior to emancipation. After the Civil War,
White congressmen declined to pass a bill first proposed in
1881 to provide equal funding to (segregated) Black and
White public schools.

The Trump Republicans' efforts to create an atmosphere
of conspiracy theories, alternative facts, disinformation, and
Great Lies to control people through ignorance have their
antecedents in the enslaving South. "In the South, ignorance
is an institution," abolitionist Henry Ward Beecher said at the
time. "They legislate for ignorance the same way we legislate
for school-houses."

Republican lawmakers drew upon two centuries of legislating
ignorance about racism. New Hampshire Republican Keith
Ammon introduced a bill on January 12, 2021, that barred
schools and organizations from endorsing "divisive concepts"
that teach New Hampshire or the United States is "fundamentally racist." By December 2021, similar legislation had

been introduced or planned in twenty states, and bills had passed in Idaho, Oklahoma, Tennessee, Texas, Iowa, New Hampshire, North Dakota, Arizona, and South Carolina. (The Arizona Supreme Court overturned that state's legislation in November 2021.)

With the exception of those in Idaho and North Dakota, these bills do not mention the words "critical race theory." Because it was never about critical race theory. Donald Trump had left the presidency in January 2021 with his Republican Party in tatters, with seemingly one viable path back to maintaining and gaining power: Exploit the racist, antidemocratic features of the American project. That meant gerrymandering to pick their own voters, racist ideas to control their own voters, voter suppression for everyone else, and the racist judges they'd appointed legalizing it all. Attacking critical race theory as the country's primary social and racial problem allowed Republican elected officials to cover up their introduction of more than 440 bills in forty-nine states to restrict voting access in 2021. Racism suffocated Breonna Taylor and George Floyd in 2020 and then democracy and schools in 2021. With racism, every day is Memorial Day.

A bill introduced in the Texas Senate dropped requirements for public schools to teach the Ku Klux Klan as "morally wrong" and for students to read materials by Dr. Martin Luther King, Jr., labor leader Cesar Chavez, and suffragist Susan B. Anthony. The bill deleted most mentions of people of color and women from the state's required curriculum. Over in Tennessee, the Williamson County chapter of Moms for Liberty used their new state law to object to two books on the life of Ruby Bridges, who at six years old in 1960 became the first Black student to desegregate a southern school. The moms called the factual images from these books—segregated water fountains, firemen hosing Black children, White parents protesting desegregation—"indoctrination" that will "sow the seeds of racial strife, neo-racism, neo-segregation, and is an affront to the ideas of Dr. Martin Luther King, Jr." Ironically, another book these parents objected to: *Martin Luther King Jr. and the March on Washington.*

One of these Moms for Liberty identified as Asian American. She has a multiracial son (her husband is White). Her son had read a story about Black high school students being attacked while trying to integrate a lunch counter. "This story is so sad," her son said. The mom took her son's compassionate reaction to injustice to mean her son is now "ashamed of his white half."

This is what children are up against. The primal fear of caregivers of White and multiracial children, mobilizing their opposition to antiracist education. By learning the enduring history of racism, they fear their children will see White people as the villains. And learning about their own race as the villains, they fear their children will learn to hate their race or be ashamed of their race. However, research tells us this is not true. One study showed that White elementary schoolers who were taught about the history of anti-Black racism demonstrated less racist ideas about Black people compared to peers who did not learn this material. Researchers found that learning about the history of anti-Black racism did *not* change White or Black children's attitudes about White people.

But fears reveal. Why do these caregivers assume that White kids reading the story of courageous little Ruby Bridges would *not* identify with Ruby Bridges? Why do these caregivers assume their kids would identify with the White segregationists who tried to stop Ruby? Don't these caregivers say their kids *don't see color*? Does that mean these caregivers have raised their kids to connect with White people—and no one else? Is that what caregivers mean when they say their kids don't see color—they don't see people of color?

Their fears reveal something these caregivers obviously *do* see: the relationship between positive and negative racial images in education and a child's conception of their own race and themselves. They seem to want White children not to be exposed to anything critical about White people. They seem to want an educational system that narrates—to White children *and children of color*—the glorious achievements of White people worldwide and in the United States (with people of color, if present at all, as supporting actors and perpetrators of harms against themselves, since no one else can be held responsible for slavery and ongoing injustice). These caregivers don't seem to care that this kind of education raises White children—*and children of color*—to think of White people as superior; to see racial injustice as normal. They don't seem to care that this kind of education quells antiracist resistance. Or—that's precisely the mission of the conservators of racism.

What's more, these caregivers seem unwilling to apply their understanding of the impact of negative and positive racial images *on children of color*. They don't seem to care about children of color at the same time they speak about MLK's children. They don't seem to care when children of color see themselves reflected negatively in textbooks. They don't seem to care that a Native child or Asian child or Middle Eastern child or Black child or Latinx child (or that poor White child) hardly sees themselves reflected in literature and lessons. These caregivers don't seem to care that children of color actually benefit from lessons about antiracists of their own races who battled settler colonialism, slavery, xenophobia, racial capitalism, eugenics, segregation, lynchings, and the prison-industrial complex. They don't seem to care that children of color are systematically taught that the racial problem today is *their race*—not racism. These caregivers don't seem to care about the children of color being raised to be "ashamed" of their own race—being raised to hate their own race. They don't seem to care that I left school and home ashamed of my own race. *Or*—that's precisely the mission of the conservators of racism.

But even in their focus on White people, they don't seem to know or care about White people. Their ignorance about White American history is stopping yet another generation of White children from learning about their own racial history. Their fearful assumption that White children would see White people as *only* the villains erases the long history of White people being antiracist across time and space. To teach about the history of slavery is to teach about the history of White abolitionists like William Lloyd Garrison, the editor of *The Liberator*. To teach about racism today is to teach about antiracist White people who are challenging structural racism and admitting their faults, like one of my U.S. senators in Massachusetts, Elizabeth Warren.

But therein lies the problem for some caregivers. If children identify with those who have identified racism—not antiracism—as the existential threat, then will those children identify with the racist politics of their caregivers? I. Think. Not.

It all goes back to the caregiver. When we claim that we're doing what's best for the child, are we in truth doing only what's best for us, as caregivers? Some caregivers don't want their children to be better than them. They want their children to *be* them. To think just like them. Anything contrary is "indoctrination."

I don't want Imani thinking of people as I did when I left home and school. I want my child to think better of people than I did. What about you?

.   .   .

In June 2000, I graduated from Stonewall Jackson High School. I did not have a racial reckoning twenty years prior to Floyd's murder. No Memorial Day of the truth for me. No anti–CRT movement to cover up the truth. Just leaving another school again. Stonewall was my eighth school since kindergarten. I had been like an army kid. My parents' war: racism. Their way of protecting me: moving me.

I know now, as a parent and educator, how disruptive and uncomfortable to their own lives my parents' decisions were to move me out of that kindergarten, out of that third grade, out of Queens. How child-centered those decisions were. And yet caregivers can do more than removing a child from harmful environments. If removing the child from racist situations is the most basic form of protection, then preparing the child for racist situations is the greater level. To prepare children to protect themselves is to raise adults. My principal job as a caregiver is to work myself out of my job by raising an adult, as author Julie Lythcott-Haims instructs us.

But in order to prepare children for racism—the most decisive form of antiracist socialization—caregivers can no longer neglect the gravity of the emergency, which became more dire when Republican state legislators and fearful school officials made it harder to deliver an antiracist education in 2021 and beyond. Color-blind socialization and denial made a comeback. Additionally, since racism doesn't exist to them, color-blind caregivers refuse to recognize that children inherit the privileges and deprivations of their caregivers. Instead, many people believe—as I did after Imani's first coo—that our biological children inherit only our positive and negative traits. This *genetic* inheritance explains racial inequity, they say, not racism.

But our children are more than a cluster of genetic inheritances—they are also who we raise them to be, influenced by the world that we raise them in. Antiracists (like racists) are bred not born, as I write in *Antiracist Baby*. Babies start seeing race between three and nine months, as noted earlier, and become partial to certain races based on their environment. That's why to raise an antiracist, caregivers must childproof the total environment for our child before they bring the child to the classroom or clinic or home—as I did *not* do for Imani to my eternal regret. "Kids make sense of the world around them through the observations they make and the interactions they have within the confines of their everyday lives," explained sociologist Margaret A. Hagerman. "What happens at schools, soccer practice, birthday parties, clarinet lessons, and in the backseat of a car driving home from summer day camp shapes children's ideas about the social world." In their social worlds, lighter people are often living on the richer end, and darker people are often dying on the poorer end. Children are trying to figure out why even before they can talk in full sentences. What is their environment telling them in verbal and nonverbal language?

But the childproofing of the racial environment is all for naught if caregivers don't pass the doll test; if caregivers don't actively raise children as early as they can to be empathetic; if caregivers don't realize that by the time children enter preschool, they already have an adultlike grasp of race; if caregivers don't inject into children the antibodies of antiracist education to protect them; if caregivers don't ensure this education is teaching children to be critical thinkers. And as they grow into more critical thinkers and become more racially aware in elementary school and start talking more about racism, caregivers can't continue shutting down those conversations. The first lesson children receive from caregivers about race can no longer be that it's unmentionable.

Because while gratifying to the caregiver, that lesson is extremely harmful to the child. Imagine being a ten-year-old experiencing or witnessing the punishing power of racism—as kids of color with disabilities like my brother do—and not having the language and freedom to talk about it with the adults in your life. It can lead to depression for the victims—and internalized racist ideas for the observers. And their caregivers won't even know. Nor do caregivers seem to know that the harm only gets worse as middle schoolers of color grow big enough to be feared. Black youth report more than five incidences of racist discrimination per day. How many do they witness? How many do their Latinx, Asian, Middle Eastern, and Native peers witness and experience? Amid all of this, where are their caregivers to protect them? Where are the caregivers to protect White youth from being recruited online by White supremacists?

With their caregivers missing in action, the fear of teens of color confines some of them in an oppositional protective posture; confines some White teens in their ignorance, leading to all sorts of distortions of ego and insecurity—or an egotistical insecurity as it did in me. I needed a humble confidence in high school to give me armor, to liberate me to join the fight against the structures of racism.

Like so many of us today, I had to learn as an adult what I could have learned as a child. I had to learn I wasn't the racial problem. I had to learn: *No racial group has more because they are more. No racial group has less because they are less.* Imagine if every child learned to see the racial inequity in their community from this antiracist point of view. How protective it would be for kids to learn about bad rules and not bad people for once.

How to Raise an Antiracist relies on decades of scientific research showing racism is the existential threat to our children. But all is not lost, like truth on another Memorial Day. Young people are ready to be antiracist like Darnella Frazier. But are their caregivers ready to raise them to be antiracist?

Preparing the child to protect herself is not enough, though. It's not enough for me as I stare into Imani's future—and my past. The ultimate way to protect our children from racism is to protect all children from racism. The ultimate way to protect all children from racism is to eliminate racism. And to do that, we have to do more than raise antiracist children, we have to raise an antiracist society.

Imani's name means "faith" in Swahili. She almost did not make it here. Sadiqa gave her life in more ways than one. Imani gave us faith.

Faith we can raise an antiracist society to protect our children.

Acknowledgments

I have many memories from the summer of 2020, when tens of millions of people demonstrated against racism and police violence in small and large towns and cities in the United States and across the world—when people realized it was no longer enough to be "not racist"; we must be antiracist. I remember the fire hose of questions coming at me about how to be antiracist—a new term for many people. But I remember by the summer's end, the questions had shifted, particularly from caregivers—and nearly every adult is a caregiver of children. Caregivers had stopped asking about how *they* could be antiracist, or their father or mother or spouse or friend or rigid uncle or old-school grandmother. They had started asking about the most precious love of their lives: their children— their daughters, their sons, their grandchildren, their nieces, their nephews, their students, their mentees, their young patients, their young clients. Caregivers kept telling me, accented with passion or tears or gravity, that they did not want the young people in their lives to be raised like them, disconnected from people of other skin colors, imagining that racial inequities are normal, controlled by the propaganda of racist ideas, and ignoring the scourge of racist policies. While the conservators of racism heard these caregivers, too, and became alarmed, and organized a movement to stop them, I became inspired. I wanted to support them. These are the caregivers who inspired me to write this book. I wanted to first and foremost acknowledge you. I wanted to first and foremost thank you.

I must thank Ayesha Pande, my literary agent, friend, and dearest advisor. What probably seemed from out of nowhere, I suddenly came to you, wanting to write this book, nervous, not knowing what you'd think. We had all these projects lined up, all these deadlines lining up, and researching and writing this book would put so much on hold. But you heard what I heard from the people, saw what I saw: the need for this book. And supported it. Pushed it. Encouraged me when I had doubts early on. This is, what, the ninth book we've done? And your encouragement, wisdom, constructive feedback, and support—it all never gets old. Still feels fresh. I thank you.

And I thank you, Chris Jackson. When Ayesha and I approached you about this book, you saw something that hadn't fully taken shape. You were game for shaping it with me, for giving me some tools to go off and shape it further myself. Our early conversations about the book were not just critical in terms of the conceptual and structural framing of the book, they boosted my confidence at times when I didn't know my confidence to write such a deeply personal book about our precious children needed boosting. Along the way, your counsel and ideas and suggestions were essential, as you know. A great editor is not merely one who is great on the page. A great editor is one who is great on the mind of the author. Thank you, Chris, for your greatness as an editor.

And I thank you, Maria Braeckel and Stacey Stein. Anything is possible for a book when you are behind it. And I thank you, Ayelet Durantt, for all the magic you make for us authors.

But I must say this book would never have gotten into Chris's great editorial hands, it would never have arrived in your hands, dear reader, without Dr. Heather Sanford. Almost as soon as you came on board to manage my research program, you started working with me to assemble and organize the scholarship and science that framed this book. I'm thankful for your thoughtfulness, tenacity, leadership, and sharing my steely commitment to precision and speaking from the evidence. Let me also send a special thanks to my wonderful colleagues Adeline Gutierrez Nunez and Tami Nguyen. Thank you for the gift of your work and friendship and support. And shout-outs to all my history department colleagues at Boston University and all my colleagues at the BU Center for Antiracist Research. And thank you, President Robert A. Brown and Provost Jean Morrison, for all your support of our center and my research.

I must thank the major characters in this book who happen to be my dearest loved ones. My brother, you are my walking and talking inspiration. You are a well of goodness. Thank you for allowing me to tell a bit of your childhood, your battle with ableism and racism as a child. Ma and Dad—thank you for sitting with me for hours reliving (and describing or corroborating) sensitive details from your lives and our lives. I learned more about each of you—and our family. I learned more about myself. I grasped how you were my rock in childhood, remain my rock in adulthood. Thank you for your constant search for safety for my brother and me. You didn't find it. The dangers of racism still lurked in each new school and neighborhood. But this book carries on your loving and longing work with your sons, and for your sons. It's on a mission to support caregivers in constructing an antiracist society of safety that protects all children.

How to Raise an Antiracist is on a mission to construct that society for your granddaughter. I guess I have to thank my parents, aka Bibi and Babu—as well as my beloved parents-in-law, aka Mimi and Baba—for allowing Sadiqa and me on occasion to hang out with their superstar granddaughter, Imani. And thank you, Uncle Cha and Aunt A, for having our backs against these feisty grandparents!

In all seriousness, as I write these words, Imani, you are five years old, in kindergarten, and learning to read words and write words. I'm tearing up thinking about how hopefully one day soon you're going to read these words. I'm also getting a bit nervous as I wonder what you are going to think about these words—how I captured your early life and my early life in this book. I hope Dad did okay.

You, too, Sadiqa, my partner, I wrote about you nervously. I know you wanted to share what happened during your pregnancy likely with racism, and those scary moments when we didn't know what was to come. But I was nervous about being the vehicle. Like when I was scared to hold one-day-old Imani after all you'd done to get her here, I was scared to hold your story after all you endured. Thank you for trusting me with your story, with Imani, with your love. Thank you for your love. Thank you for your love of all those children you take care of when there's an emergency. Thank you for being the real Dr. Kendi. Thank you for sharing this mission to raise our child—all children—to be antiracist. Thank you.

Notes

INTRODUCTION

x **microbiologist Sasha Ottey terms "health-care gaslighting"** Ashley Fetters, "The Doctor Doesn't Listen to Her. But the Media Is Starting To," *Atlantic,* August 10, 2018, www.theatlantic.com/family /archive/2018/08/womens-health-care-gaslighting/567149/.

x **The medical establishment's disregard** Linda Villarosa, "Why America's Black Mothers and Babies Are in a Life-or-Death Crisis," *New York Times Magazine,* April 11, 2018, www.nytimes.com/2018/04/11 /magazine/black-mothers-babies-death-maternal-mortality.html.

x **wealthy and powerful Black women like Serena Williams** Rob Haskell, "Serena Williams on Motherhood, Marriage, and Making Her Comeback," *Vogue,* January 10, 2018, www.vogue.com/article/serena -williams-vogue-cover-interview-february-2018.

xi **"sharing our family's story of Olympia's birth"** Serena Williams, "I didn't expect that sharing our family's story of Olympia's birth . . ." Facebook, January 15, 2018, www.facebook.com/SerenaWilliams /videos/10156086135726834/.

xi **highest maternal mortality rate among rich countries** Gianna Melillo, "Racial Disparities Persist in Maternal Morbidity, Mortality and Infant Health," *American Journal of Managed Care,* June 13, 2020, www .ajmc.com/view/racial-disparities-persist-in-maternal-morbidity -mortality-and-infant-health.

xi **Two-thirds of the annual deaths from pregnancy** Ibid.

xi **more than three times more likely to die from pregnancy** Centers for Disease Control and Prevention (CDC), "Racial and Ethnic Disparities Continue in Pregnancy-Related Deaths," press release, September 19, 2019, www.cdc.gov/media/releases/2019/p0905-racial-ethnic -disparities-pregnancy-deaths.html.

xi **a Centers for Disease Control study** Ibid.

xi **older women and women with college degrees** Ibid.

xii **"receive later or no prenatal care"** U.S. Department of Health and Human Services, Office of Minority Health, "Infant Mortality and African Americans," 2019, minorityhealth.hhs.gov/omh/browse.aspx?lvl= 4&lvlid=23.

xii **uninsured outside of pregnancy, and to lose coverage** Nina Martin, "Black Mothers Keep Dying After Giving Birth. Shalon Irving's Story Explains Why," NPR, December 7, 2017, www.npr.org/2017/12 /07/568948782/black-mothers-keep-dying-after-giving-birth-shalon -irvings-story-explains-why.

xii **to live in neighborhoods facing high air pollution** Melillo, "Racial Disparities Persist."

xii **hospitals where Black mothers give birth** Martin, "Black Mothers Keep Dying After Giving Birth."

xiv **unethical experiments he conducted on enslaved Black women** Deidre Cooper Owens, *Medical Bondage: Race, Gender, and the Origins of American Gynecology* (Athens: University of Georgia Press, 2017), 1, 38–39.

xvi **only about 6 in 10 survive** University of Utah Health Hospitals and Clinics, "When Is It Safe to Deliver Your Baby?," healthcare.utah.edu /womenshealth/pregnancy-birth/preterm-birth/when-is-it-safe-to -deliver.php.

xvi **premature babies have chronic health challenges** Krissi Danielsson, "What Is Fetal Viability?," *Verywell Family,* April 20, 2021, www .verywellfamily.com/premature-birth-and-viability-2371529.

xvi **most likely to be born premature** March of Dimes, *2020 March of Dimes Report Card,* www.marchofdimes.org/materials/US_REPORT CARD_FINAL_2020.pdf.

xvi **premature births lead to more infant deaths** Population Reference Bureau, "Premature Births Help Explain Higher U.S. Infant Mortality Rate," December 15, 2009, www.prb.org/resources/premature-births -help-explain-higher-u-s-infant-mortality-rate/.

xvi **nearly 11 Black babies** Danielle M. Ely and Anne K. Driscoll, "Infant Mortality in the United States, 2018: Data from the Period Linked Birth/ Infant Death File," *National Vital Statistics Reports* 69, no. 7 (2020), 2.

xvi **Black infants account for** Melillo, "Racial Disparities Persist."

xvi **thirty-four voter suppression bills in nineteen states** Brennan Center for Justice, "Voting Laws Roundup: December 2021," De-

cember 21, 2021, www.brennancenter.org/our-work/research-reports
/voting-laws-roundup-december-2021.

xvii **seventeen-year-old Kyle Rittenhouse** Christy Gutowski and Stacy
St. Clair, "Judge Dismisses Gun Charge Against Kyle Rittenhouse," *Chicago Tribune,* November 15, 2021, www.chicagotribune.com/news/ct
-kyle-rittenhouse-gun-charge-judge-jury-instructions-20211115
-grgmffpwsnf3tbw7ezizjkfaxa-story.html.

xvii **twenty-one-year-old Patrick Crusius** Aaron Martinez, "Suspect
Faces New Federal Charges in El Paso Walmart Mass Shooting," *El Paso
Times,* July 9, 2020, www.elpasotimes.com/story/news/crime/2020/07
/09/patrick-crusius-faces-new-federal-charges-el-paso-shooting
/3286985001/; Julio Cesar-Chavez, "Accused El Paso Mass Shooter
Charged with 90 Counts of Federal Hate Crimes," Reuters, February 6, 2020, www.reuters.com/article/us-texas-shooting/accused-el
-paso-mass-shooter-charged-with-90-counts-of-federal-hate-crimes
-idUSKBN2002PK.

xvii **nineteen-year-old Nikolas Cruz** Paul P. Murphy, "Exclusive: Group
Chat Messages Show School Shooter Obsessed with Race, Violence and
Guns," CNN, February 18, 2018, www.cnn.com/2018/02/16/us
/exclusive-school-shooter-instagram-group/index.html.

xvii **twenty-one-year-old Dylann Roof** Ray Sanchez and Ed Payne,
"Charleston Church Shooting: Who Is Dylann Roof?," CNN, December 16, 2016, www.cnn.com/2015/06/19/us/charleston-church
-shooting-suspect/index.html.

xvii **gun safety laws can prevent** A 2019 analysis of mass shootings between 1998 and 2015 found that "more permissive state gun laws" correlated to an increased number of mass shootings. Specifically, researchers
stated, "a 10 unit increase in state gun law permissiveness was associated
with a significant 11.5% higher rate of mass shootings." See Paul M.
Reeping et al., "State Gun Laws, Gun Ownership, and Mass Shootings
in the US: Cross Sectional Time Series," *BMJ* 364 (2019), L542.

xvii **The United States has been flooded with high-powered rifles**
Ibram X. Kendi, "A Lynch Mob of One," *Atlantic,* August 8, 2019, www
.theatlantic.com/ideas/archive/2019/08/a-lynch-mob-of-one
/595666/.

xvii **defunding of public safety nets** Since about 1980, there has been a
widening chasm between federal, state, and local spending for police,
prisons, and the court system and spending for welfare programs such as
Temporary Assistance for Needy Families, food stamps, and supplemental Social Security payments. Even during the COVID-19 pandemic, all
ten of the nation's largest cities allocated more money in the 2021 fiscal
year to policing than to public health, with the average police budget
standing "3.6 times greater than public health department budgets." Dis-

parities between police and public libraries are even greater. For example, Boston's budget for the 2021 fiscal year gave ten times more money to the Boston Police Department than to the Library Department. Many school districts—especially districts with predominantly Black students and students of color—continue to suffer from lack of funding compared to police budgets. See Christopher Ingraham, "U.S. Spends Twice as Much on Law and Order as It Does on Cash Welfare, Data Show," *Washington Post,* June 4, 2020, www.washingtonpost.com/business/2020/06 /04/us-spends-twice-much-law-order-it-does-social-welfare-data -show/; Ella Fassler, "10 Largest US Cities Will Spend More on Police Than Public Health This Year," *Truthout,* February 24, 2021, truthout .org/articles/10-largest-us-cities-will-spend-more-on-police-than -public-health-this-year/; Lauren Chambers, "Unpacking the Boston Police Budget," Data for Justice, June 2020, data.aclum.org/2020/06/05 /unpacking-the-boston-police-budget/; and Stephon J. Boatwright, "Defund the Police? We've Been Doing That to Education for Years," *Education Week,* July 29, 2020, www.edweek.org/leadership/opinion -defund-the-police-weve-been-doing-that-to-education-for-years /2020/07.

xviii **primarily a poverty or class issue, they say** Sociologist William Julius Wilson's book *The Declining Significance of Race: Blacks and Changing American Institutions* (Chicago: University of Chicago Press, 1978) was foundational to the narrative that class is more significant than race in shaping Black Americans' lives. This narrative persists, with serious policy implications. More recently, Kay S. Hymowitz—a senior fellow at the Manhattan Institute, a conservative think tank—repeated the claim that class was a "stronger predictor of well-being than race." Convinced of this so-called truth, she framed "race-based policies" as "a political— and moral—nonstarter." Hymowitz, "Class Is Now a Stronger Predictor of Well-Being Than Race," *New York Times,* October 10, 2016, www .nytimes.com/roomfordebate/2016/01/28/racial-reparations-and-the -limits-of-economic-policy/class-is-now-a-stronger-predictor-of-well -being-than-race.

xviii **more wealth than Black and Latinx college graduates** Michael A. Fletcher, "White High School Dropouts Are Wealthier Than Black and Hispanic College Graduates. Can a New Policy Tool Fix That?," *Washington Post,* March 10, 2015, www.washingtonpost.com/news/wonk /wp/2015/03/10/white-high-school-dropouts-are-wealthier-than -black-and-hispanic-college-graduates-can-a-new-policy-tool-fix -that/.

xviii **male millennial children of Black millionaires** Emily Badger et al., "Extensive Data Shows Punishing Reach of Racism for Black Boys,"

New York Times, March 19, 2018, www.nytimes.com/interactive/2018 /03/19/upshot/race-class-white-and-black-men.html.

xviii **dismissing the racism, they point to behavior** Blaming the behavior of Black victims of police violence, rather than the racist ideas and practices of the perpetrators of that violence, is perhaps the most prominent example of this tendency. Scholars CalvinJohn Smiley and David Fakunle identified "four major recurring themes" in media coverage of police murders of six unarmed Black men and youth: Eric Garner, Michael Brown, Jr., Akai Gurley, Tamir Rice, Tony Robinson, and Freddie Gray. Smiley and Fakunle listed the victims' behavior "at the time of their death" and "prior to their death" as the top theme, followed by appearance, location, and lifestyle. Smiley and Fakunle, "From 'Brute' to 'Thug': The Demonization and Criminalization of Unarmed Black Male Victims in America," *Journal of Human Behavior in the Social Environment* 26, nos. 3–4 (2016), 356–357.

xviii **there's something behaviorally inferior about Black people** For a discussion on this, see Ibram X. Kendi, "Stop Blaming Black People for Dying of the Coronavirus," *Atlantic,* April 14, 2020, www.theatlantic .com/ideas/archive/2020/04/race-and-blame/609946/.

xviii **core findings of my historical research on racism** See Ibram X. Kendi, *Stamped from the Beginning: The Definitive History of Racist Ideas in America* (New York: Nation Books, 2016) and *How to Be an Antiracist* (New York: One World, 2019).

xix **as domestic slave traders separated Black children** Historian Edward E. Baptist estimated that domestic slave traders marched "almost 1 million" enslaved women, men, and children from the upper South to the lower South between the 1780s and 1865. Baptist, *The Half Has Never Been Told: Slavery and the Making of American Capitalism* (New York: Basic Books, 2014), 2.

xix **as federal agents and "missionaries" separated Native children** There were 367 Indian boarding schools in 29 states between 1869 and the 1960s. About 43 percent of these schools were associated with Christian denominations. Though it is unknown exactly how many Native children were forced to attend, there were 20,000 children in these schools in 1900 and 60,889—nearly 83 percent of school-aged Native children—by 1925. Native parents only gained the right "to deny their children's placement in off-reservation schools" via the Indian Child Welfare Act of 1978. See National Native American Boarding School Healing Coalition, "Resources," boardingschoolhealing.org /education/resources/; "US Indian Boarding School History," board ingschoolhealing.org/education/us-indian-boarding-school-history/; and Northern Plains Reservation Aid, "History and Culture: Board-

ing Schools," www.nativepartnership.org/site/PageServer?pagename=
airc_hist_boardingschools.

xix **as border officials separated Latinx children** Nomaan Merchant,
"Hundreds of Children Wait in Border Patrol Facility in Texas," Associated Press, June 18, 2018, apnews.com/article/north-america-tx-state
-wire-us-news-ap-top-news-border-patrols-9794de32d39d4c6f89fbefae
a3780769.

xx **easier for children to learn spoken languages** Dana G. Smith, "At
What Age Does Our Ability to Learn a New Language Like a Native
Speaker Disappear?," *Scientific American,* May 4, 2018, www.scientific
american.com/article/at-what-age-does-our-ability-to-learn-a-new
-language-like-a-native-speaker-disappear/.

xxii **background in educational research** My first book chronicled the
antiracist activism of Black students at colleges and universities across
the United States. See *The Black Campus Movement: Black Students and the
Racial Reconstitution of Higher Education, 1965–1972* (New York: Palgrave
Macmillan, 2012).

CHAPTER 1: BIRTH OF DENIAL

6 **racially profiling, arresting, brutalizing, and killing Black people** Traffic stops offer one window into understanding racial profiling.
A recent analysis of 95 million traffic stops conducted by twenty-one
state patrol agencies and thirty-five municipal police departments across
the United States between 2011 and 2018 showed that "black drivers
were, on average, stopped more often than white drivers." However,
stop rates for Black drivers fell after dark, when police could not make
out the color of their skin—a fact that the study's authors believed was
"suggestive of racial profiling." Racial disparities bleed into arrests and
police violence. Between 2015 and 2018, Black people were arrested at
five times the rate of White people, all other demographic factors being
equal. Between 1980 and 2018, the police "disproportionately killed
Black people at a rate of 3.5 times higher than White people," and
"killed Hispanic and Indigenous people disproportionately as well." For
the analysis of traffic stops, see Emma Pierson et al., "A Large-Scale
Analysis of Racial Disparities in Police Stops Across the United States,"
Nature Human Behavior 4 (2020), doi.org/10.1038/s41562-020-0858-1.
For the study on arrests, see Pierre Thomas, John Kelly, and Tonya
Simpson, "ABC News Analysis of Police Arrests Nationwide Reveals
Stark Racial Disparity," ABC News, June 11, 2020, abcnews.go.com
/US/abc-news-analysis-police-arrests-nationwide-reveals-stark/story
?id=71188546. For the analysis of police violence, see GBD 2019, Po-
lice Violence US Subnational Collaborators, "Fatal Police Violence by
Race and State in the USA, 1980–2019: A Network Meta-Regression,"

Lancet 398, no. 10307 (October 2021), doi.org/10.1016/S0140 -6736(21)01609-3.

7 **socialize their children in the way they were socialized** Diane Hughes and Lisa Chen, "When and What Parents Tell Children About Race: An Examination of Race-Related Socialization Among African American Families," *Applied Developmental Science* 1, no. 4 (1997), 211.

7 **racist form of socialization is *promotion of mistrust*** Diane Hughes et al., "Parents' Ethnic–Racial Socialization Practices: A Review of Research and Directions for Future Study," *Developmental Psychology* 42, no. 5 (2006), 757.

8 **rare for Black parents to promote mistrust** Michael C. Thornton et al., "Sociodemographic and Environmental Correlates of Racial Socialization by Black Parents," *Child Development* 61, no. 2 (April 1990), 406. Just 2.7 percent of Black parents instructed their children to keep their distance from White people.

8 ***cultural socialization,* or "parental practices"** Hughes et al., "Parents' Ethnic–Racial Socialization Practices," 749.

8 **About eight out of twelve Black middle-class mothers** Marie-Anne Suizzo, Courtney Robinson, and Erin Pahlke, "African American Mothers' Socialization Beliefs and Goals with Young Children: Themes of History, Education, and Collective Independence," *Journal of Family Issues* 29, no. 3 (March 2008), 305.

10 **requires some level of *immersion*** Caroline Bologna, "How White Parents Can Talk to Their Kids About Race," *Huffington Post,* June 3, 2020, www.huffpost.com/entry/how-white-parents-talk-kids-race-l_5 ed522dbc5b6a2704f44c045.

10 **symbolic to transgender people** Josh Jackman, "Trans Kids' Book 'Julian Is a Mermaid' Is Winning Hearts and Awards," *PinkNews,* February 17, 2019, www.pinknews.co.uk/2019/02/17/trans-kids-book -julian-is-a-mermaid-awards/.

10 **scholars call *preparation for bias*** Hughes et al., "Parents' Ethnic–Racial Socialization Practices," 756–757.

10 **teach their adolescents about their bodies** Planned Parenthood, "New Poll: Parents Are Talking with Their Kids About Sex but Often Not Tackling Harder Issues," January 30, 2014, www.plannedparenthood .org/about-us/newsroom/press-releases/new-poll-parents-talking-their -kids-about-sex-often-not-tackling-harder-issues.

11 **about three out of four White respondents** David Chae, Leoandra Onnie Rogers, and Tiffany Yip, "There's a Right Way to Talk About Racism with Kids—And Most White Parents in the US Aren't Doing It," Ideas.Ted.Com, July 9, 2020, ideas.ted.com/theres-a-right-way-to -talk-about-racism-with-kids-and-most-white-parents-in-the-us-arent -doing-it/.

11 **fewer than half see unequal opportunity** Ibid.

12 **does not cause them to engage in sexual intercourse** Cora C. Breuner and Gerri Mattson, "Sexuality Education for Children and Adolescents," *Pediatrics* 138, no. 2 (2016), e6–e7.

14 **"never seemed to notice or care"** Jennifer Harvey, *Raising White Kids: Bringing Up Children in a Racially Unjust America* (Nashville: Abingdon Press, 2017), 23.

14 *color blindness,* **whereby caregivers actively** Hughes et al., "Parents' Ethnic–Racial Socialization Practices," 757. Though Hughes et al. labeled this form of racial socialization as "egalitarianism or silence about race," many scholars deploy the term "color blindness." See, for example, Jill V. Hamm, "Barriers and Bridges to Positive Cross-Ethnic Relations: African American and White Parent Socialization Beliefs and Practices," *Youth & Society* 33, no. 1 (September 2001), 62–98; Erin Pahlke, Rebecca S. Bigler, and Marie-Anne Suizzo, "Relations Between Color-blind Socialization and Children's Racial Bias: Evidence from European American Mothers and Their Preschool Children," *Child Development* 83, no. 4 (July/August 2012), 1164–1179; Margaret A. Hagerman, "White Families and Race: Colour-Blind and Colour-Conscious Approaches to White Racial Socialization," *Ethnic and Racial Studies* 37, no. 14 (2014), 2598–2614; and Brigitte Vittrup, "Color Blind or Color Conscious? White American Mothers' Approaches to Racial Socialization," *Journal of Family Issues* 39, no. 3 (2018), 668–692.

15 **"I don't see color"** Vittrup, "Color Blind or Color Conscious?," 671.

15 **only 8.2 percent of Black parents** Thornton et al., "Sociodemographic and Environmental Correlates of Racial Socialization by Black Parents," 406.

15 **"only a small minority"** Hughes and Chen, "When and What Parents Tell Children About Race, 206.

15 **stress the importance of hard work (22.2 percent) or emphasize racial pride** Thornton et al., "Sociodemographic and Environmental Correlates of Racial Socialization by Black Parents," 405. See also Hughes et al., "Parents' Ethnic–Racial Socialization Practices," 757.

15 **only a sixth of Black middle-class mothers** Suizzo, Robinson, and Pahlke, "African American Mothers' Socialization Beliefs," 300.

16 **still more likely than any other racial group** Jennifer Kotler, Tanya Haider, and Michael H. Levine, *Parents' and Educators' Perceptions of Children's Social Identity Development* (New York: Sesame Workshop, 2019), 27.

16 **least likely to engage their kids** Ibid.

16 **about two-thirds of White respondents** Chae, Rogers, and Yip, "There's a Right Way to Talk About Racism with Kids."

16 *Little Eva* American Antiquarian Society, "African American Resources

at the American Antiquarian Society," www.americanantiquarian.org /african-american-resources. The character of Little Eva originally appeared in Harriet Beecher Stowe's *Uncle Tom's Cabin* (1852). This proslavery adaptation, which changed several of Little Eva's personal details and transformed her into a supporter of slavery, was a children's book version of the "Anti-Tom" novels released in opposition to Stowe's novel. For more, see *"Uncle Tom* as Children's Book," *Uncle Tom's Cabin & American Culture,* utc.iath.virginia.edu/childrn/cbhp.html.

16 **"the only daughter of a wealthy planter"** *Aunt Mary's Picture Book: Little Eva. The Flower of the South* (New York: Phil. J. Cozans, c. 1853; Stereotyped by Vincent L. Dill), 1, John Hay Library, Brown University, utc.iath.virginia.edu/childrn/gallambf.html.

16 **"all love Eva"** Ibid., 2.

17 **"never left them, he loved them all too well"** Ibid., 7.

17 **from teaching "that one race is the unique oppressor"** Ben Felder, "As Critical Race Theory Stirs National Debate, Oklahoma Bill Seeks to Alter Teaching of Slavery," *Oklahoman,* December 16, 2021, www.oklahoman.com/story/news/2021/12/16/critical-race-theory -oklahoma-rep-jim-olsen-bill-teaching-slavery/8912667002/.

17 **"He has lots of Black friends"** Harvey, *Raising White Kids,* 17.

17 **"She is just too young now"** Vittrup, "Color Blind or Color Conscious?," 680.

17 **"form this kind of preconceived notion"** Hamm, "Barriers and Bridges to Positive Cross-Ethnic Relations," 76.

18 **"I cannot see what I would do"** Linda P. Juang et al., "Reactive and Proactive Ethnic-Racial Socialization Practices of Second-Generation Asian American Parents," *Asian American Journal of Psychology* 9, no. 1 (2018), 9.

18 **"fatal inventions"** Dorothy Roberts, *Fatal Invention: How Science, Politics, and Big Business Re-create Race in the Twenty-first Century* (New York: New Press, 2011).

18 *assimilationist* **racist ideas suggest** For a fuller explanation of assimilationist and segregationist ideas, see Kendi, *Stamped from the Beginning.*

18 **"race is the child of racism"** Ta-Nehisi Coates, *Between the World and Me* (New York: Spiegel & Grau, 2015), 7.

CHAPTER 2: NEWBORN NATURE

22 **the benefits of kangaroo care** Cleveland Clinic, "Kangaroo Care," June 29, 2020, my.clevelandclinic.org/health/treatments/12578-kangaroo-care.

23 **more comfortable addressing gender than race** Phyllis A. Katz, "Racists or Tolerant Multiculturalists? How Do They Begin?," *American Psychologist* 58, no. 11 (2003), 904.

23 **"a lens, a prism, for seeing the way"** Kimberlé Crenshaw quoted in

Katy Steinmetz, "She Coined the Term 'Intersectionality' over 30 Years Ago. Here's What It Means to Her Today," *TIME,* February 20, 2020, time.com/5786710/kimberle-crenshaw-intersectionality/.

24 **babies coo about eight weeks** Mayo Clinic, "Infant Development: Birth to 3 Months," June 25, 2020, www.mayoclinic.org/healthy-lifestyle /infant-and-toddler-health/in-depth/infant-development/art -20048012.

25 **like disproportionate numbers of Black kids** Non-White school districts receive $23 billion less than White school districts, largely due to the reliance on property taxes. Black students are more likely than students of any other racial group to attend schools with police and are arrested at disproportionate rates. See EdBuild, "$23 Billion," February 2019, edbuild.org/content/23-billion/full-report.pdf; and Evie Blad and Alex Harwin, "Black Students More Likely to Be Arrested at School," *Education Week,* January 24, 2017, www.edweek.org/leadership/black -students-more-likely-to-be-arrested-at-school/2017/01.

25 **creates its own harmful distortions** See Ijeoma Oluo, *Mediocre: The Dangerous Legacy of White Male America* (New York: Seal Press, 2020); and Anti-Defamation League, *When Women Are the Enemy: The Intersection of Misogyny and White Supremacy,* www.adl.org/media/11707/download.

26 **longer life spans for White people** CDC data showed that the average White American in 2020 lived to age seventy-eight, while the average Black American lived to age seventy-two. Inequitable socioeconomic conditions and healthcare access contribute to this gap, beginning before Black Americans are even born. Farah Yousry, "Black Americans Face Widening Life Expectancy Gap, Biggest Since 1998," WFYI, March 29, 2021, www.wfyi.org/news/articles/black-americans-face-widening-life -expectancy-gap-biggest-since-1998.

27 **One article listed five things** "5 Things to Know About the DNA You Pass on to Your Children," All Pro Dad, www.allprodad.com /5-things-know-dna-pass-children/.

27 *Talent* **and** *aptitude* **are defined** See "talent," Merriam-Webster.com, www.merriam-webster.com/dictionary/talent; and "aptitude," Merriam-Webster.com, www.merriam-webster.com/dictionary/aptitude.

27 **He argued nature** Wendy Kline, *Building a Better Race: Gender, Sexuality, and Eugenics from the Turn of the Century to the Baby Boom* (Berkeley: University of California Press, 2001), 13; Raymond E. Fancher, "Scientific Cousins," *The American Psychologist* 64, no. 2 (2009), 84.

27 **"average intellectual standard of the negro race"** Francis Galton, *Hereditary Genius: An Inquiry into Its Laws and Consequences* (New York: D. Appleton, 1869), 338.

28 **lower "stock" of people** Kline, *Building a Better Race,* 13.

28 **meaning "good in birth"** Ibid.

28 **"all the testing says not really"** James Watson quoted in Associated Press, "Race Remarks Get Nobel Winner in Trouble," NBC News, October 18, 2007, www.nbcnews.com/id/wbna21362732# .XDxfJFVKhQJ.

28 **"no scientific basis for such a belief"** James Watson quoted in Cornelia Dean, "Nobel Winner Issues Apology for Comments About Blacks," *New York Times,* October 19, 2007, www.nytimes.com/2007 /10/19/science/19watson.html.

28 **"I haven't seen any knowledge"** James Watson quoted in Meagan Flynn, "The Father of DNA Says He Still Believes in a Link Between Race, Intelligence. His Lab Just Stripped Him of His Titles," *Washington Post,* January 14, 2019, www.washingtonpost.com/nation/2019/01/14 /father-dna-says-he-still-believes-link-between-race-intelligence-his -lab-just-stripped-him-his-titles/.

28 **disproved that IQ scores are a reliable measure** Adam Hampshire et al., "Fractionating Human Intelligence," *Neuron* 76, no. 6 (December 2012), 1225–1237; Michelle Castillo, "IQ Scores Not Accurate Marker of Intelligence, Study Shows," CBS News, December 21, 2012, www .cbsnews.com/news/iq-scores-not-accurate-marker-of-intelligence -study-shows/.

28 **disproved the long-standing idea** Noah A. Rosenberg et al., "Genetic Structure of Human Populations," *Science* 298 (December 2002), 2381–2385.

28 **more genetic variation *within* Africa** Ning Yu et al., "Larger Genetic Differences Within Africans Than Between Africans and Eurasians," *GENETICS* 161, no. 1 (May 2002), 269–274.

29 **"condemns the misuse of science to justify prejudice"** Bruce Stillman and Marilyn Simons quoted in Flynn, "The Father of DNA Says He Still Believes."

29 **poisoning the purity** Kline, *Building a Better Race,* 8–11.

29 **Nazis inspired by American eugenicists** James Q. Whitman, *Hitler's American Model: The United States and the Making of Nazi Race Law* (Princeton: Princeton University Press, 2017).

29 ***Positive* eugenics encouraged** Kline, *Building a Better Race,* 3, 13, 32–60.

29 ***Negative* eugenics discouraged** Ibid., 3, 13, 124–156.

29 **"the science of the improvement of the human race by better breeding"** Charles Benedict Davenport, *Heredity in Relation to Eugenics* (New York: H. Holt, 1911), 1.

29 **Granddaughters of the formerly prized breeders** Kline, *Building a Better Race,* 5–6, 8–11, 25, 32. For more on twentieth-century sterilization campaigns, see Kline, *Building a Better Race,* 118; Alexandra Minna Stern, *Eugenic Nation: Faults and Frontiers of Better Breeding in Modern America* (Berkeley: University of California Press, 2005); and Stern,

"Forced Sterilization Policies in the US Targeted Minorities and Those with Disabilities—And Lasted into the 21st Century," *The Conversation,* August 26, 2020, theconversation.com/forced-sterilization-policies-in -the-us-targeted-minorities-and-those-with-disabilities-and-lasted-into -the-21st-century-143144.

30 **in more than thirty states** Erika Lee, *America for Americans: A History of Xenophobia in the United States* (New York: Basic Books, 2019), 113– 115, 137–143; Social Sciences and Humanities Research Council of Canada, "Miscegenation," *Eugenics Archive,* eugenicsarchive.ca/discover /connections/52329c0e5c2ec5000000000b; Lutz Kaelber, "Eugenics: Compulsory Sterilization in 50 American States," www.uvm.edu /~lkaelber/eugenics/.

30 **"Sterilization protects future generations"** Harry Olson, preface to Harry Hamilton Laughlin, *Eugenical Sterilization in the United States* (Chicago: Psychopathic Laboratory of the Municipal Court of Chicago, 1922), v–vi.

30 **The nation's first adoption agencies** University of Oregon Department of History, "Eugenics," *The Adoption History Project,* pages.uoregon .edu/adoption/topics/eugenics.htm.

30 **"Not babies merely, but better babies"** Ibid.

30 **Better Baby contests** Francine Uenuma, " 'Better Babies' Contests Pushed for Much-Needed Infant Health but Also Played into the Eugenics Movement," *Smithsonian Magazine,* January 17, 2019, www .smithsonianmag.com/history/better-babies-contests-pushed-infant -health-also-played-eugenics-movement-180971288/.

30 **children, who were scrutinized like livestock** Laura L. Lovett, *Conceiving the Future: Pronatalism, Reproduction, and the Family in the United States, 1890–1938* (Chapel Hill: University of North Carolina Press, 2007), 136.

31 **intelligence correlates to over five hundred genes** W. D. Hill et al., "A Combined Analysis of Genetically Correlated Traits Identifies 187 Loci and a Role for Neurogenesis and Myelination in Intelligence," *Molecular Psychiatry* 24, no. 2 (February 2019), 169–181.

31 **aggression is tied to forty genes** Yanli Zhang-James et al., "An Integrated Analysis of Genes and Functional Pathways for Aggression in Human and Rodent Models," *Molecular Psychiatry* 24, no. 11 (November 2019), 1655–1667.

31 **spoken language is related to several genes** Sarah A. Graham and Simon E. Fisher, "Decoding the Genetics of Speech and Language," *Current Opinion in Neurobiology* 23, no. 1 (February 2013), 43. Graham and Fisher specified, "[T]he evolution of language is unlikely to be accounted for by only a single gene" (45).

31 **sexual orientation is influenced by "many" genes** Andrea Ganna

et al., "Large-Scale GWAS Reveals Insights into the Genetic Architecture of Same-Sex Sexual Behavior," *Science* 365, no. 6456 (August 2019), doi/10.1126/science.aat7693.

31 **typically only partly responsible** For example, aggression is "around 50%" hereditary, and genes contribute to at most 25 percent of same-sex sexual behaviors. Zhang-James et al., "An Integrated Analysis of Genes and Functional Pathways for Aggression," 1655; Ganna et al., "Large-Scale GWAS Reveals Insights"; Jonathan Lambert, "No 'Gay Gene': Massive Study Homes in on Genetic Basis of Human Sexuality," *Nature,* August 29, 2019, www.nature.com/articles/d41586-019-02585-6.

31 **often point us to environmental explanations** In "An Integrated Analysis of Genes and Functional Pathways for Aggression," a study on genes associated with aggression, Zhang-James et al. noted "its complex genetic architecture interacts with environmental factors" (1655). Simon E. Fisher and Constance Scharff, "FOXP2 as a Molecular Window into Speech and Language," *Trends in Genetics* 25, no. 4 (April 2009), acknowledged the role of "environmental input" in children's acquisition of spoken language (166). Regarding human sexuality, Ganna et al., "Large-Scale GWAS Reveals Insights," stated "the importance of sociocultural context" in same-sex sexual behavior.

33 **innate "evaluative or attitudinal system"** Yarrow Dunham, Andrew S. Baron, and Mahzarin R. Banaji, "The Development of Implicit Intergroup Cognition," *Trends in Cognitive Sciences* 12, no. 7 (July 2008), 252.

33 **demonstrate "no spontaneous preference"** David J. Kelly et al., "Three-Month-Olds, but Not Newborns, Prefer Own-Race Faces," *Developmental Science* 8, no. 6 (2005), F31.

33 **Portuguese began justifying the racist policies** Kendi, *Stamped from the Beginning,* 23.

33 **"No one is born hating another person"** "Nelson Mandela's Most Inspirational Quotes," ABC News, December 5, 2013, abcnews.go.com /International/nelson-mandelas-inspirational-quotes/story?id= 8879848.

CHAPTER 3: BABY NURTURE

37 **the number one cause of death in children** CDC, "Injuries Among Children and Teens," September 22, 2021, www.cdc.gov/injury/features /child-injury/index.html.

38 **parental influence is *the* major element** Gordon W. Allport, *The Nature of Prejudice* (Cambridge, MA: Addison-Wesley, 1954), 291–294, 297–300, 307–308.

38 **"empty vessels into which adults put their own ideas"** Debra Van Ausdale and Joe R. Feagin, *The First R: How Children Learn Race and Racism* (Lanham, MD: Rowman & Littlefield, 2001), 17.

38 **apply specific racial knowledge** Van Ausdale and Feagin, ibid., referred to children "doing racism" (28). Margaret A. Hagerman, in "Reproducing and Reworking Colorblind Racial Ideology: Acknowledging Children's Agency in the White Habitus," *Sociology of Race and Ethnicity* 2, no. 1 (2016), 58–71, characterized children as active participants in their own racial socialization.

38 **the "smog" our children breathe** Beverly Daniel Tatum, *"Why Are All the Black Kids Sitting Together in the Cafeteria?" And Other Conversations About Race* (New York: Basic Books, 1999), 6.

39 **"are starting to become proficient"** Sandy Sangrigoli and Scania de Schonen, "Recognition of Own-Race and Other-Race Faces by Three-Month-Old Infants," *Journal of Child Psychology and Psychiatry* 45, no. 7 (2004), 1225.

39 **"preference for own-race faces is present"** Yair Bar-Haim et al., "Nature and Nurture in Own-Race Face Processing," *Psychological Science* 17, no. 2 (2006), 159.

40 **"experience-dependent"** Sangrigoli and de Schonen, "Recognition of Own-Race and Other-Race Faces," 1225.

40 **"predominantly homogenous own-race environments"** Bar-Haim et al., "Nature and Nurture in Own-Race Face Processing," 162.

40 **most likely to live in predominantly homogeneous own-race environments** William H. Frey, "Even as Metropolitan Areas Diversify, White Americans Still Live in Mostly White Neighborhoods," Brookings Institution, March 23, 2020, www.brookings.edu/research/even-as-metropolitan-areas-diversify-white-americans-still-live-in-mostly-white-neighborhoods/.

40 **"significant preference for faces"** Kelly et al., "Three-Month-Olds, but Not Newborns, Prefer Own-Race Faces," F31.

40 **recognize an individual White face but not an individual Asian face** Sangrigoli and de Schonen, "Recognition of Own-Race and Other-Race Faces," 1222.

40 **recognize an individual Asian face** Ibid., 1223.

40 **rapidly increase their face-processing skills** Ibid., 1225; Gizelle Anzures et al., "Categorization, Categorical Perception, and Asymmetry in Infants' Representation of Face Race," *Developmental Science* 13, no. 4 (2010), 561.

40 **"have preverbal concepts of both gender and race"** Katz, "Racists or Tolerant Multiculturalists? How Do They Begin?," 904.

40 **categorize own-race faces** Anzures et al., "Categorization, Categorical Perception, and Asymmetry in Infants' Representation of Face Race," 561.

41 **"approximately ninety-four percent of cases"** Linda Tropp quoted

in Heather C. McGhee, *The Sum of Us: What Racism Costs Everyone and How We Can Prosper Together* (New York: One World, 2021), 175.

41 **majority of Black Americans** Douglas S. Massey, "Residential Segregation and Neighborhood Conditions in U.S. Metropolitan Areas," in *America Becoming: Racial Trends and Their Consequences*, eds. Neil J. Smelser, William Julius Wilson, and Faith Mitchell (Washington, DC: The National Academies Press, 2001), vol. 1, 393.

41 **red lines were for mortgage lenders** Richard Rothstein, *The Color of Law: A Forgotten History of How Our Government Segregated America* (New York: Liveright, 2017), 64; Keeanga-Yamahtta Taylor, *Race for Profit: How Banks and the Real Estate Industry Undermined Black Homeownership* (Chapel Hill: University of North Carolina Press, 2019).

42 **"alongside some big black buck"** Dwight Eisenhower quoted in Sylvia Gonzalez-Gorman, *Political Speech as a Weapon: Microaggression in a Changing Racial and Ethnic Environment* (Santa Barbara: Praeger, 2018), 69.

42 **living in relatively homogeneous neighborhoods** Massey, "Residential Segregation and Neighborhood Conditions in U.S. Metropolitan Areas," 395–398.

42 **From 2014 to 2018 in the hundred largest metropolitan areas** Frey, "Even as Metropolitan Areas Diversify."

42 **"seldom or never" interact** McGhee, *The Sum of Us,* 175.

42 **"the most segregated people in America"** Ibid., 68.

42 **especially high among middle-income White residents** Samuel H. Kye, "The Persistence of White Flight in Middle-Class Suburbia," *Social Science Research* 72 (2018), 48–49.

42 **discontinued an Obama-era program** Annie Karni, Maggie Haberman, and Sydney Ember, "Trump Plays on Racist Fears of Terrorized Suburbs to Court White Voters," *New York Times,* July 29, 2020, www.nytimes.com/2020/07/29/us/politics/trump-suburbs-housing-white-voters.html.

43 **"People living their Suburban Lifestyle Dream"** Donald Trump tweet quoted in Karni, Haberman, and Ember, "Trump Plays on Racist Fears."

43 **"living in hell in the inner cities"** Donald Trump campaign speech quoted in Candace Smith, "Trump Warns of Inner City 'Hell' for Blacks Where Trayvon Martin Was Shot," *ABC News*, October 25, 2016, abcnews.go.com/Politics/trump-warns-city-hell-blacks-trayvon-martin-shot/story?id=43057914.

43 **about 47 percent White** McGhee, *The Sum of Us,* 175–176.

43 **less desirable than White neighborhoods** Ibid., 176.

43 **slightly Whiter neighborhoods** University of Southern California,

"White Families with Children Drawn to Less Diverse Neighborhoods, Schools," *ScienceDaily,* March 23, 2017, www.sciencedaily.com/releases /2017/03/170323105810.htm.

43 **"a wealthier and whiter neighborhood"** Heather Beth Johnson, *The American Dream and the Power of Wealth: Choosing Schools and Inheriting Inequality in the Land of Opportunity,* 2nd ed. (New York: Routledge, 2015), 56.

43 **rate Black perpetrators more harshly** Heidi McGlothlin and Melanie Killen, "How Social Experience Is Related to Children's Intergroup Attitudes," *European Journal of Social Psychology* 40, no. 4 (2010), 630.

43 **Test scores aren't lower** U.S. Department of Education, National Assessment of Educational Progress, *School Composition and the Black-White Achievement Gap* (2015), 1, nces.ed.gov/nationsreportcard/subject /studies/pdf/school_composition_and_the_bw_achievement_gap_2015 .pdf.

44 **score higher on standardized tests** McGhee, *The Sum of Us,* 181.

44 **best fostered in diverse classrooms** Kristina Rizga, "3 Ways White Kids Benefit Most from Racially Diverse Schools," *Mother Jones,* January 15, 2016, www.motherjones.com/politics/2016/01/white-kids-benefits -diverse-schools/.

44 **Graduates of diverse schools** Rizga, "3 Ways White Kids Benefit Most from Racially Diverse Schools."

44 **make all our kids smarter** Amy Stuart Wells, Lauren Fox, and Diana Cordova-Cobo, *How Racially Diverse Schools and Classrooms Can Benefit All Students* (The Century Foundation, February 9, 2016), 2, production -tcf.imgix.net/app/uploads/2016/02/09142501/HowRaciallyDiverse _AmyStuartWells-11.pdf.

44 **zero weeks of federally guaranteed paid maternity leave** Miranda Bryant, "Maternity Leave: US Policy Is Worst on List of the World's Richest Countries," *Guardian,* January 27, 2020, www.theguardian.com /us-news/2020/jan/27/maternity-leave-us-policy-worst-worlds-richest -countries.

44 **Only 16 percent of private U.S. employees** Warren Fiske, "Fact-Check: Is U.S. the Only Industrialized Country Without Paid Family Medical Leave?," *Austin American-Statesman,* January 29, 2021, www .statesman.com/story/news/politics/politifact/2021/01/29/united -states-industrialized-nation-no-paid-family-medical-leave-plan /4313107001/.

46 **policy outcomes familial and societal caregivers can pursue** Poverty & Race Research Action Council, "An Anti-Racist Agenda for State and Local Housing Agencies" (PRRAC, July 2020), prrac.org/an-anti -racist-agenda-for-state-and-local-housing-agencies/; Andre M. Perry and Stuart Yasgur, "Dismantling White Privilege Starts with Undoing

Racist Housing Policies," Brookings Institution, January 14, 2021, www
.brookings.edu/blog/the-avenue/2021/01/14/dismantling
-white-privilege-starts-with-undoing-racist-housing-policies/; Ta-Nehisi
Coates, "The Case for Reparations," *Atlantic,* June 2014, www.theatlantic
.com/magazine/archive/2014/06/the-case-for-reparations/361631/;
Ibram X. Kendi, interview with Mariame Kaba, *Be Antiracist* podcast,
July 28, 2021, www.pushkin.fm/episode/prison-police-abolition-finding
-true-safety/; Nicole Friedman, "How to Make the Housing Market
More Equitable," *Wall Street Journal,* December 8, 2020, www.wsj.com
/articles/how-to-make-the-housing-market-more-equitable
-11607457660; Jason Grotto, "How Unfair Property Taxes Keep Black
Families from Gaining Wealth," *Bloomberg,* March 9, 2021, www.bloomberg
.com/news/features/2021-03-09/racial-inequality-broken-property-tax
-system-blocks-black-wealth-building?srnd=equality&sref=aUgb5sAb.

47 **watching TV before eighteen months can have lasting effects**
David L. Hill, "Why to Avoid TV for Infants & Toddlers," *Healthy Chil-
dren,* October 21, 2016, www.healthychildren.org/English/family-life
/Media/Pages/Why-to-Avoid-TV-Before-Age-2.aspx.

47 **books that reflect the full range of humanity** Ebony Elizabeth
Thomas, "Stories Still Matter: Rethinking the Role of Diverse Children's Literature Today," *Language Arts* 94, no. 2 (November 2016), 115.
Thomas powerfully stated, "If today's children grow up with literature
that is multicultural, diverse, and decolonized, we can begin the work of
healing our nation and world through humanizing stories."

47 **channel their child's attention** Katz, "Racists or Tolerant Multiculturalists? How Do They Begin?," 904.

47 **"most pronounced"** Ibid.

47 **Childproofing our circle of friends** Van Ausdale and Feagin, in *The
First R,* highlighted the importance of parental friendships with people
of different racial and ethnic backgrounds. They made the essential point
to "not place these friends in the position of being 'experts' on racial and
ethnic issues" (211).

47 **White Americans are less likely** Deborah L. Plummer et al., "Pat-
terns of Adult Cross-Racial Friendships: A Context for Understanding
Contemporary Race Relations," *Cultural Diversity and Ethnic Minority
Psychology* 22, no. 4 (October 2016), 479, 484.

47 **more likely than White and Black individuals** Ibid., 479.

47 **twice as likely as White people** Ibid., 484.

48 **more influenced by *perceptions*** Brigitte Vittrup and George W.
Holden, "Exploring the Impact of Educational Television and Parent–
Child Discussions on Children's Racial Attitudes," *Analyses of Social Issues
and Public Policy* 11, no. 1 (2011), 99.

48 **when parents and teachers fail to talk directly** Ibid.

CHAPTER 4: INFANT'S DOLL

50 **the quality of time** Brigid Schulte, "Making Time for Kids? Study Says Quality Trumps Quantity," *Washington Post,* March 28, 2015, www .washingtonpost.com/local/making-time-for-kids-study-says-quality -trumps-quantity/2015/03/28/10813192-d378-11e4-8fce -3941fc548f1c_story.html.

51 **Regular time spent taking care of grandkids** American Heart Association News, "Time with Grandkids Could Boost Health—Even Lifespan," August 30, 2019, www.heart.org/en/news/2019/08/30/time -with-grandkids-could-boost-health-even-lifespan.

51 **2.5 and 3 million grandparents** Ibid.

53 **mass-produced toys first entered American homes** Americans first imported mass-produced toys from Germany. American manufacturers began to make toys in the 1840s, but production significantly expanded after the Civil War. American-made iron toys boomed beginning in the late 1870s. Even so, Americans still relied on the German toy industry— at the turn of the twentieth century, the United States imported a quarter of all German toys. See Antonia Fraser, *A History of Toys* (New York: Delacorte Press, 1966), 200–202. Mamie Phipps Clark's parents were born around this time; her father, Harold, was born in the West Indies around 1883, and her mother, Katy, was born in Arkansas around 1893. "United States Census, 1930," database with images, *FamilySearch* (familysearch.org/ark:/61903/1:1:XML3-4V8), Harold H. Phipps, Hot Springs, Garland, Arkansas, United States; citing enumeration district (ED) ED 14, sheet 4B, line 56, family 102, NARA microfilm publication T626 (Washington, DC: National Archives and Records Administration, 2002), roll 75; FHL microfilm 2,339,810.

53 **"Always Did 'Spise a Mule" mechanical bank** Pamela B. Nelson, "Toys as History: Ethnic Images and Cultural Change," Jim Crow Museum of Racist Memorabilia, Ferris State University, www.ferris.edu /HTMLS/news/jimcrow/links/essays/toys.htm; Christopher P. Barton and Kyle Somerville, "Play Things: Children's Racialized Mechanical Banks and Toys, 1880–1930," *International Journal of Historical Archaeology* 16, no. 1 (March 2012), 60–63, 68.

53 **"Paddy and the Pig" mechanical bank** Nelson, "Toys as History: Ethnic Images and Cultural Change"; Barton and Somerville, "Play Things: Children's Racialized Mechanical Banks and Toys," 55–58.

54 **"Reclining Chinaman" mechanical bank** Nelson, "Toys as History: Ethnic Images and Cultural Change"; Barton and Somerville, "Play Things: Children's Racialized Mechanical Banks and Toys," 58–60.

54 **"fair hair and blue eyes are the favorites"** G. Stanley Hall and Alex-

ander Caswell Ellis, *A Study of Dolls* (New York: E. L. Kellogg, 1897), 11.

54 **"'funny' or exceptional"** Ibid., 16.

54 **"a certain kind of protective armor"** Mamie Clark quoted in Leila McNeill, "How a Psychologist's Work on Race Identity Helped Overturn School Segregation in 1950s America," *Smithsonian Magazine,* October 26, 2017, www.smithsonianmag.com/science-nature/psychologist-work-racial-identity-helped-overturn-school-segregation-180966934/.

55 **"race prejudice" was not an "inborn trait"** Bruno Lasker, *Race Attitudes in Children* (New York: Henry Holt, 1929), 55.

55 **inspired Eugene and Ruth Horowitz** John P. Jackson, *Social Scientists for Social Justice Making the Case against Segregation* (New York: New York University Press, 2001), 29–31.

55 **"Give me the doll you like to play with"** Kenneth B. Clark and Mamie P. Clark, "Racial Identification and Preference in Negro Children" (1947), in *Readings in Social Psychology,* eds. Eugene L. Hartley, Eleanor E. Maccoby, and Theodore M. Newcomb (New York: Holt, Rinehart, and Winston, 1958), 169.

55 **gave them a White doll** Ibid., 175–177.

55 **mostly gave them the White doll** Ibid., 169, 175–177.

55 **asked a child in rural Arkansas** Interview with Dr. Kenneth Clark, conducted by Blackside, Inc., on November 4, 1985, for *Eyes on the Prize: America's Civil Rights Years (1954–1965),* Washington University Libraries, Film and Media Archive, Henry Hampton Collection, way back.archive-it.org/8967/20171023214228/http://digital.wustl.edu/cgi/t/text/text-idx?c=eop;cc=eop;rgn=main;view=text;idno=cla0015.0289.020.

55 **refused to answer which doll** NAACP Legal Defense Fund, "A Revealing Experiment: Brown v. Board and 'The Doll Test,'" www.naacpldf.org/ldf-celebrates-60th-anniversary-brown-v-board-education/significance-doll-test/.

55 **burst into tears** Ibid.

56 **presented the available research** See Kenneth Clark, "The Effects of Prejudice and Discrimination," in *Personality in the Making: The Fact-Finding Report of the Midcentury White House Conference on Children and Youth,* eds. Helen Leland Witmer and Ruth Kotinsky (New York: Harper and Brothers, 1952), 135–158.

56 **"Segregation, prejudices and discriminations"** Robert L. Carter, "The Effects of Segregation and the Consequences of Desegregation: A Social Science Statement," *Journal of Negro Education* 22, no. 1 (Winter 1953), 69–70.

56 **"Segregation of white and colored children"** Brown v. Board of Education, 347 U.S. 483 (1954).

57 **"being drawn closer" together** E. Franklin Frazier, *The Negro Family in the United States*, 2nd ed. (Chicago: University of Chicago Press, 1940), 488.

57 **assimilating into the broader racial category of White** See Erika Lee, *America for Americans: A History of Xenophobia in the United States* (New York: Basic Books, 2019); Nell Irvin Painter, *The History of White People* (New York: W. W. Norton, 2010); Matthew Frye Jacobson, *Whiteness of a Different Color: European Immigrants and the Alchemy of Race* (Cambridge: Harvard University Press, 1999). While Irish were encompassed under the umbrella of whiteness around the turn of the twentieth century, prejudice boxed out Jews and Italians for another half century.

57 **"White men with Black skins"** Kenneth M. Stampp, *The Peculiar Institution: Slavery in the Ante-Bellum South* (New York: Vintage Books, 1956), vii–ix.

57 **The myth of American homogeneity** Nelson, "Toys as History: Ethnic Images and Cultural Change."

57 **largely stopping production** Ibid.

57 **"Chutes and Ladders" and "Candyland"** Ibid.

58 **exclusively White Barbie doll** Ibid.

58 **toy makers assimilated nearly all toys into Whiteness** Ibid.

58 **stereotypical portrayals of Native Americans** Ibid.

58 **"Who taught you to hate"** African Docs Project, "Malcolm X— Who Taught You to Hate Yourself (Powerful Speech), Los Angeles, May 5, 1962," YouTube video, 22:16–22:45, March 3, 2021, www.youtube .com/watch?v=QVidxSuQvDQ.

58 **the Black Power movement, which inspired** For more on the connections between the Black Power, Red Power, Brown Power, and Yellow Power movements, and for overviews of each of these movements, see Jeffrey O. G. Ogbar, *Black Power: Radical Politics and African American Identity,* rev. ed. (Baltimore: Johns Hopkins University Press, 2019), 159–189; Van Gosse, *Rethinking the New Left: An Interpretive History* (New York: Palgrave Macmillan, 2005), 131–151; Paul Chaat Smith and Robert Allen Warrior, *Like a Hurricane: The Indian Movement from Alcatraz to Wounded Knee* (New York: New Press, 1996); Marc S. Rodriguez, *Rethinking the Chicano Movement* (New York: Routledge, 2015); Daryl J. Maeda, *Rethinking the Asian American Movement* (New York: Routledge, 2012).

58 **Remco's line of Black dolls** "The Advent of Soul Toys," *Ebony* (November 1968), 165.

58 **Black, Asian, and Latinx Barbies** "40th Anniversary First Black Barbie Doll," *Barbie,* barbie.mattel.com/shop/en-us/ba/all-signature-dolls /40th-anniversary-black-barbie-doll-glg35#:~:text=The%20original %20Black%20Barbie%C2%AE,hailed%20as%20Barbie%C2%AE %20herself; Natasha Piñon, "She's a Barbie Girl, in a New World," *Mash-*

able, December 23, 2019, mashable.com/feature/barbie-diverse-inclusive
/#:~:text=The%20first%20apparent%20East%20Asian,countries%20like
%20Italy%20and%20Scotland; Talia Lakritz, "Here's What Barbie
Looked Like the Year You Were Born," *Insider,* August 9, 2020, www
.insider.com/how-barbie-dolls-changed-evolution-2018-3.

58 **Black and Asian G.I. Joe figurines** Carlos D. Morrison, "The Evolution of an Identity: G.I. Joe and Black Masculinity," in *Communicating Marginalized Masculinities: Identity Politics in TV, Film, and New Media,* eds. Ronald L. Jackson II and Jamie E. Moshin (New York: Routledge, 2013), 106; Brian Cronin, "Owning Is Half the Battle: The 15 Most Expensive G.I. Joe Figures," *Comic Book Resource,* September 23, 2017, www.cbr.com/most-expensive-g-i-joe-figures/; Sig Christenson, "G.I. Joe Doll Is the Spitting Image of Real-Life Hispanic Hero," South Florida *Sun-Sentinel,* July 28, 2001, www.sun-sentinel.com/news/fl-xpm -2001-07-28-0107270543-story.html.

59 **explicitly Latinx G.I. Joe figurine** Christenson, "G.I. Joe Doll Is the Spitting Image."

59 **"Fashionista" line of Barbies** Piñon, "She's a Barbie Girl, in a New World."

59 **new body sizes, skin tones, and hair textures** Eliana Dockterman, "Why Ken's Got a New Body, Too," *TIME,* June 20, 2017, time.com /4825191/ken-dolls-new-body-mattell-2017/.

59 **first Barbie to wear a hijab** Erica Gonzales, "Barbie Just Released Its First Doll Wearing a Hijab to Honor American Olympian Ibtihaj Muhammad," *Harper's Bazaar,* November 13, 2017, www.harpersbazaar.com /culture/features/a13529557/first-barbie-wearing-hijab/.

59 **"the world's first gender-neutral doll"** Eliana Dockterman, " 'A Doll for Everyone': Meet Mattel's Gender-Neutral Doll," *TIME,* September 25, 2019, time.com/5684822/mattel-gender-neutral-doll/.

59 **dolls with wheelchairs and prosthetic limbs** Michelle Lou and Brandon Griggs, "Barbie Introduces Dolls with Wheelchairs and Prosthetic Limbs," CNN, February 12, 2019, www.cnn.com/2019/02/12 /us/barbie-doll-disabilities-trnd/index.html.

59 **55 percent of all dolls sold** Piñon, "She's a Barbie Girl, in a New World."

59 **old stereotype of "jovial Italians"** Nelson, "Toys as History: Ethnic Images and Cultural Change." To better understand how Mario's representation has changed over time, see "Mario Through the Years," Nintendo, mario.nintendo.com/history/.

59 **toy box reflects the multiracial, multiethnic, multicultural world** Shanicia Boswell, "How to Diversify Your Toy Box," *New York Times,* August 3, 2020, www.nytimes.com/2020/08/03/parenting/multiracial -toys-diversity-play.html.

60 **the follower as much as the leader** Ibid.

60 **there aren't bad or good people** Mariame Kaba subscribes to wisdom bequeathed by her mother: "My mother said that there was no such thing as bad people, only people who sometimes did a bad thing." See Kaba, *We Do This 'til We Free Us: Abolitionist Organizing and Transforming Justice,* ed. Tamara K. Nopper (Chicago: Haymarket Books, 2021), 160.

60 **displayed what researchers called *White bias*** "Study: White and Black Children Biased Toward Lighter Skin," CNN, May 14, 2010, www.cnn.com/2010/US/05/13/doll.study/index.html.

62 **a report by the Board on Children, Youth, and Families** Board on Children, Youth, and Families, National Academies of Sciences, Engineering, and Medicine, *Child Development and Early Learning: A Foundation for Professional Knowledge and Competencies* (Washington, DC: National Academies of Sciences, Engineering, and Medicine, 2015), 4.

63 **"I know that we don't look the same"** Grace Byers and Keturah A. Bobo (illustrator), *I Am Enough* (New York: Balzer Bray, 2018).

63 **"open[s] dialogue around prejudice"** Sian Jones, "One Like Me! Toying with the Doll Industry," Goldsmiths, University of London, sites .gold.ac.uk/psychology/2016/06/06/one-like-me-toying-with-the -doll-industry/.

CHAPTER 5: EMPATHETIC TODDLER

65 **Only 14 percent of people diagnosed with Stage 4 colon cancer** Colon Cancer Coalition, "Get the Facts About Colon Cancer," colon-cancercoalition.org/get-educated/what-you-need-to-know/colon -cancer-facts/.

66 **Between fourteen months and two and a half years** Daniel Goleman, "Researchers Trace Empathy's Roots to Infancy," *New York Times,* March 28, 1989, www.nytimes.com/1989/03/28/science/researchers -trace-empathy-s-roots-to-infancy.html.

67 **"mental-state understanding"** Henry M. Wellman, David Cross, and Julianne Watson, "Meta-Analysis of Theory-of-Mind Development: The Truth About False Belief," *Child Development* 72, no. 3 (May/June 2001), 655; Nicole M. McDonald and David Messinger, "The Development of Empathy: How, When, and Why," in *Free Will, Emotions, and Moral Actions: Philosophy and Neuroscience in Dialogue,* eds. Ariberto Acerbi, José Angel Lombo, and Juan José Sanguineti (Rome, Italy: IF Press, 2011), 5.

67 **"Dare to be the adults"** Brené Brown, *Daring Greatly: How the Courage to Be Vulnerable Transforms the Way We Live, Love, Parent, and Lead* (New York: Avery, 2012), 177.

67 **"overall life situation"** Goleman, "Researchers Trace Empathy's Roots to Infancy."

67 **"hardwired" for empathy** Helen Riess, "The Science of Empathy," *Journal of Patient Experience* 4, no. 2 (2017), 75.

68 **the same areas of our brains** Ibid. Riess gave the example of another person's hand muscle being pricked by a needle.

68 **"empathy is a mutable trait"** Helen Riess quoted in Jane E. Brody, "How to Foster Empathy in Children," *New York Times,* December 10, 2018, www.nytimes.com/2018/12/10/well/live/how-to-foster -empathy-in-children.html.

68 **avoid dismissing our children's questions** Brody, "How to Foster Empathy in Children."

68 **hardly raising them to be empathetic** Psychologists Maayan Davidov and Joan W. Grusec found that children between ages six and eight whose mothers exhibited positive responses to distress (e.g., comforting and helping the child instead of dismissing or reacting with hostility) were more empathetic and likely to engage in prosocial behaviors (e.g., help). See Davidov and Grusec, "Untangling the Links of Parental Responsiveness to Distress and Warmth to Child Outcomes," *Child Development* 77, no. 1 (January–February 2006), 44–58.

68 **"Are you afraid?"** Paraphrase of Riess quoted in Brody, "How to Foster Empathy in Children."

68 **"Why do you feel that way?"** Ibid.

68 **teach and model empathetic action** Brody, "How to Foster Empathy in Children."

68 **with markedly less empathy** Sara H. Konrath, Edward H. O'Brien, and Courtney Hsing, "Changes in Dispositional Empathy in American College Students over Time: A Meta-Analysis," *Personality and Social Psychology Review* 15, no. 2 (2011), 180. Specifically, these researchers found that over time, American college students scored lower levels of empathic concern and perspective taking, "which are the most central components of empathy" (185).

69 **"multidimensional" concept of empathy** Mark H. Davis, "A Multidimensional Approach to Individual Differences in Empathy," *JSAS Catalog of Selected Documents in Psychology* 85, no. 10 (1980), 1–19.

69 *Fantasy* **is "the tendency"** Ibid., 2.

69 *Perspective taking* **refers to "spontaneous attempts"** Ibid.

69 *Empathic concern* **describes "feelings of warmth"** Ibid.

69 *Personal distress* **is characterized by "personal feelings"** Ibid.

69 **"Higher empathy countries"** William J. Chopik, Ed O'Brien, and Sara H. Konrath, "Differences in Empathic Concern and Perspective Taking Across 63 Countries," *Journal of Cross-Cultural Psychology* 48, no. 1 (2017), 23. With the understanding that there might be cultural variations to empathy, Chopik, O'Brien, and Konrath studied empathy in more than 100,000 adults in 63 countries (though 74.3 percent lived in

the United States). They concluded, "The countries with the highest Total Empathy scores were Ecuador, Saudi Arabia, Peru, Denmark, and the United Arab Emirates. The countries with the lowest Total Empathy scores were Lithuania, Venezuela, Estonia, Poland, and Bulgaria" (30).

69 **higher rates of regular (rather than episodic) volunteerism** Lynette S. Unger and Lakshmi K. Thumuluri, "Trait Empathy and Continuous Helping: The Case of Voluntarism," *Journal of Social Behavior and Personality* 12, no. 3 (1997), 796.

69 **tend to be more altruistic** Willa Litvak-Miller, Daniel McDougall, and David M. Romney, "The Structure of Empathy During Middle Childhood and Its Relationship to Prosocial Behavior," *Genetic, Social, and General Psychology Monographs* 123, no. 3 (1997), 303–324.

69 **"enhanced levels" of cognitive and affective empathy** Tirza H. J. van Noorden et al., "Empathy and Involvement in Bullying in Children and Adolescents: A Systematic Review," *Journal of Youth and Adolescence* 44, no. 3 (2014), 652.

69 **"ability to *comprehend* another person's emotions"** Ibid., 638. Authors' emphasis.

70 **"capacity to *experience* another person's emotions"** Ibid. Authors' emphasis.

70 **Bullies generally have less** Ibid., 651–652. Van Noorden et al. explained, "Whether or not bullies *understand* what others feel, they do not *experience* what others feel" (652). In another study, researchers found that when accounting for other influential factors, e.g., socioeconomic status, single-parent household, and levels of parental supervision, male adolescents (ages thirteen to seventeen) who bullied others had lower levels of affective empathy than peers who did not bully. See Darrick Jolliffe and David P. Farrington, "Is Low Empathy Related to Bullying After Controlling for Individual and Social Background Variables?," *Journal of Adolescence* 34, no. 1 (2011), 59–71.

70 **"I can hurt others with"** Susan Verde and Peter H. Reynolds (illustrator), *I Am Human: A Book of Empathy* (New York: Abrams, 2018).

70 **can all teach empathic skills** Amanda B. Nickerson, Danielle Mele, and Dana Princiotta, "Attachment and Empathy as Predictors of Roles as Defenders or Outsiders in Bullying Interactions," *Journal of School Psychology* 46, no. 6 (2008), 698.

70 **prioritize social and emotional learning** Kaitlin Luna, interview with Sara Konrath, "Episode 95: The Decline of Empathy and the Rise of Narcissism," *Speaking of Psychology* (American Psychological Association), podcast transcript, December 4, 2019, www.apa.org/research /action/speaking-of-psychology/empathy-narcissism.

70 **the "criminal punishment system"** Kaba, *We Do This 'til We Free Us*.

70 **"power-assertive discipline"** See, for example, Julia Krevans and John

C. Gibbs, "Parents' Use of Inductive Discipline: Relations to Children's Empathy and Prosocial Behavior," *Child Development* 67, no. 6 (December 1996), 3263–3277. Krevans and Gibbs defined "power-assertive discipline" as characterized by "power assertions, that is, discipline which attempts to change the child's behavior through use of the parents' power over the child (e.g., 'Tell him that he'll be punished for what he's done')" (3266).

70 **"inductive discipline"** Krevans and Gibbs, in "Parents' Use of Inductive Discipline: Relations to Children's Empathy and Prosocial Behavior," framed "inductive discipline" as "discipline which directs the child to attend to his or her victims' perspectives (e.g., 'Point out how his friend must feel,' and 'Tell him I never expected to hear that sort of thing from him')" (3266). Krevans and Gibbs observed that children in sixth and seventh grades (ages eleven to fourteen) whose parents used other-oriented inductive discipline (e.g., point out how injured/victimized friend must feel) rather than power-assertive discipline (e.g., you will be punished for what you've done) were more empathic and likely to engage in prosocial behavior.

71 **suspension rates were cut in half** Jason A. Okonofua, David Paunesku, and Gregory M. Walton, "Brief Intervention to Encourage Empathic Discipline Cuts Suspension Rates in Half Among Adolescents," *Proceedings of the National Academy of Sciences of the United States of America* 113, no. 19 (May 2016), 5221.

71 **inductive discipline involved** Ibid., 5222.

71 **Adults with low levels of empathy** Felicia Pratto et al., "Social Dominance Orientation: A Personality Variable Predicting Social and Political Attitudes," *Journal of Personality and Social Psychology* 67, no. 4 (1994), 744, 754.

71 **Adults with high levels of empathy** Ibid., 755.

71 **"principle of care"** Mark Ottoni Wilhelm and René Bekkers, "Helping Behavior, Dispositional Empathic Concern, and the Principle of Care," *Social Psychology Quarterly* 73, no. 1 (March 2010), 11.

71 **"spontaneous, short-term helping"** Ibid., 25–26.

71 **"planned, long-term helping"** Ibid.

72 **not perceived as "responsible" for their condition** Saerom Lee, Karen Page Winterich, and William T. Ross, Jr., "I'm Moral, but I Won't Help You: The Distinct Roles of Empathy and Justice in Donations," *Journal of Consumer Research* 41, no. 3 (October 2014), 685–688, 693.

73 **support for (or opposition to) government assistance programs** Lauren D. Appelbaum, "The Influence of Perceived Deservingness on Policy Decisions Regarding Aid to the Poor," *Political Psychology* 22, no. 3 (September 2001), 429–430.

73 **considered deserving of welfare in the 1950s** For an excellent history of the racialized and gendered framing of welfare recipients, see Premilla Nadasen, *Welfare Warriors: The Welfare Rights Movement in the United States* (New York: Routledge, 2005).

73 **considered deserving of treatment in 2016** Julie Netherland and Helena B. Hansen, "The War on Drugs That Wasn't: Wasted Whiteness, 'Dirty Doctors,' and Race in Media Coverage of Prescription Opioid Misuse," *Culture, Medicine, and Psychiatry* 40, no. 4 (December 2016), 664–686, doi.org/10.1007/s11013-016-9496-5.

74 **wealthy people (who are disproportionately White)** Neil Bhutta et al., "Disparities in Wealth by Race and Ethnicity in the 2019 Survey of Consumer Finances," FEDS Notes (Washington, DC: Board of Governors of the Federal Reserve System, September 28, 2020), doi.org/10.17016/2380-7172.2797. "White families have the highest level of both median and mean family wealth: $188,200 and $983,400, respectively. . . . Black families' median and mean wealth is less than 15 percent that of White families, at $24,100 and $142,500, respectively. Hispanic families' median and mean wealth is $36,100 and $165,500, respectively. Other families—a diverse group that includes those identifying as Asian, American Indian, Alaska Native, Native Hawaiian, Pacific Islander, other race, and all respondents reporting more than one racial identification—have lower wealth than White families but higher wealth than Black and Hispanic families."

74 **capitalist policy that makes it cheap to be rich** For an overview of government benefits for the rich, see Emily Badger and Christopher Ingraham, "The Rich Get Government Handouts Just Like the Poor. Here Are 10 of Them," *Washington Post,* April 9, 2015, www.washingtonpost.com/news/wonk/wp/2015/04/09/the-rich-get-government-handouts-just-like-the-poor-here-are-10-of-them/.

74 **"most empathy for others who look or act like them"** Riess, "The Science of Empathy," 75.

75 **Black, Brown, and Native people dying at the highest rates from COVID-19** The COVID Racial Data Tracker, "COVID-19 is affecting Black, Indigenous, Latinx, and other people of color the most," 2021, covidtracking.com/race.

CHAPTER 6: PRESCHOOLER'S RACE

82 **incredible 91 percent** Stephen Sawchuk, "School Resource Officers (SROs), Explained," *Education Week,* November 16, 2021, www.edweek.org/leadership/school-resource-officer-sro-duties-effectiveness.

82 **more likely to see students as a threat** Mark Keierleber, "'The Students Were the Danger': In Racially Diverse Schools, Police Were More Likely to View Students as Threats, Study Shows," *The 74,* June 16,

2020, www.the74million.org/the-students-were-the-danger-in-racially
-diverse-schools-police-were-more-likely-to-view-students-as-threats
-study-shows/.

82 **tend to feel less safe** Matthew T. Theriot and John G. Orme, "School Resource Officers and Students' Feelings of Safety at School," *Youth Violence and Juvenile Justice* 14, no. 2 (2016), 139–140.

82 **"People who often know little to nothing"** Monique W. Morris, *Pushout: The Criminalization of Black Girls in Schools* (New York: New Press, 2016), 4.

82 **primed to expect "challenging behavior"** S. Gilliam et al., *Do Early Educators' Implicit Biases Regarding Sex and Race Relate to Behavior Expectations and Recommendations of Preschool Expulsions and Suspensions?* (New Haven: Yale Child Study Center, 2016), 11–14.

83 **53 percent of female suspensions** Valerie Strauss, "New Federal Data Shows Black Preschoolers Still Disciplined at Far Higher Rates Than Whites," *Washington Post,* November 26, 2020, www.washingtonpost .com/education/2020/11/26/new-federal-data-shows-black -preschoolers-still-disciplined-far-higher-rates-than-whites/.

83 **41 percent of the male suspensions** Ibid.

83 **pipeline begins in preschool** Mackenzie Chakara, "From Preschool to Prison: The Criminalization of Black Girls," Center for American Progress, December 8, 2017, www.americanprogress.org/article /preschool-prison-criminalization-black-girls/.

83 **particularly those children with disabilities** Cristina Novoa and Rasheed Malik, "Suspensions Are Not Support: The Disciplining of Preschoolers with Disabilities," Center for American Progress, January 17, 2018, www.americanprogress.org/article/suspensions-not-support/.

83 **an end to preschool exclusionary punishment** U.S. Department of Health and Human Services (HHS) and U.S. Department of Education (ED), Policy Statement on Expulsion and Suspension Policies in Early Childhood Settings, 2014, www2.ed.gov/policy/gen/guid/school -discipline/policy-statement-ece-expulsions-suspensions.pdf. Specifically, HHS and ED made recommendations "to prevent, severely limit, and work toward eventually eliminating the expulsion and suspension" (1).

83 **at least nineteen states** Strauss, "New Federal Data Shows Black Preschoolers."

83 **racial disparities remained stark** Ibid.

83 **the latter remained neglected** Ibid. Strauss explained, "The many states that have passed reforms focused on limiting exclusionary discipline did so without ever mentioning race or disparity."

85 **associate negative traits like anger with *other* racial groups** Yarrow Dunham, Eva E. Chen, and Mahzarin R. Banaji, "Two Signatures of Implicit Intergroup Attitudes: Developmental Invariance and Early En-

culturation," *Psychological Science* 24, no. 6 (2013), 860–868. Dunham, Chen, and Banaji performed a study with White American children between the ages of three and fourteen, as well as Taiwanese children between four and twelve, to examine the emergence of implicit intergroup attitudes and the preference for one's racial in-group. Among White children in the United States between three and fourteen, "angry faces were 1.32 times as likely to be categorized as Black as were happy faces" (862). Among White children in the United States between five and twelve, "[a]ngry faces were 1.38 times as likely to be categorized as belonging to the Asian out-group as were happy faces" (864). Recognizing the racist hierarchies entrenched in the United States, researchers performed an identical assessment of intergroup bias with children between four and twelve in Taiwan (a comparatively racially homogeneous country). Similar to the results in the U.S. context, among Taiwanese children, "angry faces were 1.24 times more likely to be categorized as White than Asian faces" (865). The researchers concluded that children associate anger with a racial out-group without significant change with age, which points to "rapid social orienting, in which children map membership and status onto existing social groups while simultaneously acquiring representations of those groups" (866).

85 **"choose a Black person as looking 'bad'"** Frances E. Aboud, *Children and Prejudice* (Oxford, UK: Basil Blackwell, 1988), 29.

85 **think "race is fixed-at-birth"** Lawrence A. Hirschfeld, "Children's Developing Conceptions of Race," in *Handbook of Race, Racism, and the Developing Child*, eds. Stephen M. Quintana and Clark McKown (Hoboken, NJ: John Wiley & Sons, 2008), 48–49.

85 **confuse race and ethnicity** Louise Derman-Sparks and the A.B.C. Task Force, *Anti-Bias Curriculum: Tools for Empowering Young Children* (Washington, DC: National Association for the Education of Young Children, 1989), 34–35. Derman-Sparks provides the example of a child named Anita who claimed she is not Mexican because her skin is white. Her teacher told her, "You are Mexican because your family is Mexican American. Do you know that Mexican is not a color? Mexican people have many different skin colors, from dark brown to very light. All those are good colors to be."

86 **learning at a faster pace** Rishi Sriram, "Why Ages 2-7 Matter So Much for Brain Development," *Edutopia,* June 24, 2020, www.edutopia .org/article/why-ages-2-7-matter-so-much-brain-development.

87 **kids who attend preschool** Maia Szalavitz, "How to Cut Crime, Alcoholism and Addiction? It's Not Elementary, But Preschool," *TIME,* June 9, 2011, healthland.time.com/2011/06/09/how-to-cut-crime -alcoholism-and-addiction-its-not-elementary-but-preschool/. See also Dana Charles McCoy et al., "Impacts of Early Childhood Education on

Medium- and Long-Term Educational Outcomes," *Educational Researcher* 46, no. 8 (2017), 474–487; National Education Association, "Early Childhood Education," www.nea.org/student-success/smart-just-policies /funding-public-schools/early-childhood-education; and Diane Whitmore Schanzenbach and Lauren Bauer, "The Long-Term Impact of the Head Start Program," Brookings Institution, August 19, 2016, www .brookings.edu/research/the-long-term-impact-of-the-head-start -program/.

87 **do not discuss race with their three-year-olds** Katz, "Racists or Tolerant Multiculturalists? How Do They Begin?," 907.

87 **"hadn't noticed before"** Ibid.

87 **"notice physical differences"** Tatum, *"Why Are All the Black Kids Sitting Together in the Cafeteria?" And Other Conversations About Race,* 32.

87 **less reluctance than White parents** Katz, "Racists or Tolerant Multiculturalists? How Do They Begin?," 907.

88 **opportunities to teach** Bologna, "How White Parents Can Talk to Their Kids About Race."

88 **bad rules making life harder** Ibid.

88 **right and wrong, fairness and unfairness** Roger R. Harrison, "Talking to Kids About Race and Racism," *KidsHealth,* June 2020, kids health.org/en/parents/talk-about-race.html.

88 **research the answers with children** Meghan Holohan, "How to Talk to Kids About Racism, Protests and Injustice," *TODAY,* June 1, 2020, www.today.com/parents/how-talk-kids-about-racism-protests-injustice -t182929.

88 **admit the times we are being racist** Brita Belli, "It's Never Too Early to Talk with Children About Race," *YaleNews,* June 15, 2020, news.yale .edu/2020/06/15/its-never-too-early-talk-children-about-race.

89 **thought their mothers would be sad or angry** Valeria Lovelace et al., "Making a Neighbourhood the Sesame Street Way: Developing a Methodology to Evaluate Children's Understanding of Race," *Journal of Educational Television* 20, no. 2 (January 1994), 69–78.

89 **are far more likely than Black three-year-olds** Katz, "Racists or Tolerant Multiculturalists? How Do They Begin?," 905.

89 **the *number* of interracial friendships** Pahlke, Bigler, and Suizzo, "Relations Between Colorblind Socialization and Children's Racial Bias," 1177. Pahlke, Bigler, and Suizzo concluded, "Children's racial attitudes were related to the percentage of non-European Americans among their mothers' own friend groups, suggesting that children are observing—and influenced by—their mothers' race-related behavior."

89 **White caregiver's positive nonverbal behavior** Luigi Castelli, Cristina De Dea, and Drew Nesdale, "Learning Social Attitudes: Children's Sensitivity to the Nonverbal Behaviors of Adult Models During Inter-

racial Interactions," *Personality and Social Psychology Bulletin* 34, no. 11 (November 2008), 1504–1513. Castelli, De Dea, and Nesdale explained, "The White adult's nonverbal behaviors influenced both the children's attitudes and their predictions of the White adult's attitudes and behaviors toward the Black adult. . . . Even when verbal behavior was positive, children were nonetheless influenced by nonverbal behaviors, consistent with the view that the expression of positive verbal statements cannot override the effects of nonverbal cues that signal interpersonal discomfort" (1511).

89 **even in the complete absence of explicitly judgmental messages** Megan M. Patterson and Rebecca S. Bigler, "Preschool Children's Attention to Environmental Messages About Groups: Social Categorization and the Origins of Intergroup Bias," *Child Development* 77, no. 4 (July/August 2006), 858.

CHAPTER 7: CRITICAL KINDERGARTENER

92 **laying off teachers during the U.S. recession** Historian Kim Phillips-Fein estimates that approximately six thousand New York City teachers lost their job during the recession. Phillips-Fein, "The Legacy of the 1970s Fiscal Crisis," *Nation,* April 16, 2013, www.thenation.com /article/archive/legacy-1970s-fiscal-crisis/.

92 **the Family and Medical Leave Act in 1993** The Family and Medical Leave Act of 1993, Public Law 103-3, U.S. Department of Labor Wage and Hour Division, www.dol.gov/agencies/whd/laws-and-regulations /laws/fmla.

93 **re-created the very neighborhoods that the structures of racism had largely made for them** Lovelace et al., "Making a Neighbourhood the Sesame Street Way," 69–78.

95 **Caregivers must model** In a study of middle schoolers' reactions to bullying, psychologists Amanda B. Nickerson, Danielle Mele, and Dana Princiotta wrote, "Children who can trust, seek advice from, and communicate openly with their mothers may be in a better position to help others in need because this type of behavior has been modeled for them. Secure attachment predicts more open discussion about potentially threatening topics and associated feelings between mothers and preschool children" (697). See Nickerson, Mele, and Princiotta, "Attachment and Empathy as Predictors of Roles as Defenders or Outsiders in Bullying Interactions," 687–703.

96 **"Knowledge emerges only through"** Paulo Freire, *Pedagogy of the Oppressed,* 30th Anniversary ed. (New York: Continuum, 2000), 72.

97 **"antithesis of prejudicial thinking"** Debbie Walsh, "Critical Thinking to Reduce Prejudice," *Social Education* 52, no. 4 (April/May 1988), 280–282, quoted in Maureen McBride, *What Works to Reduce Prejudice*

and Discrimination? A Review of the Evidence (Edinburgh: Produced for the Scottish Government by APS Group Scotland, 2015), 17.

97 **"skills and dispositions"** Philip C. Abrami et al., "Strategies for Teaching Students to Think Critically: A Meta-Analysis," *Review of Educational Research* 85, no. 2 (June 2015), 306.

97 **"willingness to reconsider and revise views"** Ibid.

97 **"seek and find confirmations"** Mark Weinstein, "Critical Thinking and the Psycho-Logic of Race Prejudice," Institute for Critical Thinking, Resource Publication, 3rd ser., no. 1 (1990), 7–8.

97 **White children better remember** Rebecca S. Bigler and Lynn S. Liben, "A Cognitive-Developmental Approach to Racial Stereotyping and Reconstructive Memory in Euro-American Children," *Child Development* 64, no. 5 (October 1993), 1507–1518. Bigler and Liben noted, "In the present study, children scoring in the highest quartile for stereotyped responding (i.e., who stereotyped 80% of the traits) remembered only 58% of the counterstereotypic story information, compared to 87% of the stereotypic story information" (1516).

97 **"gap between teachers' values and their practices"** Abrami et al., "Strategies for Teaching Students to Think Critically: A Meta-Analysis," 276.

99 **three instructional methods most effective** Ibid., 302.

99 **Dialogue is particularly effective when** Ibid.

99 **student problem-solving and role-playing** Ibid.

99 **draw clear connections** Weinstein, "Critical Thinking and the Psycho-Logic of Race Prejudice," 16–17.

100 **reported lower levels of anti-immigrant attitudes** Mikael Hjerm, Ingemar Johansson Sevä, and Lena Werner, "How Critical Thinking, Multicultural Education and Teacher Qualification Affect Anti-Immigrant Attitudes," *International Studies in Sociology of Education* 27, no. 1 (2018), 54.

100 **defined instruction in critical thinking** Ibid., 44.

100 **"better equips students to overcome stereotypical thinking"** Ibid., 54.

100 **"direct teaching of prejudice-reduction techniques"** Walsh, "Critical Thinking to Reduce Prejudice," 18.

101 **nurturing the racist perceptions of the children** Nathaniel Bryan, "White Teachers' Role in Sustaining the School-to-Prison Pipeline: Recommendations for Teacher Education," *Urban Review* 49, no. 2 (2017), 326–345. Bryan, an expert in early childhood education, drew on sociologist Dan C. Lortie's concept of the apprenticeship of observation in teaching, and found that White teachers influence White children's perception of Black boys through their disproportionate targeting and disciplining of Black male students for minor and subjective school

disciplinary infractions. Specifically, Bryan posited that White children's apprenticeship of observation creates a "cycle of intergenerational legacies of negative view[s] and disproportionate disciplining of Black boys, which perpetuate the School To Prison Pipeline" (338).

101 **"significant degrees of pro-White, anti-Black bias"** Katz, "Racists or Tolerant Multiculturalists? How Do They Begin?," 897.

101 **85 percent held racist ideas** Anna Beth Doyle and Frances E. Aboud, "A Longitudinal Study of White Children's Racial Prejudice as a Social-Cognitive Development," *Merrill-Palmer Quarterly* 41, no. 2 (April 1995), 217–219.

101 **at least two-thirds of White children** Aboud, *Children and Prejudice,* 29.

101 **highest expectations for Asian students** Harriet R. Tenenbaum and Martin D. Ruck, "Are Teachers' Expectations Different for Racial Minority Than for European American Students? A Meta-Analysis," *Journal of Educational Psychology* 99, no. 2 (2007), 253.

101 **higher expectations for White students** Ibid.

102 **more referrals for gifted programs and fewer referrals for special education and punishment** Ibid., 265–267.

103 **"significantly increased the math and reading achievement"** Thomas S. Dee, "Teachers, Race, and Student Achievement in a Randomized Experiment," *Review of Economics and Statistics* 86, no. 1 (February 2004), 195. See also Anna J. Egalite, Brian Kisida, and Marcus A. Winters, "Representation in the Classroom: The Effect of Own-Race Teachers on Student Achievement," *Economics of Education Review* 45, Issue C (2015), 44–52. Egalite, Kisida, and Winters analyzed a dataset of 2.9 million Florida public school students in grades three through ten and 92,000 teachers for each year from 2001–2002 through 2008–2009 and explained, "Assignment to an own-race/ethnicity teacher has positive and potentially policy relevant reading achievement impacts for black and white students, and significant math achievement impacts for black, white, and Asian/Pacific Island students" (50).

103 **most significant among "lower-performing black and white students"** Egalite, Kisida, and Winters, "Representation in the Classroom: The Effect of Own-Race Teachers on Student Achievement," 44.

103 **reduces the likelihood he drops out** Seth Gershenson et al., "The Long-Run Impacts of Same-Race Teachers," *IZA Institute of Labor Economics Discussion Paper Series* (March 2017), 16–19. Gershenson et al. estimated, "On average, having had at least one black teacher in grades 3-5 reduces [Black] males' dropout probability by about eight percentage points, effectively halving the black male dropout rate" (15–16).

103 **"99.7 percent of white students"** Laura Meckler and Kate Rabinowitz, "America's Schools Are More Diverse Than Ever. But the Teachers

Are Still Mostly White," *Washington Post,* December 27, 2019, www
.washingtonpost.com/graphics/2019/local/education/teacher
-diversity/.

103 **higher expectations for the same Black student** Seth Gershenson,
Stephen B. Holt, and Nicholas W. Papageorge, "Who Believes in Me?
The Effect of Student–Teacher Demographic Match on Teacher Expectations," *Economics of Education Review* 52 (2016), 209. Racial disparities
in expectations are drastic: Non-Black (mostly White) teachers were almost 40 percent higher than average in their expectations for "Black
students to complete a high school diploma or less" (220) and "12 percentage points less likely to expect black students to complete a four-year
college degree" (222).

103 **favorable assessments to the abilities of their same-race students**
Amine Ouazad, "Assessed by a Teacher Like Me: Race and Teacher Assessments," *Education Finance and Policy* 9, no. 3 (2014), 368.

103 **translate into greater high school and collegiate completion
rates** "After controlling for student demographics, teacher expectations
were more predictive of college success than many major factors, including student motivation and student effort," suggesting that "teacher expectations are powerful predictors of future success." Ulrich Boser,
Megan Wilhelm, and Robert Hanna, *The Power of the Pygmalion Effect:
Teacher Expectations Strongly Predict College Completion* (Washington, DC:
Center for American Progress, 2014), 3.

CHAPTER 8: AWARE KID

105 **in 1956 to cater to White Americans** Jon C. Teaford, *The Metropolitan Revolution: The Rise of Post-Urban America* (New York: Columbia
University Press, 2006), 91–93.

105 **designed to halt poor people and people of color** Robert A. Caro,
The Power Broker: Robert Moses and the Fall of New York (New York: Alfred
A. Knopf, 1974), 7–10, 546.

106 **Low-clearance bridges** Ibid., 546; Ashish Valentine, "'The Wrong
Complexion for Protection': How Race Shaped America's Roadways
and Cities," NPR, July 5, 2020, www.npr.org/2020/07/05/887386869
/how-transportation-racism-shaped-america.

106 **the Reagan administration was assaulting the community's
safety net** The Omnibus Budget Reconciliation Act of 1981 alone "cut
AFDC rolls by 400,000 individuals, reduced benefits for hundreds of
thousands more." And 70 percent of Reagan's budget cuts impacted programs that assisted poor Americans, despite the fact that "welfare" spending constituted just 4 percent of the federal budget. Marisa Chappell, *The
War on Welfare: Family, Poverty, and Politics in Modern America* (Philadelphia: University of Pennsylvania Press, 2010), 202.

106 **cultural and social-cognitive skills** Christia Spears Brown and Rebecca S. Bigler, "Children's Perceptions of Discrimination: A Developmental Model," *Child Development* 76, no. 3 (May–June 2005), 544.

106 **move from being relatively unaware of the racist ideas** Clark McKown and Rhona S. Weinstein, "The Development and Consequences of Stereotype Consciousness in Middle Childhood," *Child Development* 74, no. 2 (March/April 2003), 510–511.

108 **"Mothering you is not a problem"** Imani Perry, *Breathe: A Letter to My Sons* (Boston: Beacon Press, 2019), 1–2.

108 **"earlier and greater awareness of broadly held stereotypes"** McKown and Weinstein, "The Development and Consequences of Stereotype Consciousness in Middle Childhood," 498, 511.

108 **"stereotype threat"** Ibid., 500–501, 506–510.

109 **Nearly 30 percent** Anita Jones Thomas and Sha'Kema M. Blackmon, "The Influence of the Trayvon Martin Shooting on Racial Socialization Practices of African American Parents," *Journal of Black Psychology* 41, no. 1 (2015), 83.

109 **14.7 percent** Ibid.

110 **13.1 percent** Ibid.

110 **about 10 percent** Ibid.

110 **twelve reported discussing it** Megan R. Underhill, "Parenting During Ferguson: Making Sense of White Parents' Silence," *Ethnic and Racial Studies* 41, no. 11 (2018), 1935.

110 **ten out of the twelve adopted** Ibid., 1942–1943.

110 **Only two of the study's participants** Ibid., 1946.

110 **curate a "worry-free" racial life** Ibid.,1947.

111 **White children with higher levels of racial prejudice** Frances E. Aboud, Morton J. Mendelson, and Kelly T. Purdy, "Cross-Race Peer Relations and Friendship Quality," *International Journal of Behavioral Development* 27, no. 2 (2003), 170.

111 **Black and White elementary schoolers both** Ibid., 169–170.

111 **defer the responsibility for widening their child's social life** Hamm, "Barriers and Bridges to Positive Cross-Ethnic Relations," 82–83, 88. Hamm, an educational psychologist, observed that White parents of children in elementary school (fifth grade) or high school "rarely assumed direct responsibility for broadening or facilitating cross-[race] contact" or relationships, and felt it was the school's responsibility to do so; yet, even among those White parents who expressed a desire for their children to have cross-racial friendships, "few parents . . . reported efforts to seek ethnically diverse activities for their youth."

111 **teachers in such schools defer this responsibility** Kotler, Haider, and Levine, *Parents' and Educators' Perceptions of Children's Social Identity Development,* documented, "Discussions about race and ethnicity are

more likely to occur in classrooms with higher proportions of Black and Hispanic students at least sometimes" (23). Specifically, "Fifty-eight percent of teachers in classrooms with fewer than 50% Hispanic students say they often or sometimes discuss race and ethnicity, compared with 75% of teachers in classrooms with 50% or more Hispanic students. Similarly, 61% of teachers in classrooms with fewer than 50% Black students say they discuss race and ethnicity compared with 81% of teachers in classrooms with 50% or more Black students."

113 **declining between ages six and nine** Aboud, *Children and Prejudice,* 30; Doyle and Aboud, "A Longitudinal Study of White Children's Racial Prejudice as a Social-Cognitive Development," 222–223.

113 **a behavior learned from caregivers** Evan P. Apfelbaum et al., "Learning (Not) to Talk About Race: When Older Children Underperform in Social Categorization," *Developmental Psychology* 44, no. 5 (2008), 1513–1518. By age ten, White children avoid acknowledging race, while children ages eight and nine more readily acknowledge race.

113 **just don't express them aloud** Adam Rutland et al., "Social Norms and Self-Presentation: Children's Implicit and Explicit Intergroup Attitudes," *Child Development* 76, no. 2 (March/April 2005), 453, 458.

113 **"externally motivated"** Ibid., 458.

113 **"internally motivated"** Ibid.

113 **"the tendency to avoid acknowledging race altogether"** Apfelbaum et al., "Learning (Not) to Talk About Race," 1516.

113 **Pre-seven-year-old children** Aboud, *Children and Prejudice,* 128.

113 **Post-seven-year-old children** Ibid.

114 **receives $2,226 less per student than the average White school district** EdBuild, "$23 Billion."

114 **receiving about $1,500 *more* per student** Ibid.

114 **up to 4.6 times more likely** Nick Noel et al., *The Economic Impact of Closing the Racial Wealth Gap* (New York: McKinsey, 2019), 9.

114 **died prematurely from exposure** Lara P. Clark, Dylan B. Millet, and Julian D. Marshall, "Changes in Transportation-Related Air Pollution Exposures by Race-Ethnicity and Socioeconomic Status: Outdoor Nitrogen Dioxide in the United States in 2000 and 2010," *Environmental Health Perspectives* 125, no. 9 (September 2017), 097012-8. These researchers found that, in general, non-White populations experienced 37 percent higher exposures to NO_2 than Whites, and concentrations of NO_2 in neighborhoods with the highest proportion of non-White residents were 2.7 times higher than in neighborhoods with the lowest proportion of non-White residents. NO_2 is associated with low birth weight, asthma in children, and cardiovascular deaths.

114 **more likely to be diagnosed with asthma** Asthma and Allergy Foundation of America, *Asthma Disparities in America: A Roadmap to Re-*

ducing Burden on Racial and Ethnic Minorities (Landover, MD: Asthma and Allergy Foundation of America, 2020), 37.

114 **the problem of how the high cost of healthy food** Lindsey Haynes-Maslow, *The Devastating Consequences of Unequal Food Access* (Cambridge, MA: Union of Concerned Scientists, April 2016), www.ucsusa.org/sites /default/files/attach/2016/04/ucs-race-income-diabetes-2016.pdf?utm _source=twitter&utm_medium=social&utm_campaign=tw. Haynes-Maslow, a food systems and health analyst, identified a direct correlation between racially and economically disparate food access and disproportionate rates of type 2 diabetes, obesity, and heart disease among Native Americans and Alaska Natives, Black Americans, and Latinx Americans.

115 **associate White people with superiority and wealth** Anna-Kaisa Newheiser and Kristina R. Olson, "White and Black American Children's Implicit Intergroup Bias," *Journal of Experimental Social Psychology* 48, no. 1 (2012), 267. Strikingly, "Black children with a high explicit preference for the rich showed an implicit bias favoring Whites comparable in magnitude to White children's implicit ingroup bias."

115 **less likely than White families to receive an inheritance** Noel et al., *The Economic Impact of Closing the Racial Wealth Gap,* 11. "Only 8 percent of black families receive an inheritance, compared with 26 percent of white families. When an inheritance does come, it is 35 percent of the value of that of a white family."

116 **provide teachers with only one or two courses** Christine E. Sleeter, "Critical Race Theory and the Whiteness of Teacher Education," *Urban Education* 52, no. 2 (2017), 156.

116 **the multicultural education courses that are taught** Paul C. Gorski, "What We're Teaching Teachers: An Analysis of Multicultural Teacher Education Coursework Syllabi," *Teaching and Teacher Education* 25, no. 2 (2009), 312.

116 **teachers blamed the students** Sleeter, "Critical Race Theory and the Whiteness of Teacher Education," 156.

118 **what English teacher Matthew R. Kay called the** *ecosystem* Matthew R. Kay, *Not Light, but Fire: How to Lead Meaningful Race Conversations in the Classroom* (Portsmouth, NH: Stenhouse, 2018), 13.

CHAPTER 9: PRETEEN DISABILITY

120 **Black boys entering the fourth grade** Hakim Rashid, "From Brilliant Baby to Child Placed at Risk: The Perilous Path of African American Boys in Early Childhood Education," *Journal of Negro Education* 78, no. 3 (Summer 2009), 347.

121 **the passage of the Americans with Disabilities Act (ADA)** Americans with Disabilities Act, Public Law 101-336, U.S. Department of Justice Civil Rights Division, www.ada.gov/ada_intro.htm.

122 **strangled low-income Black urban communities** The struggles faced by Black people in cities in the North and West at this time were inseparable from the racist backlash to the Great Migration (1915–70) that significantly increased the Black population in those areas. See Isabel Wilkerson, *The Warmth of Other Suns: The Epic Story of America's Great Migration* (New York: Random House, 2010).

122 **the age when kids increasingly experience or witness racism** Ronald L. Simons et al., "Discrimination, Crime, Ethnic Identity, and Parenting as Correlates of Depressive Symptoms Among African American Children: A Multilevel Analysis," *Development and Psychopathology* 14, no. 2 (2002), 372–373.

123 **A disability is "any mental or physical"** Ibram X. Kendi, interview with Rebecca Cokley, *Be Antiracist*, podcast transcript, June 9, 2021, share.descript.com/view/OhggnmprRFb. The audio for this episode can be found at www.pushkin.fm/episode/ableism-racism-roots-of-the -same-tree/, or wherever you get your podcasts.

123 **acquiring a disability during the trauma of incarceration** Pediatricians Maria Trent, Danielle G. Dooley, and Jacqueline Dougé, American Academy of Pediatrics Section on Adolescent Health, American Academy of Pediatrics Committee on Adolescence, "The Impact of Racism on Child and Adolescent Health," *Pediatrics* 144, no. 2 (2019), 2–3, explained that Black, Latinx, and Native youth are disproportionately represented in the juvenile punishment system, and are thus subjected to "additional adverse experiences, such as solitary confinement and abuse, that have the potential to undermine socioemotional development and general developmental outcomes."

123 **were "dramatically" being *over*diagnosed** Martha J. Coutinho, Donald P. Oswald, and Al M. Best, "The Influence of Sociodemographics and Gender on the Disproportionate Identification of Minority Students as Having Learning Disabilities," *Remedial and Special Education* 23, no. 1 (January/February 2002), 55.

123 **deeper poverty correlating to fewer diagnoses** Ibid., 54.

123 **School districts with large populations of students of color** Ibid.

123 **diagnosed at about the same rate as White students** Ibid., 55.

124 **lower odds of disability diagnosis and special education receipt** Rachel Elizabeth Fish, "Standing Out and Sorting In: Exploring the Role of Racial Composition in Racial Disparities in Special Education," *American Educational Research Journal* 56, no. 6 (December 2019), 2573, 2585–2588.

124 **more likely to receive disability diagnoses** Ibid.

124 **lowest odds overall of being diagnosed** The most common (25 percent) disability for Asian children served under the Individuals with Disabilities Education Act (IDEA) is autism. By contrast, "for most racial/

ethnic groups, specific learning disabilities and speech or language impairments were the two most common types of disabilities, accounting for at least 43 percent of students receiving IDEA services." Scholar Kim Fong Poon-McBrayer suggested that this underdiagnosis of learning disabilities is directly correlated to the "model minority" stereotype, whereby teachers and other specialists performing the assessments that lead to such diagnoses assume that Asian Americans and Asian immigrants are a "hardworking, successful, and law-abiding ethnic minority which has overcome discrimination, adversity, and oppression to achieve great success." See U.S. Department of Education, National Center for Education Statistics, "Students with Disabilities," May 2021, and Kim Fong Poon-McBrayer, "Model Minority and Learning Disabilities: Double Jeopardy for Asian Immigrant Children in the USA," *Global Studies of Childhood* 1, no. 2 (2011), 152.

124 **diversity of the Asian American Pacific Islander (AAPI) community** Poon-McBrayer, "Model Minority and Learning Disabilities," 153–156.

124 **scholar Kim Fong Poon-McBrayer explains** Ibid., 155.

125 **sociologist Rachel Fish found** Rachel Elizabeth Fish, "Teacher Race and Racial Disparities in Education," *Remedial and Special Education* 40, no. 4 (2019), 221.

125 **More teachers of color decrease the likelihood** Ibid., 219. In 2019, U.S. Department of Education data showed that Black or African American students between six and twenty-one who received special education services were most likely to be assigned the "emotional disturbance" disability category. See U.S. Department of Education, Office of Special Education and Rehabilitative Services, Office of Special Education Programs, *41st Annual Report to Congress on the Implementation of the Individuals with Disabilities Education Act, 2019* (Washington, DC, 2020), xxvi, 49.

125 **decrease Latinx students being referred** Fish, "Teacher Race and Racial Disparities in Education," 221.

125 **only 7 percent of teachers are Black, compared with 15 percent** U.S. Department of Education, National Center for Education Statistics, "Characteristics of Public School Teachers," May 2021, nces.ed.gov /programs/coe/indicator/clr and "Racial/Ethnic Enrollment in Public Schools," May 2021.

125 **9 percent of teachers are Latinx, compared with 27 percent** Ibid.

125 **2 percent of teachers are Asian, compared with 5 percent** Ibid.

125 **1 percent of teachers and students are Native** Ibid.

125 **79 percent of teachers are White, compared with 47 percent** Ibid.

125 **a "system that places value on people's bodies and minds"** Talila A. Lewis, "January 2021 Working Definition of Ableism," January 1,

2021, www.talilalewis.com/blog/january-2021-working-definition-of
-ableism.

126 **The system of ableism** Simmons University Library, "Anti-Oppression:
Anti-Ableism," September 15, 2021, simmons.libguides.com/anti
-oppression/anti-ableism.

126 **83 percent of polling places not being fully accessible** U.S. Government Accountability Office (GAO), *Voters with Disabilities: Observations on Polling Place Accessibility and Related Federal Guidance,* GAO-18-4
(Washington, DC: October 2017), 15, www.gao.gov/assets/gao-18-4.
pdf.

126 **effectively barred from marriage** U.S. Social Security Administration, "FAQS: If I Get Married, Will It Affect My Benefits?," May 14,
2021, faq.ssa.gov/en-US/Topic/article/KA-02172; U.S. Social Security
Administration, "Understanding Supplemental Social Security Income
(SSI) and Other Government Programs," 2021, www.ssa.gov/ssi/text
-other-ussi.htm; Richard Balkus and Susan Wilschke, Office of Policy,
Office of Disability and Income Assistance Policy, "Treatment of Married Couples in the SSI Program," Issue Paper No. 2003-001 (December
2003), www.ssa.gov/policy/docs/issuepapers/ip2003-01.html.

126 **facing unemployment rates nearly double** U.S. Bureau of Labor
Statistics, *Persons with a Disability: Labor Force Characteristics—2020,*
USDL-21-0316 (Washington, DC: February 2021), 4, www.bls.gov
/news.release/pdf/disabl.pdf. In 2019, the unemployment rate for people with a disability was 7.3 compared with 3.5 for people with no disability. In 2020, the COVID-19 pandemic exacerbated unemployment;
the unemployment rate for people with a disability was 12.6 compared
with 7.9 for people with no disability.

126 **nearly 20 percentage points lower** Laura Schifter, "The ADA Has
Fallen Short for Black Students. It's Past Time to Fix That," *Education
Week,* July 24, 2020, www.edweek.org/teaching-learning/opinion-the
-ada-has-fallen-short-for-black-students-its-past-time-to-fix-that/2020
/07.

126 **1.5 times more likely to drop out** Ibid.

126 **at least 38 percent of the people populating American prisons**
U.S. Department of Justice, *Disabilities Reported by Prisoners,* by Laura M.
Maruschak, Jennifer Bronson, and Mariel Alper, NCJ252642 (Washington, DC: March 2021), 2, bjs.ojp.gov/content/pub/pdf/drpspi16st.pdf.
I say "at least" because though this study is based on incarcerated people's
self-reports, this method often results in underrepresentation. For example, in 2019, a study by the Center for Talent Innovation (now known
as Coqual) surveyed employees with disabilities about whether or not
they had informed their employer about their disability. Researchers
found, "Only 39% of employees with disabilities have disclosed to their

manager. Even fewer have disclosed to their teams (24%) and HR (21%). Almost none (4%) have revealed their disability to clients." See Pooja Jain-Link and Julia Taylor Kennedy, "Why People Hide Their Disabilities at Work," *Harvard Business Review,* June 3, 2019, hbr.org/2019/06 /why-people-hide-their-disabilities-at-work.

126 **26 percent of the U.S. general population** CDC, "Disability Impacts All of Us," September 16, 2020, www.cdc.gov/ncbddd/disabilityandhealth /infographic-disability-impacts-all.html#:~:text=26%20percent %20(one%20in%204,is%20highest%20in%20the%20South.

126 **between one-third and one-half of the people being killed by police** Abigail Abrams, "Black, Disabled and At Risk: The Overlooked Problem of Police Violence Against Americans with Disabilities," *TIME,* June 25, 2020, time.com/5857438/police-violence-black-disabled/.

126 **arrested by their twenty-eighth birthday** Erin J. McCauley, "The Cumulative Probability of Arrest by Age 28 Years in the United States by Disability Status, Race/Ethnicity, and Gender," *American Journal of Public Health* (December 2017), ajph.aphapublications.org/doi/10.2105/AJPH .2017.304095.

126 **believe people when they disclose** Ashley Eisenmenger, "Ableism 101: What It Is, What It Looks Like, and What We Can Do to Fix It," Access Living, December 12, 2019, www.accessliving.org/newsroom /blog/ableism-101/.

126 **Anti-ableism means using words like** For a more comprehensive list of anti-ableist alternatives to ableist language, see Ariane Resnick, "Types of Ableist Language and What to Say Instead," *Verywell Mind,* December 5, 2021, www.verywellmind.com/types-of-ableist-language-and-what -to-say-instead-5201561.

127 **value and extend worthiness to every human being** Ibram X. Kendi, interview with Rebecca Cokley, *Be Antiracist,* podcast transcript, June 9, 2021, share.descript.com/view/OhggnmprRFb.

127 **Kids as young as one and a half or two** "How to Teach Children About Disabilities and Inclusion," Baylor University, Online Graduate Programs, December 3, 2019, onlinegrad.baylor.edu/resources/teaching -children-disabilities-inclusion/.

127 **one in four people around me with disabilities** CDC, "1 in 4 US Adults Live with a Disability," press release, August 16, 2018, www.cdc .gov/media/releases/2018/p0816-disability.html.

127 **"as long as the tools are in place"** Kristen Parisi, "How to Teach Children About Disability, at Every Age," *TODAY,* July 28, 2020, www .today.com/parents/how-teach-children-about-disability-every-age -t187942.

128 **overrepresented in the receipt of services for speech** Paul L. Morgan et al., "Cross-Cohort Evidence of Disparities in Service Receipt for

Speech or Language Impairments," *Exceptional Children* 84, no. 1 (2017), 27–41.

128 **the most clearly stigmatized forms of disability** Black and Latinx children are overrepresented in more stigmatized categories like intellectual disability and emotional disturbance, while White children are overrepresented in less stigmatized categories like attention-deficit/hyperactivity disorder and autism. Speech and language impairment does not fit neatly into either a more stigmatized or less stigmatized category, partly because diagnosis can rely on both objective and subjective methods of assessment. See Thomas M. Skrtic, Argun Saatcioglu, and Austin Nichols, "Disability as Status Competition: The Role of Race in Classifying Children," *Socius* 7 (2021), 1–20.

128 **for 87 percent of students enrolled** Beth Harry and Mary G. Anderson, "The Disproportionate Placement of African American Males in Special Education Programs: A Critique of the Process," *Journal of Negro Education* 63, no. 4 (Autumn 1994), 609.

130 **"segregated in self-contained classrooms or in separate schools"** National Council on Disability, *The Segregation of Students with Disabilities* (Washington, DC: National Council on Disability, 2018), 1, 52. During the 2015–2016 school year, 62.7 percent of all students with disabilities were educated at least 80 percent of the time in general education classrooms. However, Native Hawaiian/Pacific Islander students (55.3 percent), Asian/Pacific Islander students (56.5 percent), Black students (58.0 percent), and Hispanic students (61.0 percent) with disabilities were included at below average rates, while White students (65.5 percent) and American/Alaskan Native students (64.1 percent) were included at above average rates.

130 **White students with disabilities (59.1 percent)** Ibid., 52.

130 **Black students with disabilities (43.9 percent)** Ibid.

130 **most likely to be integrated** Ibid.

130 **sued the Georgia Network for Educational and Therapeutic Support** The case stalled in a U.S. District Court in 2017, so disability advocacy groups and families filed a separate class action lawsuit. The DOJ case also resumed in 2020. See Allie Gross, "Georgia Is Illegally Segregating Students with Behavioral Problems. There's a Better Way," *Mother Jones,* July 30, 2015, www.motherjones.com/politics/2015/07 /behavior-segregation-georgia-doj/; U.S. Department of Justice, "Justice Department Sues Georgia for Unnecessarily Segregating Students with Disabilities," news release, August 23, 2016, www.justice.gov/opa /pr/justice-department-sues-georgia-unnecessarily-segregating-students -disabilities; Ashley Dejean, "Will Trump's Justice Department Pay Attention to Disability Rights?," *Mother Jones,* October 13, 2017, www .motherjones.com/politics/2017/10/will-trumps-justice-department

-pay-attention-to-disability-rights/; Center for Public Representation, Georgia Advocacy Office, et al. v. The State of Georgia, et al., www .centerforpublicrep.org/court_case/gao-v-georgia/.

131 **"all-White middle-class area"** Constance L. Hays, "July 4 Racial Clash Leaves Rosedale Split over Its Image and Its Reality," *New York Times,* July 30, 1989, www.nytimes.com/1989/07/30/nyregion/july -4-racial-clash-leaves-rosedale-split-over-its-image-and-its-reality.html.

131 **named Restore Our American Rights (ROAR)** Ibid.

131 **"This is our park"** Ibid.

131 **later arrested five of them** Joseph P. Fried, "Leniency Due as 5 Whites Plead Guilty in Racial Attack in Queens," *New York Times,* April 10, 1990, www.nytimes.com/1990/04/10/nyregion/leniency-due -as-5-whites-plead-guilty-in-racial-attack-in-queens.html.

131 **called for the return of the death penalty** Jan Ransom, "Trump Will Not Apologize for Calling for Death Penalty over Central Park Five," *New York Times,* June 18, 2019, www.nytimes.com/2019/06/18 /nyregion/central-park-five-trump.html.

132 **murdered a young Black man** Robert D. McFadden, "Black Man Dies After Beating by Whites in Queens," *New York Times,* December 21, 1986, www.nytimes.com/1986/12/21/nyregion/black-man-dies -after-beating-by-whites-in-queens.html; Sam Roberts, "Jon Lester, Convicted in Howard Beach Race Attack, Dies at 48," *New York Times,* October 23, 2017, www.nytimes.com/2017/10/23/obituaries/jon -lester-convicted-in-howard-beach-race-attack-dies-at-48.html.

132 **educator Jonathan Kozol visited schools** Jonathan Kozol, *Savage Inequalities: Children in America's Schools* (New York: Crown, 1991), 2.

132 **resembled the school my brother attended in Queens** My parents remember my brother's classroom being predominantly Black.

132 **700 "mainstream" and "gifted" students** Kozol, *Savage Inequalities,* 93–94.

132 **the twelve special education classrooms** Ibid., 93, 95.

132 **"can usually be traced to neurological damage"** Ibid., 95.

132 **In one "gifted" class** Ibid., 94.

133 **"a well-known statistic that should long since have aroused"** Ibid., 119.

133 **report experiencing racist discrimination** Simons et al., "Discrimination, Crime, Ethnic Identity, and Parenting as Correlates of Depressive Symptoms," 381. A near majority (48 percent) of these Black preteens also reported that family members had experienced discrimination.

133 **more likely to have symptoms of depression** Tumaini R. Coker et al., "Perceived Racial/Ethnic Discrimination Among Fifth-Grade Students and Its Association with Mental Health," *American Journal of Public Health* 99, no. 5 (2009), 881.

133 **become withdrawn and struggle to pay attention** Ana K. Marcelo and Tuppett M. Yates, "Young Children's Ethnic–Racial Identity Moderates the Impact of Early Discrimination Experiences on Child Behavior Problems," *Cultural Diversity and Ethnic Minority Psychology* 25, no. 2 (2019), 256–257. Marcelo and Yates, both psychologists, found that the internalizing behavior problems—including feeling withdrawn and depressed—that followed Black, Latinx, and multiethnic-racial children's experiences of discrimination were "buffered" by a greater commitment to one's racial or ethnic group. See pp. 258–260 of the study for further explanation.

133 **twice as likely as non-Black students** U.S. Department of Education, Office of Special Education and Rehabilitative Services, Office of Special Education Programs, *41st Annual Report to Congress on the Implementation of the Individuals with Disabilities Education Act, 2019* (2020), xxvi, 49.

134 **White students are more likely** Daniel Losen et al., "Disturbing Inequities: Exploring the Relationship Between Racial Disparities in Special Education Identification and Discipline," *Journal of Applied Research on Children* 5, no. 2 (2014), 7. According to a CDC analysis of data from 2014, White children were 1.1 times more likely than Black children and 1.2 times more likely than Latinx children to be diagnosed with autism spectrum disorder (ASD). See CDC, "Spotlight On: Racial and Ethnic Differences in Children Identified with Autism Spectrum Disorder (ASD)," *Autism Spectrum Disorder*, August 27, 2019, www.cdc.gov/ncbddd /autism/addm-community-report/differences-in-children.html.

134 **much higher than the suspension risk of students with autism** Losen et al., "Disturbing Inequities," 7, 15.

134 **lose seventy-seven more days of instruction** Daniel J. Losen, *Disabling Punishment: The Need for Remedies to the Disparate Loss of Instruction Experienced by Black Students with Disabilities* (Los Angeles and Cambridge, MA: UCLA Civil Rights Project and Charles Hamilton Houston Institute for Race & Justice, April 2018), 2.

134 **at least three times more likely** Matthew C. Fadus et al., "Racial Disparities in Elementary School Disciplinary Actions: Findings from the ABCD Study," *Journal of the American Academy of Child and Adolescent Psychiatry* 60, no. 8 (2021), 1001. "Specifically, Black children had 3.5 times greater odds of receiving a suspension or a detention than White children. Multiracial Black youth had 3.0 times higher odds of receiving a suspension or detention."

CHAPTER 10: FEARED MIDDLE SCHOOLER

136 **the reverse Great Migration** Demographer William H. Frey wrote, "The reversal of the Great Migration out of the South began as a trickle

in the 1970s, increased in the 1990s, and turned into a virtual evacuation from many northern areas in the first decade of the 2000s." Frey, *Diversity Explosion: How New Racial Demographics Are Remaking America* (Washington, DC: Brookings Institution Press, 2015), 107.

136 **"Negroes and whites don't mix"** Frederick H. Ecker quoted in Charles V. Bagli, "A New Light on a Fight to Integrate Stuyvesant Town," *New York Times,* November 21, 2010, www.nytimes.com/2010 /11/22/nyregion/22stuyvesant.html.

136 **veterans returning from World War II** Charles V. Bagli, "$5.4 Billion Bid Wins Complexes in New York Deal," *New York Times,* October 18, 2006, www.nytimes.com/2006/10/18/nyregion/18stuyvesant .html.

136 **served their country but were not served by their country** See Rothstein, *The Color of Law.*

137 **upheld MetLife's "right"** Dorsey v. Stuyvesant Town Corp., 190 Misc. 187, 74 N.Y.S.2d 220 (N.Y. Sup. Ct. 1947).

137 **declined to review the case** Amy Fox, "Battle in Black and White," *New York Times,* March 26, 2006, www.nytimes.com/2006/03/26 /nyregion/thecity/battle-in-black-and-white.html.

137 **Town and Village Tenants Committee to End Discrimination in Stuyvesant Town** Bagli, "A New Light on a Fight to Integrate Stuyvesant Town."

137 **successfully desegregated the new development** Ibid.; Fox, "Battle in Black and White."

137 **aware of the development's racist origins and stayed away** Fox, "Battle in Black and White."

138 **equally or less innocent than White boys** Phillip Atiba Goff et al., "The Essence of Innocence: Consequences of Dehumanizing Black Children," *Journal of Personality and Social Psychology* 106, no. 4 (2014), 529.

138 **less in need of protection and care, and more likely to be a danger** Ibid.

138 **by an average of about 4.6 years** Ibid., 534.

138 **the more often they used force** Ibid., 535.

138 **"more similar to adults"** Aneeta Rattan et al., "Race and the Fragility of the Legal Distinction between Juveniles and Adults," *PLOS One* 7, no. 5 (May 2012), 2–4.

139 **the "adultification" of Black girls** Rebecca Epstein, Jamilia J. Blake, and Thalia González, *Girlhood Interrupted: The Erasure of Black Girls' Childhood* (Washington, DC: Georgetown Law Center on Poverty and Inequality, August 2017), 1–2.

140 **six times more likely to be expelled, four times more likely to be arrested, and three times more likely to be suspended** Julian

Glover, "Pushed Out: How Excessive School Discipline Against Black Girls Leads to Drop Out, Incarceration," ABC7 News, March 10, 2021, abc7news.com/black-girls-suspended-more-than-white-pushed-out-school-to-prison-pipeline-school-pushout/10405118/.

141 more "appropriate target for police violence" Goff et al., "The Essence of Innocence: Consequences of Dehumanizing Black Children," 526.

142 Black *and* *White* adolescents with African American "culture-related movements" La Vonne I. Neal et al., "The Effects of African American Movement Styles on Teachers' Perceptions and Reactions," *Journal of Special Education* 37, no. 1 (2003), 55–56.

142 "more troubled" Jason A. Okonofua and Jennifer L. Eberhardt, "Two Strikes: Race and the Disciplining of Young Students," *Psychological Science* 26, no. 5 (2015), 619.

142 far more likely to recommend "more severe" punishment Ibid., 619–620.

142 "indicative of a pattern" Ibid., 621.

143 "as challenging to authority, loud, and not ladylike" Edward W. Morris, "'Ladies' or 'Loudies'? Perceptions and Experiences of Black Girls in Classrooms," *Youth & Society* 38, no. 4 (2007), 501.

143 most likely to police "ladylike" behavior Ibid., 503–505. Morris explained that other research suggested that "Black women teachers are particularly conscious of stereotypes of Black women, and may actively try to rid Black girls of behavior corresponding to these stereotypes."

143 misperceptions were worse Ibid., 504–505.

143 not policing and punishing and pushing out Black girls For more, see Morris, *Pushout: The Criminalization of Black Girls in Schools.*

144 more than five incidences of racist discrimination *per day* Devin English et al., "Daily Multidimensional Racial Discrimination Among Black U.S. American Adolescents," *Journal of Applied Developmental Psychology* 66 (2020), 1–12.

144 oppositional social identity Tatum, *"Why Are All the Black Kids Sitting Together in the Cafeteria?" And Other Conversations About Race,* 60–61.

144 "For as long as their youthful energies hold out" John Dilulio, "The Coming of the Super-Predators," *Washington Examiner,* November 27, 1995, www.washingtonexaminer.com/weekly-standard/the-coming-of-the-super-predators.

144 all unleashed on Black youth See Michelle Alexander, *The New Jim Crow: Mass Incarceration in the Age of Colorblindness,* rev. ed. (New York: New Press, 2012).

145 rapid expansion of "zero tolerance" policies in schools Nicholas P. Triplett, Ayana Allen, and Chance W. Lewis, "Zero Tolerance, School Shootings, and the Post-Brown Quest for Equity in Discipline Policy:

An Examination of How Urban Minorities Are Punished for White Suburban Violence," *Journal of Negro Education* 83, no. 3 (2014), 353.

145 **urban kids of color felt the brunt** Ibid., 354–355.

145 **"objective criminal activities"** Ibid., 354.

145 **"subjectively defined behaviors that have little impact on school safety"** Ibid.

147 **more likely than light-skinned kids to be suspended** Lance Hannon, Robert DeFina, and Sarah Bruch, "The Relationship Between Skin Tone and School Suspension for African Americans," *Race and Social Problems* 5, no. 4 (2013), 287. Hannon, DeFina, and Bruch calculated "it is about 3.4 times as likely for a young African American woman with the darkest skin tone to be suspended compared to one with the lightest skin, and 2.5 times as likely for a young African American male."

147 **be conscious of colorism** Tatum, *"Why Are All the Black Kids Sitting Together in the Cafeteria?" And Other Conversations About Race,* 43–45.

CHAPTER 11: CONFINED HIGH SCHOOLER

149 **his role in securing religious liberty** Bowne House Historical Society, "The Bownes," Bowne House, www.bownehouse.org/the-bownes.

149 **enslaved at least two people** Jim O'Grady, "Neighborhood Report: Flushing; For a Beacon of Freedom, a Troubling New Light," *New York Times,* February 22, 2004, www.nytimes.com/2004/02/22/nyregion /neighborhood-report-flushing-for-a-beacon-of-freedom-a-troubling -new-light.html.

149 **likely to assume their friends share their racial beliefs** P. Neal Ritchey and Harold D. Fishbein, "The Lack of an Association Between Adolescent Friends' Prejudices and Stereotypes," *Merrill-Palmer Quarterly* 47, no. 2 (April 2001), 200. Ritchey and Fishbein found little correlation between the prejudices and stereotypes of White adolescents and their friends. They cited existing research to offer a possible explanation: "A number of studies have found that even in the domain of behaviors or activities such as grade point average, substance use, and academically disruptive behavior, adolescents overestimate the similarity of their friends to themselves. Thus, if prejudice and stereotyping are rarely discussed, adolescents can comfortably assume that their own beliefs are supported by those of their friends."

149 **White supremacist recruitment on college campuses** White supremacist propaganda on college campuses increased every year between 2017 and 2019. In 2020, on-campus propaganda dropped while off-campus propaganda reached "the highest number ever recorded." The Anti-Defamation League said that the disparity between on-campus and off-campus incidents was likely a strategic shift in response to "the pandemic and lack of students on campus." Anti-Defamation League,

"White Supremacists Increase College Campus Recruiting Efforts for Third Straight Year," June 27, 2019, www.adl.org/news/press-releases /white-supremacists-increase-college-campus-recruiting-efforts-for -third; "White Supremacist Propaganda Spikes in 2020," 2021, www.adl .org/white-supremacist-propaganda-spikes-2020.

149 **typical age range of most extremist recruits** Caitlin Gibson, "'Do You Have White Teenage Sons? Listen Up.' How White Supremacists Are Recruiting Boys Online," *Washington Post,* September 17, 2019, www.washingtonpost.com/lifestyle/on-parenting/do-you-have-white -teenage-sons-listen-up-how-white-supremacists-are-recruiting-boys -online/2019/09/17/f081e806-d3d5-11e9-9343-40db57cf6abd_story .html. For a personal account of teenage recruitment, see Arno Michae- lis, *My Life After Hate* (Milwaukee: La Prensa de LAH, 2010).

149 **Christian Picciolini was fourteen years old** Gibson, "'Do You Have White Teenage Sons? Listen Up.'"

150 **more likely to happen online** Ibid.

150 **Ten percent of the teens between the ages of thirteen and seven-teen who play** Anti-Defamation League, "Results," *Hate Is No Game: Harassment and Positive Social Experiences in Online Games 2021,* www.adl .org/hateisnogame#results, and "Executive Summary," *Hate Is No Game,* www.adl.org/hateisnogame#executive-summary.

150 **most common threat (17 percent) of exposure to racist ideas** Anti-Defamation League, "Results." Participating thirteen- to seventeen- year-olds identified the following sources of exposure to White suprem- acist views (in descending order): social media (17 percent), in person (11 percent), chat app (10 percent), online video game (10 percent), online forum (6 percent).

150 **White children beginning at age eleven** Gibson, "'Do You Have White Teenage Sons? Listen Up.'"

150 **turn impressionable White teens into White supremacists** Ibid.

150 **"inundated by memes"** Joanna Schroeder (@iproposethis), "It's a sys- tem I believe is purposefully created to disillusion white boys away from progressive/liberal perspectives," Twitter, August 13, 2019, 12:23 A.M., twitter.com/iproposethis/status/1161131164477771776.

150 **"White-nationalist and alt-right groups use jokes and memes"** Lindsay Schubiner quoted in Gibson, "'Do You Have White Teenage Sons? Listen Up.'"

150 **Not seeing the nuance** Joanna Schroeder (@iproposethis), "It's a sys- tem I believe is purposefully created."

150 **"people are too sensitive"** Joanna Schroeder (@iproposethis), "The second step is the boys consuming media with the 'people are too sensitive' and 'you can't say anything anymore!' themes," Twitter, August 13, 2019, 12:28 A.M., twitter.com/iproposethis/status/1161132334868942849.

150 **"These boys are being set up"** Joanna Schroeder (@iproposethis), "And who is their anger with?," Twitter, August 13, 2019, 12:30 A.M., twitter.com/iproposethis/status/1161132790038978561.

151 **"trying to pull the wool over your eyes"** Joanna Schroeder quoted in Gibson, "'Do You Have White Teenage Sons? Listen Up.'"

151 **the best approach in these situations** Gibson, "'Do You Have White Teenage Sons? Listen Up.'"

151 **"kids have a big developmental shift, cognitively"** Alice LoCicero quoted in Gibson, "'Do You Have White Teenage Sons? Listen Up.'"

152 **78.9 percent of them consider racism to be an interpersonal** Youths' articulations of intrapersonal/interpersonal racism were "unassociated with youths' race/ethnicity," though youths whose parents had completed some high school or less were more likely to articulate racism in this way. For the full study, see Josefina Bañales et al., "Something You Can See, Hear, and Feel: A Descriptive, Exploratory Mixed-Methods Analysis of Youths' Articulations About Racism," *Journal of Adolescent Research* (December 2021), 1–35.

153 **"embedding oneself in the contexts where the students are from"** Christopher Emdin, *For White Folks Who Teach in the Hood . . . and the Rest of Y'all Too: Reality Pedagogy and Urban Education* (Boston: Beacon Press, 2016), 139–143.

154 **"collective deficit terms"** Bryan K. Hotchkins, "African American Males Navigate Racial Microaggressions," *Teachers College Record* 118, no. 6 (June 2016), 2–3, 15–16.

154 **"often entering the profession with a lifetime of hegemonic reinforcement"** Bree Picower, "The Unexamined Whiteness of Teaching: How White Teachers Maintain and Enact Dominant Racial Ideologies," *Race Ethnicity and Education* 12, no. 2 (July 2009), 211.

154 **"pathologizes individual students"** Marilyn Cochran-Smith and Curt Dudley-Marling, "Diversity in Teacher Education and Special Education: The Issues That Divide," *Journal of Teacher Education* 63, no. 4 (2012), 239–240. "Deficit thinking" and the "medical model" of disability dominate special education practice, emphasizing diagnosis and treatment. Instead, Cochran-Smith and Dudley-Marling advocated for a "sociocultural theory of learning," which accounts for the sociocultural context in which students are situated and its impact on how children learn. David M. Perry and Lawrence Carter-Long, authors of *The Ruderman White Paper on Media Coverage of Law Enforcement Use of Force and Disability* (Newton, MA: Ruderman Family Foundation, March 2016), articulated the lethal consequences of the "medical model" of disability during interactions between police and people with disabilities, especially Black people with disabilities. Perry and Carter-Long, like Cochran-Smith and Dudley-Marling, advanced a "social model" of dis-

ability that includes a consideration of "societal factors" that might contribute to a "given problem, occurrence, or incident" (10).

154 **some teachers lash out emotionally** Picower, "The Unexamined Whiteness of Teaching," 205–209.

154 **what education scholar Lisa Delpit calls the "deadly fog"** Lisa Delpit, *Other People's Children: Cultural Conflict in the Classroom*, 2nd ed. (New York: New Press, 2006), xxiii.

155 **dropout rates** U.S. Department of Education, National Center for Education Statistics, "Total Number 16- to 24-Year-Old High School Dropouts (Status Dropouts) and Percentage of Dropouts Among Persons 16 to 42 Years Old (Status Dropout Rate), by Selected Characteristic: 2006 Through 2018, *Digest of Education Statistics*, 2019, nces.ed.gov /programs/digest/d19/tables/dt19_219.80.asp.

155 **twice as likely to be arrested** *that same month* Katherine C. Monahan et al., "From the School Yard to the Squad Car: School Discipline, Truancy, and Arrest," *Journal of Youth and Adolescence* 43, no. 7 (July 2014), 1116.

155 **Twelve years later, suspended youth** Janet Rosenbaum, "Educational and Criminal Justice Outcomes 12 Years After School Suspension," *Youth & Society* 52, no. 4 (2020), 527–529. Suspended youth were "6% less likely to have earned a high school diploma," "24% less likely to have earned a BA," "30% more likely to have been arrested once, 51% more likely to have been arrested two or more times, 23% more likely to have been in prison, and 49% more likely to have been on probation."

156 **enslaver of six people and a general in the Confederate States Army** Jessie Knadler, "New Research Sheds Light on Slaves Owned by Stonewall Jackson," WVTF, May 15, 2018, www.wvtf.org/news/2018-05 -15/new-research-sheds-light-on-slaves-owned-by-stonewall-jackson.

156 **Confederate vice president Alexander Stephens declared "our new government"** Alexander H. Stephens, "Cornerstone Speech," March 21, 1861, in *The Civil War and Reconstruction: A Documentary Reader*, ed. Stanley Harrold (Malden, MA: Blackwell, 2008), 61.

156 **branded the school with Jackson's name** Jill Palermo, "Big Names Behind 'Stonewall Jackson' Include Colgan, Pattie, Beville, Wood," *Fauquier Times*, August 24, 2017, www.fauquier.com/prince_william_times /news/big-names-behind-stonewall-jackson-include-colgan-pattie -beville-wood/article_83998d44-8881-11e7-a5a3-2fe4c4a24c27.html.

156 **like a middle finger to the civil rights movement** Fatima Bhojani, "What's in a Name? Virginia School Enters Confederate Symbols Battle," Reuters, August 18, 2017, www.reuters.com/article/us-usa-protests -school-idUSKCN1AY2C1.

156 **voted six to one to continue Jackson's commemoration** Palermo, "Big Names Behind 'Stonewall Jackson.'"

156 **did not change until 2020** Michelle Basch, "Prince William County Votes to Rename Schools Honoring Stonewall Jackson," WTOP News, June 29, 2020, wtop.com/prince-william-county/2020/06/prince -william-county-votes-to-rename-schools-honoring-stonewall -jackson/.

157 **the College Board found that** Jamaal Abdul-Alin, "Report: AP Courses Not Available for Black Students," *Diverse: Issues in Higher Education,* February 8, 2012, www.diverseeducation.com/demographics /african-american/article/15091144/report-ap-courses-not-available -for-black-students.

157 **"The intellectual superiority of our Nordic group"** Carl C. Brigham, *A Study of American Intelligence* (Princeton: Princeton University Press, 1923), 191–192.

157 **don't necessarily correlate with success in college** Researchers have found that grade point average (GPA) better predicts college success than standardized tests like the SAT and ACT. See Michal Kurlaender and Kramer Cohen, *Predicting College Success: How Do Different High School Assessments Measure Up?* (Stanford, CA: PACE, March 2019); and Elaine M. Allensworth and Kallie Clark, "High School GPAs and ACT Scores as Predictors of College Completion: Examining Assumptions About Consistency Across High Schools," *Educational Researcher* 49, no. 3 (2020): 198–211.

157 **do correlate with the wealth of the parents** Abigail Johnson Hess, "Rich Students Get Better SAT Scores—Here's Why," CNBC, October 3, 2019, www.cnbc.com/2019/10/03/rich-students-get-better-sat -scores-heres-why.html.

157 **nearly ten times more wealth than Black people** Kriston McIntosh et al., "Examining the Black-White Wealth Gap," Brookings Institution, February 27, 2020, www.brookings.edu/blog/up-front/2020/02/27 /examining-the-black-white-wealth-gap/.

157 **preferential treatment to students who take these classes** IB students have an 18 percent higher acceptance rate into Ivy League universities and a 22 percent higher acceptance rate into universities outside the Ivy League. See Crimson Education, *IB Student Acceptance Rates at the Top 25 U.S. Universities* (2018), pages.crimsoneducation.org/rs/039 -NBM-750/images/FL-10-2018-ib-student-acceptance-rates-at-top-us -universities.pdf?mkt_tok=eyJpIjoiWTJaalltRTJOV0kzT1.

158 **require letters of recommendation** Accredited Schools Online, "Choosing an International Baccalaureate or IB Program," May 28, 2021, www.accreditedschoolsonline.org/resources/international-bacca laureate/.

158 **least likely of any racial or ethnic group to be enrolled in privi- leged classes** U.S. Department of Education, National Center for Edu-

cation Statistics, "Percentage of Public School Students Enrolled in Gifted and Talented Programs, by Sex, Race/Ethnicity, and State: Selected Years, 2004 through 2013-14," *Digest of Education Statistics,* 2018, nces.ed.gov/programs/digest/d18/tables/dt18_204.90.asp.

159 **Black students in privileged classes** Malik S. Henfield, James L. Moore III, and Chris Wood, "Inside and Outside Gifted Education Programming: Hidden Challenges for African American Students," *Exceptional Children* 74, no. 4 (2008), 440–441.

161 **"drawing on the imagination"** Bettina L. Love, *We Want to Do More Than Survive: Abolitionist Teaching and the Pursuit of Educational Freedom* (Boston: Beacon Press, 2019), 2.

162 **more likely to be selected for the privileged classes** Kathleen Barlow and C. Elaine Dunbar, "Race, Class, and Whiteness in Gifted and Talented Identification: A Case Study," *Berkeley Review of Education* 1, no. 1 (2010), 73.

163 **author James Patterson once wrote** James Patterson (@JP_Books), "There's no such thing as a kid who hates reading," Twitter, January 9, 2014, 1:16 P.M., twitter.com/jp_books/status/421344811224817664.

AFTERWORD: LEAVING THE NEST

165 **"Man Dies After Medical Incident During Police Interaction"** Minneapolis Police Department, "Man Dies After Medical Incident During Police Interaction," press release, May 25, 2020, web.archive.org /web/20210331182901/https://www.insidempd.com/2020/05/26 /man-dies-after-medical-incident-during-police-interaction/.

165 **cellphone video by seventeen-year-old Darnella Frazier** Giulia McDonnell Nieto del Rio, "Darnella Frazier, the Teenager Who Recorded George Floyd's Murder, Speaks Out," *New York Times,* May 25, 2021, www.nytimes.com/2021/05/25/us/darnella-frazier.html.

165 **"I can't breathe," cried out for his mother** Richard A. Oppel, Jr., and Kim Barker, "New Transcripts Detail Last Moments for George Floyd," *New York Times,* April 1, 2021, www.nytimes.com/2020/07/08 /us/george-floyd-body-camera-transcripts.html.

165 **nearly eight out of ten Americans had seen some or all** Cameron Easley, "Floyd Protests Are Backed by Most Americans as More Say Racism Isn't Taken Seriously Enough," *Morning Consult,* June 1, 2020, morningconsult.com/2020/06/01/floyd-protests-are-backed-by-most -americans-as-more-say-racism-isnt-taken-seriously-enough/.

166 **between 15 and 26 million Americans in all fifty states** Larry Buchanan, Quoctrung Bui, and Jugal K. Patel, "Black Lives Matter May Be the Largest Movement in U.S. History," *New York Times,* July 3, 2020, www.nytimes.com/interactive/2020/07/03/us/george-floyd-protests -crowd-size.html.

166 **After Floyd's murder, just 34 percent of White parents** Chae, Rogers, and Yip, "There's a Right Way to Talk About Racism with Kids." Of these White parents, 27 percent said they "never" talked about "the need for racial equality," and another 15 percent said such conversations were "rare."

166 **Only 14 percent of teachers** Denisa R. Superville, "Principals Need Help Building Anti-Racist Schools," *Education Week,* September 23, 2020, www.edweek.org/leadership/principals-need-help-building-anti-racist-schools/2020/09.

166 **One popular textbook, *The American Pageant*** Jon Hale, "The Problem in the Classroom," *American Scholar,* July 30, 2020, theamerican scholar.org/the-problem-in-the-classroom/.

166 **A Florida middle school textbook, *Discovering Our Past*** Ibid.

167 **often "center on the white experience"** Southern Poverty Law Center, *Teaching Hard History: American Slavery* (2018), 11, www.splcenter.org/sites/default/files/tt_hard_history_american_slavery.pdf.

167 **"All instruction is culturally responsive"** Gloria Ladson-Billings quoted in Maya Kaul, "Reimagining Assessment: Keeping Students at the Center with Culturally Relevant Performance Assessments," *Next Generation Learning Challenges,* June 4, 2019, www.nextgenlearning.org/articles/keeping-students-at-the-center-with-culturally-relevant-performance-assessments.

167 **have adopted the Common Core standards** Terry Nguyen, "Student Activists Want Change—And They're Starting in the Classroom," *Vox,* July 29, 2020, www.vox.com/identities/2020/7/29/21345114/students-diversify-curriculum-change-antiracist.

167 **curriculum materials in the New York City public school system** Ibid.

167 **roughly seventeen hundred students across two hundred school districts** Ibid.

168 **about a thousand young people at the Baltimore School for the Arts** Lauren Lumpkin, "Baltimore Students Protest for Anti-Racist Curriculum: 'We Don't Know the Truth,'" *Washington Post,* June 19, 2020, www.washingtonpost.com/local/education/george-floyd-protests-curriculum-reform/2020/06/18/79170a2a-ac2a-11ea-a9d9-a81c1a491c52_story.html.

168 **Gladwyne Elementary School in suburban Philadelphia** Tyler Kingkade, Brandy Zadrozny, and Ben Collins, "Critical Race Theory Battle Invades School Boards—With Help from Conservative Groups," NBC News, June 15, 2021, www.nbcnews.com/news/us-news/critical-race-theory-invades-school-boards-help-conservative-groups-n1270794.

168 **"reprehensible resources designed to inoculate Caucasian chil-**

dren" Elana Yaron Fishbein quoted in Eric Hananoki, "No Left Turn in Education, a Leading Anti-Critical Race Theory Group, Frequently Pushes Toxic Rhetoric in Media," *Media Matters for America,* June 22, 2021, www.mediamatters.org/education/no-left-turn-education-leading-anti-critical-race-theory-group-frequently-pushes-toxic.

169 **Trained in social work** Kingkade, Zadrozny, and Collins, "Critical Race Theory Battle Invades School Boards."

169 **named her group No Left Turn in Education** Ibid.

169 **advocating against teaching about sex and climate change** Julia Carrie Wong, "The Fight to Whitewash US History: 'A Drop of Poison Is All You Need,'" *Guardian,* May 25, 2021, www.theguardian.com /world/2021/may/25/critical-race-theory-us-history-1619-project.

169 **fewer than two hundred Facebook followers** Kingkade, Zadrozny, and Collins, "Critical Race Theory Battle Invades School Boards."

169 **"was totally taken by the harsh criticism" of her letter** "PA Parent Says School's 'Cultural Proficiency' Curriculum Turns Martin Luther King's Teachings 'Upside Down,'" *Yahoo!,* September 16, 2020, www .yahoo.com/now/pa-parent-says-schools-cultural-014310651.html.

169 **"this teaching turns Martin Luther King's teaching upside down"** Ibid.

169 **"forced to teach the Negro"** Martin Luther King, Jr., "Where Do We Go from Here?," August 16, 1967, Martin Luther King, Jr. Research and Education Institute, Stanford University, kinginstitute.stanford.edu /where-do-we-go-here.

169 **producing documentaries, mostly abroad** Benjamin Wallace-Wells, "How a Conservative Activist Invented the Conflict over Critical Race Theory," *New Yorker,* June 18, 2021, www.newyorker.com/news/annals -of-inquiry/how-a-conservative-activist-invented-the-conflict-over -critical-race-theory.

170 **outraged looking at the racial trainings for his city's employees** Christopher F. Rufo, "Cult Programming in Seattle," *City Journal,* July 8, 2020, www.city-journal.org/seattle-interrupting-whiteness-training.

170 **had expanded to the federal government** Fabiola Cineas, "Critical Race Theory, and Trump's War on It, Explained," *Vox,* September 24, 2020, www.vox.com/2020/9/24/21451220/critical-race-theory-diversity -training-trump.

170 **banned these trainings** Russell Vought, "Training in the Federal Government," official memorandum (Washington, DC: Office of Management and Budget, September 4, 2020), www.whitehouse.gov/wp -content/uploads/2020/09/M-20-34.pdf.

170 **announced the creation of the 1776 Commission** Donald Trump, "Remarks by President Trump at the White House Conference on

American History," White House, September 17, 2020, trumpwhite house.archives.gov/briefings-statements/remarks-president-trump -white-house-conference-american-history/.

170 **while calling slavery "a necessary evil"** Tom Cotton quoted in Frank E. Lockwood, "Bill by Sen. Tom Cotton Targets Curriculum on Slavery," *Arkansas Democrat-Gazette,* July 26, 2020, www.arkansasonline .com/news/2020/jul/26/bill-by-cotton-targets-curriculum-on-slavery /?utm_campaign=snd-autopilot&utm_medium=social&utm_source= twitter_ArkansasOnline.

170 **peaceful 96.3 percent of the time** Erica Chenoweth and Jeremy Pressman, "This Summer's Black Lives Matter Protesters Were Overwhelmingly Peaceful, Our Research Finds," *Washington Post,* October 16, 2020, www .washingtonpost.com/politics/2020/10/16/this-summers-black-lives -matter-protesters-were-overwhelming-peaceful-our-research-finds/.

170 **"left-wing rioting and mayhem"** Trump, "Remarks by President Trump at the White House Conference on American History."

170 **The manufactured problem** Jasmine Banks, "The Radical Capitalist Behind the Critical Race Theory Furor," *Nation,* August 13, 2021, www .thenation.com/article/politics/charles-koch-crt-backlash/.

171 **74 electoral votes and more than 7 million popular votes** Mark Sherman, "Electoral College Makes It Official: Biden Won, Trump Lost," Associated Press, December 14, 2020, apnews.com/article/joe-biden -270-electoral-college-vote-d429ef97af2bf574d16463384dc7cc1e.

171 **cities with large Black and Brown populations** Ashley Nguyen, Kayla Ruble, and Tim Craig, "Anger Builds in Black Community over Trump's Claims of Voter Fraud in Big Cities," *Washington Post,* November 20, 2020, www.washingtonpost.com/national/2020/11/20 /f0d11954-2b71-11eb-9b14-ad872157ebc9_story.html; Jonathan J. Cooper, "AP FACT CHECK: Trump Makes False Claims About Arizona Audit," Associated Press, July 17, 2021, apnews.com/article /technology-joe-biden-arizona-government-and-politics-ap-fact-check -0e7fad7e5bdf02d953c6b90a474267cc; Ken Ritter, "Campaign Attorney: Trump Won Nevada, Despite Biden Results," Associated Press, November 17, 2020, apnews.com/article/jesse-binnall-trump-won-nevada -040283b5e5e2ffe64ffb3a80609005aa.

171 **violently stormed the United States Capitol** Maura Judkis and Ellen McCarthy, "The Capitol Mob Desecrated a Historical Workplace—And Left Behind Some Disturbing Artifacts," *Washington Post,* January 8, 2021, www.washingtonpost.com/lifestyle/style/the-capitol-mob-desecrated -a-historical-workplace--and-left-behind-some-disturbing-artifacts/2021 /01/08/e67b3c88-51d1-11eb-83e3-322644d82356_story.html.

171 **littered with their feces and the broken glass** Devon Link, "Fact Check: Photo Shows U.S. Capitol Cleanup After Rioters Left American

Flag Among Debris," *USA Today,* February 3, 2021, www.usatoday.com /story/news/factcheck/2021/02/03/fact-check-u-s-capitol-riot-cleanup -photo-lacks-context/4346608001/.

171 **Five people died** Kenya Evelyn, "Capitol Attack: The Five People Who Died," *Guardian,* January 8, 2021, www.theguardian.com/us-news /2021/jan/08/capitol-attack-police-officer-five-deaths.

171 **more than one hundred police officers, four of whom later died by suicide** Tim Fitzsimmons, Geoff Bennett, and Phil Helsel, "Four Officers Who Responded to Capitol Riot Have Died by Suicide," NBC News, August 2, 2021, www.nbcnews.com/news/us-news/third-d-c -officer-who-responded-capitol-riot-dies-suicide-n1275740.

171 **the most devastating assault on the Capitol since the British burned Washington in 1814** Dalton Bennett et al., "41 Minutes of Fear: A Video Timeline from Inside the Capitol Siege," *Washington Post,* January 16, 2021, www.washingtonpost.com/investigations/2021/01 /16/video-timeline-capitol-siege/.

171 **inside the Capitol for the first time in history** Maria Cramer, "Confederate Flag an Unnerving Sight in Capitol," *New York Times,* January 9, 2021, www.nytimes.com/2021/01/09/us/politics/confederate -flag-capitol.html.

171 **held off the Confederate rebels from seizing the Capitol** See Robert Knox Sneden, Plan of the Rebel Attack on Washington, D.C., July 11th and 12th, 1864, www.loc.gov/item/gvhs01.vhs00256/.

171 **calls for "unity" and "healing"** Joseph R. Biden, "Inaugural Address by President Joseph R. Biden, Jr.," January 20, 2021, White House, www .whitehouse.gov/briefing-room/speeches-remarks/2021/01/20 /inaugural-address-by-president-joseph-r-biden-jr/.

172 **"a way of looking at the law's role"** Kimberlé Crenshaw quoted in "What Is Critical Race Theory, and Why Is Everyone Talking About It?," *Columbia News,* July 1, 2021, news.columbia.edu/news/what-critical -race-theory-and-why-everyone-talking-about-it-0.

172 **"Critical race theory says every white person is a racist"** Ted Cruz quoted in Alexandra Hutzler, "Ted Cruz Says Critical Race Theory Is 'Every Bit as Racist as Klansmen in White Sheets,'" *Newsweek,* June 18, 2021, www.newsweek.com/ted-cruz-says-critical-race-theory -every-bit-racist-klansmen-white-sheets-1602105.

172 **Republican think tanks and periodicals** Wong, "The Fight to Whitewash US History."

172 **"one of the most innocent little girls in the whole world"** Jason Lemon, "Video of Mom Insisting She Isn't Racist for Opposing Racial Justice Lessons Viewed over 500K Times," *Newsweek,* May 2, 2021, www .newsweek.com/video-mom-insisting-she-isnt-racist-opposing-racial -justice-lessons-viewed-over-500k-times-1588167.

172 **a clip of her speech went viral** Gramps (@capetownbrown), "A racist," Twitter, May 1, 2021, 5:33 P.M., twitter.com/capetownbrown/status /1388607612023885826.

172 **"perhaps the most potent reactionary figure in this country"** Esther Wang, "Angry White Parents Are Once Again Winning the Battle for the American Classroom," *New Republic,* July 14, 2021, newrepublic.com /article/162976/critical-race-theory-fox-news-angry-white-parents.

173 **After mentioning "critical race theory" 132 times in 2020** Ibram X. Kendi, "There Is No Debate over Critical Race Theory," *Atlantic,* July 9, 2021, www.theatlantic.com/ideas/archive/2021/07/opponents -critical-race-theory-are-arguing-themselves/619391/.

173 **expanded rapidly in 2021 to thirty chapters in twenty-three states** Kingkade, Zadrozny, and Collins, "Critical Race Theory Battle Invades School Boards."

173 **At least 165 local and national groups** Ibid.

173 **Educational Liberty Alliance** Frederick M. Hess, "A New Group Battling for Freedom of Thought in Education," American Enterprise Institute, September 24, 2021, www.aei.org/op-eds/a-new-group -battling-for-freedom-of-thought-in-education/.

173 **Critical Race Training in Education** Critical Race Training in Education, "About This Website," criticalrace.org/critical-race-theory -today/.

173 **Rich Lowry, the editor of the *National Review,* urged** Rich Lowry quoted in Wang, "Angry White Parents Are Once Again Winning the Battle for the American Classroom."

173 **"Families did not ask for this divisive nonsense"** "READ: McConnell Letter to the Education Department Regarding '1619 Project' Programs," CNN, April 30, 2021, www.cnn.com/2021/04/30/politics /mitch-mcconnell-miguel-cardona-letter/index.html.

173 **the Southern Manifesto of 1956** U.S. Congress, *Congressional Record,* 84 Cong., 2nd Sess., 102, part 4 (March 12, 1956), 4515–4516, 4460– 4461.

174 **passed a series of bans and censorship laws** Keri Leigh Merritt, *Masterless Men: Poor Whites and Slavery in the Antebellum South* (Cambridge: Cambridge University Press, 2017), 144.

174 **railed against Webster's dictionary for its accurate definition** Paula T. Connolly, *Slavery in American Children's Literature, 1790–2010* (Iowa City: University of Iowa Press, 2013), 76.

174 **John Abbott observed in 1860** John S. C. Abbott, *South and North; Impressions Received During a Trip to Cuba and the South* (New York: Abbey & Abbott, 1860), 157–158; Merritt, *Masterless Men,* 144.

174 **resisted the establishment of free public schools** Nikole Hannah-Jones, "Our Democracy's Founding Ideals Were False When They Were

Written. Black Americans Have Fought to Make Them True," *New York Times Magazine,* August 14, 2019, www.nytimes.com/interactive/2019 /08/14/magazine/black-history-american-democracy.html.

174 **illegal to teach enslaved Black people to read and write** For more on anti-literacy laws and the strategies that enslaved people used to circumvent them, see Heather Andrea Williams, *Self-Taught: African American Education in Slavery and Freedom* (Chapel Hill: University of North Carolina Press, 2005).

174 **declined to pass a bill first proposed in 1881 to provide equal funding** The so-called Blair Education Bill was introduced by Sen. Henry W. Blair (R-NH). Jeffery A. Jenkins and Justin Peck, "The Erosion of the First Civil Rights Era: Congress and the Redemption of the White South, 1877–1891," paper presented at the 2015 Annual Congress & History Conference, 30–47.

174 **"In the South, ignorance is an institution"** Henry Ward Beecher quoted in Merritt, *Masterless Men,* 143.

174 **New Hampshire Republican Keith Ammon introduced a bill** Adam Harris, "The GOP's 'Critical Race Theory' Obsession," *Atlantic,* May 7, 2021, www.theatlantic.com/politics/archive/2021/05/gops -critical-race-theory-fixation-explained/618828/.

174 **By December 2021** Rashawn Ray and Alexandra Gibbons, "Why Are States Banning Critical Race Theory?," Brookings Institution, November 2021, www.brookings.edu/blog/fixgov/2021/07/02/why-are-states -banning-critical-race-theory/.

175 **do not mention the words "critical race theory"** Ibid.

175 **more than 440 bills in forty-nine states** Brennan Center for Justice, "Voting Laws Roundup: December 2021," December 21, 2021.

175 **dropped requirements for public schools to teach** Minyvonne Burke and the Associated Press, "Texas Senate Passes Bill That Removes Requirement to Teach Ku Klux Klan as 'Morally Wrong,'" NBC News, July 21, 2021, www.nbcnews.com/politics/politics-news/texas-senate -passes-bill-removes-requirement-teach-ku-klux-klan-n1274610.

175 **deleted most mentions of people of color and women** Isabella Zou, "Texas Senate Bill Seeks to Strip Required Lessons on People of Color and Women from 'Critical Race Theory' Law," *Texas Tribune,* July 9, 2021, www.texastribune.org/2021/07/09/texas-critical-race-theory-schools -legislation/. The bill (SB 3), introduced by Texas state senator Bryan Hughes (R), passed the Senate but never became law. To view all actions on this bill, see "SB 3," Legislative Session 87 (1), Texas Legislature Online, capitol.texas.gov/BillLookup/History.aspx?LegSess=871&Bill=SB3.

175 **the Williamson County chapter of Moms for Liberty** Tori Keafer, "Local Parent Group Submits Grievance to State Concerning Wit & Wisdom Curriculum," *Williamson Herald,* July 11, 2021, www

.williamsonherald.com/news/local-parent-group-submits-grievance-to
-state-concerning-wit-wisdom-curriculum/article_cde5870a-e11e
-11eb-9a39-4fa4aae7de48.html.

176 **"ashamed of his white half"** Wang, "Angry White Parents Are Once
Again Winning the Battle for the American Classroom."

176 **taught about the history of anti-Black racism** Julie M. Hughes,
Rebecca S. Bigler, and Sheri R. Levy, "Consequences of Learning
About Historical Racism Among European American and African
American Children," *Child Development* 78, no. 6 (November–December
2007), 1689–1705.

179 **author Julie Lythcott-Haims instructs us** Julie Lythcott-Haims, *How
to Raise an Adult: Break Free of the Overparenting Trap and Prepare Your Kid
for Success* (New York: Henry Holt, 2015).

180 **"Kids make sense of the world around them"** Margaret A. Hagerman, *White Kids: Growing Up with Privilege in a Racially Divided America*
(New York: New York University Press, 2020), 19–20.

Index

ABOUT THE AUTHOR

Dr. Ibram X. Kendi is the Andrew W. Mellon Professor in the Humanities at Boston University and the founding director of the BU Center for Antiracist Research. He is a contributing writer at *The Atlantic* and a CBS News racial justice contributor. Dr. Kendi is the author of many highly acclaimed books including *Stamped from the Beginning: The Definitive History of Racist Ideas in America*, which won the National Book Award for Nonfiction, making him the youngest-ever winner of that award. He has also produced five #1 *New York Times* bestsellers, including *How to Be an Antiracist*, *Antiracist Baby*, and *Stamped: Racism, Antiracism, and You*, co-authored by Jason Reynolds. In 2020, *Time* magazine named Dr. Kendi one of the 100 Most Influential People in the world. He was awarded a 2021 MacArthur Fellowship, popularly known as the Genius Grant.

ibramxkendi.com
Facebook.com/ibramxkendi
Twitter: @dribram
Instagram: @ibramxk

To inquire about booking Ibram X. Kendi for a speaking engagement, please contact the Penguin Random House Speakers Bureau at speakers@penguinrandomhouse.com.

A discussion guide is available at ibramxkendi.com/how-to-raise.

ABOUT THE TYPE

This book was set in Bembo, a typeface based on an old-style Roman face that was used for Cardinal Pietro Bembo's tract *De Aetna* in 1495. Bembo was cut by Francesco Griffo (1450–1518) in the early sixteenth century for Italian Renaissance printer and publisher Aldus Manutius (1449–1515). The Lanston Monotype Company of Philadelphia brought the well-proportioned letterforms of Bembo to the United States in the 1930s.